CW00373394

Literature and Visual Technologies

Literature and Visual Technologies

Writing After Cinema

Edited by

Julian Murphet

and

Lydia Rainford

Introduction, editorial matter and selection © Julian Murphet and Lydia
Rainford 2003
Chapter 1 © Colin MacCabe 2003
All other chapters © Palgrave Macmillan 2003

All rights reserved. No reproduction, copy or transmission of this
publication may be made without written permission.

No paragraph of this publication may be reproduced, copied or transmitted
save with written permission or in accordance with the provisions of the
Copyright, Designs and Patents Act 1988, or under the terms of any licence
permitting limited copying issued by the Copyright Licensing Agency, 90
Tottenham Court Road, London W1T 4LP.

Any person who does any unauthorised act in relation to this publication
may be liable to criminal prosecution and civil claims for damages.

The authors have asserted their rights to be identified as the authors of
this work in accordance with the Copyright, Designs and Patents Act 1988.

First published 2003 by
PALGRAVE MACMILLAN
Houndmills, Basingstoke, Hampshire RG21 6XS and
175 Fifth Avenue, New York, N. Y. 10010
Companies and representatives throughout the world

PALGRAVE MACMILLAN is the global academic imprint of the Palgrave
Macmillan division of St. Martin's Press, LLC and of Palgrave Macmillan Ltd.
Macmillan® is a registered trademark in the United States, United Kingdom
and other countries. Palgrave is a registered trademark in the European
Union and other countries.

ISBN 1–4039–1308–0

This book is printed on paper suitable for recycling and made from fully
managed and sustained forest sources.

A catalogue record for this book is available from the British Library.

Library of Congress Cataloging-in-Publication Data
Literature and visual technologies : writing after cinema / edited by Julian
Murphet and Lydia Rainford.
        p. cm.
    Includes bibliographical references and index.
    ISBN 1–4039–1308–0
      1. Motion pictures and literature. 2. Television and literature.
    I. Murphet, Julian. II. Rainford, Lydia, 1972–

    PN1995.3.L565 2003
    791.43′6—dc21

                                                            2003053612

10   9   8   7   6   5   4   3   2   1
12   11   10   09   08   07   06   05   04   03

Printed and bound in Great Britain by
Antony Rowe Ltd, Chippenham and Eastbourne

For Nathaniel Oliver

List of Contents

After the Modern

List of Illustrations

Plates appear between pp. 66-67.

Notes on Contributors

Tim Armstrong is Reader in Modern English and American Literature at Royal Holloway, University of London. His recent publications include *Modernism, Technology and the Body: A Cultural Study* (1998) and *Haunted Hardy: Poetry, History, Memory* (2000).

Rachel Connor is a lecturer in the Department of English Literature at the University of Glasgow. She is the author of a monograph, *H.D. and the image* (forthcoming from Manchester University Press) and is currently working on a critical edition of H.D.'s unpublished prose manuscript, 'Majic Ring'. She has also published on contemporary American writing and on European cinema.

Paula Geyh is an assistant professor of English at Yeshiva University, where she teaches 20th-century American and European literature and literary theory. She is a co-editor of *Postmodern American Fiction: A Norton Anthology* and is presently at work on a book on representations of the postmodern city and cyberspace.

Elena Gualtieri lives in Brighton, where she lectures in English at the University of Sussex. She is the author of *Virginia Woolf's Essays: Sketching the Past* (London: Macmillan, 2000). Her work on Proust and Musil is part of a wider project on the intersection between writing and photography in the first half of the twentieth century.

Colin MacCabe is Distinguished Professor of English and Film at the University of Pittsburgh where he has taught since 1985. He has also taught as Professor of English at the University of Exeter since 1998. His most recent publication is *Godard: A Portrait of the Artist at 70* (Bloomsbury 2003)

Laura Marcus is Reader in English at the University of Sussex. She has published books on theories of auto/biography, psychoanalysis, and Virginia Woolf. She is currently co-editing the *Cambridge History of Twentieth-Century English Literature*, and working on a study of cinema and modernism.

Julian Murphet is a lecturer at the Department of English, University of Sydney. He has published on Los Angeles fiction and postmodernism.

Michael North is Professor of English at the University of California, Los Angeles. His most recent books are *Reading 1922: A Return to the Scene of the Modern* (Oxford, 1999) and the Norton Critical Edition of T. S. Eliot's *The Waste Land* (2001). He is currently at work on a new study of the visual arts, spectatorship, and modern literature.

Arkady Plotnitsky is a Professor of English and a University Faculty Scholar at Purdue University, where he is also a Director of Theory and Cultural Studies Program. His most recent book is *The Knowable and the Unknowable: Modern Science, Nonclassical Thought, and 'The Two Cultures'* (2002). He is currently completing two books, *Minute Particulars: Romanticism, Science,* and *Epistemology* and *Reading Bohr: Physics and Philosophy.*

Lydia Rainford is a Junior Research Fellow at St. Hugh's College, Oxford. She has published on Samuel Beckett, modern literature and theory.

Eric Robertson is Senior Lecturer in French at Royal Holloway, University of London. He is the author of *Writing Between the Lines* (1995), a study of the bilingual novelist René Schickele, and co-editor of *Yvan Goll – Claire Goll: Texts and Contexts* (1997), and has published various articles and book chapters on twentieth-century poetry and visual arts. He is currently completing a book on the artist, sculptor and poet Hans Jean Arp, to be published by Yale University Press.

Keith Williams is Senior Lecturer in English at the University of Dundee. He has published widely on aspects of Modernism and visual technology and culture, including *British Writers and the Media 1930-45* (1996). He is currently working on studies of film and the work of both James Joyce and H.G. Wells.

Acknowledgements

The editors would like to acknowledge the assistance of St John's College, Oxford for supporting the initial idea of this book. Professor John Kelly was an indispensable ally in these early stages.

Katy Mullin deserves many thanks for all her help and extensive involvement in this project. Dominic Oliver has been an invaluable helpmate throughout.

Chapter 7 by Tim Armstrong appeared first in the *Forum for Modern Language Studies*, vol. XXXVII (2), 2001. We are grateful to Oxford University Press for granting permission to republish this material.

Introduction

Julian Murphet and Lydia Rainford

By way of introduction to this volume, we give you a prophesy from 1908:

> You will see that this little clicking contraption with the revolving handle will make a revolution in our life – in the life of writers. It is a direct attack on the old methods of literary art. We shall have to adapt ourselves to the shadowy screen and to the cold machine. A new form of writing will be necessary. I have thought of that and I can see what is coming.
>
> But I rather like it. This swift change of scene, this blending of emotion and experience – it is much better than the heavy, long-drawn-out kind of writing to which we are accustomed. It is closer to life. In life, too, changes and transitions flash by before our eyes, and emotions of the soul are like a hurricane. The cinema has divined the mystery of motion. And that is its greatness.[1]

So Tolstoy, little more than a year away from his death, foretold the crisis of the greatest narrative form of the nineteenth century – the Realist novel – and the supremacy of a new mechanical one in the twentieth. We might expect such a pronouncement on these lips to be offered as a lament; but there is something unrepentant about the old man's enthusiasm: 'But the films! They are wonderful! Drr! and a scene is ready! Drr! and we have another! We have the sea, the coast, the city, the palace...' His excitement was for the momentous formal challenge at hand: nothing less than the invention of 'a new form of writing'. The 'heavy, long-drawn-out kind of writing' was now, overnight, an anachronism. The lightness and speed of scenic transitions in the films would forever alter the method of literary narrative composition and the style of its discourse.

Was Tolstoy right? Indubitably, yes, and this volume of essays seeks to testify to the changes he predicted. For in spite of more than a century of film technology, there has still been relatively little written about its impact on literary culture. Plenty of analysis of film has ensued, and of cinematic adaptations of literature, but the ways in which film infiltrated, contaminated and altered literary forms has yet to receive the scholarly attention it deserves. Why this should be is a question several of the essays included here will tackle; but the answer is clearly embedded in the complex history of cinema's cultural reception.

The history of the relation of literary and visual technologies has frequently taken unexpected routes. Just as Tolstoy's excitement at the prospect of cinematic writing was surprising for a realist writer, so the consequences of the new technology for literature seemed, at first glance, unlikely. The most immediate changes provoked by this medium of the masses were, arguably, to be seen in the more elitist realms of 'literary art', and the most radical adjustments to literary forms came not in the light of cinema's representational facilities (photographic realism), so much as its constructive ones. Literary narrative had always had a 'problem' with transitions: what rhetorical prestidigitation could really justify the reader's forcible relocation from, in *The Arcadia* say, the blinding of Drialus on one page, to the song of Amphialus to Philoclea on another? In such 'early' prose fiction, this mattered rather less than the display of rhetoric *per se*. But as the conception of 'organic form' really took root in the eighteenth and nineteenth centuries, the tonal rebalancing of the narrative voice that was forever being demanded became more awkward. The notebook may simply have read 'get from London to Bourton', but prior to the films, the novel would be forced to indulge in occasionally agonizing circumlocutions in order to reach its destination. In the cinema, this clumsy, or comic, or hyper-conscious late-Jamesian *pause* over narrative transitions was obviated at a stroke. Drr! and we're at Bourton! Drr! and back in London! It was the longer, syntactical periods of transitional verbiage (not only between scenes, but also within them) that the cinema finally put to rest; so that, by 1925, Virginia Woolf could 'get us' from London to Bourton with no noise at all. Let Woolf herself describe the possibilities:

> The past could be unrolled, distances annihilated, and the gulfs which dislocate novels (when, for instance, Tolstoy has to pass from Levin to Anna and in doing so jars his story and wrenches and arrests our sympathies) could by the sameness of the background, by the repetition of some scene, be smoothed away.[2]

It is worth pondering the typical stylistic and architectural devices of Modernism as so many reactions to a narrative medium untroubled by the rhetoric of transitions. Of course, *transition* by that very token became the greatest of form-problems for the Moderns, since without that thick texture of conventional discourse developed for getting us from A to B, it becomes a hair-raising experience to navigate the now isolated scenes or images within some overall form. We may recall Woolf describing the effect of reading T. S. Eliot in terms of a high-wire act:

> …how intolerant he is of the old usages and politenesses of society…! As I sun myself upon the intense and ravishing beauty of one of his lines, and reflect

that I must make a dizzy and dangerous leap to the next, and so on from line to line, like an acrobat flying precariously from bar to bar, I cry out, I confess, for the old decorums, and envy the indolence of my ancestors who, instead of spinning madly through mid-air, dreamt quietly in the shade with a book.[3]

The assimilation of cinematic transitionality – a trick which by now we have all come to call 'montage' – meant looking for the logic of transitions elsewhere, in the genius of the design or the felicities of the style. The basic pleasures of narrative had migrated to the silver screen; and in spite of Woolf's hankerings after the dreamy verbosity of the old narrative technology, there was little room for nostalgia.

The new literature 'will be harder and saner, it will be ... "nearer the bone." It will be as much like granite as it can be, its force will lie in its truth.... We will have fewer painted adjectives impeding the shock and stroke of it. At least for myself, I want it so, austere, direct, free from emotional slither.'[4] Thus Ezra Pound, whose intolerance towards Victorian sentimentality was aligned with a distate for clutter and rhetoric, as though the persistence of excess verbiage, in poetics as in prose, amounted to that very Mauberlian vice of pumping up '"the sublime"/in the old sense'. Paring away conventional jargon from the bare austerity of the thing was, moreover, not simply an option; it was 'what the age demanded': 'an image of its accelerated grimace... a prose kinema'. The death-sentence pronounced by Imagism over the twitching body of literary rhetoric was, unlike Wordsworth's and Coleridge's a century before, announced in the name of a machine, not the common man. Gertrude Stein also made her revolution against the dead language of Literature in the name of the rhetoric-free cinema;[5] and her principal disciple, Ernest Hemingway would memorably write:

> There were many words that you could not stand to hear and finally only the names of places had dignity. Certain numbers were the same way and certain dates and these with the names of the places were all you could say and have them mean anything. Abstract words such as glory, honor, courage, or hallow were obscene beside the concrete names of villages, the numbers of roads, the names of rivers, the numbers of regiments and the dates.[6]

Harder, saner, nearer the bone; dismissive of weary abstractions and the insidious ideologies that lurked within them; machinic, free of sentimentality, and able to be assembled in new and unpredictable ways: how much Modernist literature owes to the cinema, its techniques and forms, is still a long way from being properly ascertained. As the merest token, we can note that Marshall McLuhan wrote to Ezra Pound in 1943 at St Elizabeth's, in reply to his gift copy of the Pisan Cantos: 'Your Cantos I now judge to be the first and only serious use of the great technical possibilities of the cinematograph.'[7] It was not an idea, surely, at which Pound would have brightened, but it powerfully underscored the nature of the revolution Pound and Stein had started many years before.

Nevertheless, the initial ecstasy of inspiration was constantly being interrupted by other factors, above all the cinema's persistent recourse to the novel itself. We can stay with Woolf here, who, a year after *Mrs Dalloway*, was ironically and yet painfully bemoaning this carnivorous assault:

> All the famous novels of the world, with their well-known characters and their famous scenes, only asked, it seemed, to be put on the films. What could be easier and simpler? The cinema fell upon its prey with immense rapacity, and to the moment largely subsists upon the body of its unfortunate victim. But the results are disastrous to both. The alliance is unnatural. Eye and brain are torn asunder ruthlessly....[8]

This is the instinctual, defensive posture of the writer who, almost twenty years after Tolstoy's excitement, has seen the effects of industrialised cinema on literate culture: parasitism, infantilization, objectification, depthlessness, commodification. Her very metaphor of a rapacious beast of prey tearing into the defenseless ecosystem of literature suggests a worthwhile model for the comprehension of what has been a century-long struggle for position on the cultural food chain: a media ecology. It really was not until sound cinema hit its tyrannosaurus-stride in the 1930s that the devastating impact of the new narrative beast was fully appreciated, and by F. Scott Fitgerald more than anybody – an early enthusiast for, and later wage-slave of, the cinema:

> I saw that the novel, which at my maturity was the strongest and supplest medium for conveying thought and emotion from one human being to another, was becoming subordinated to a mechanical and communal art that, whether in the hands of Hollywood merchants or Russian idealists, was capable of reflecting only the tritest thought, the most obvious emotion. It was an art in which words were subordinate to images, where personality was worn down to the inevitable low gear of collaboration. As long past as 1930, I had a hunch that the talkies would make even the best selling novelist as archaic as silent pictures. People still read ... but there was a rankling indignity, that to me had become almost an obsession, in seeing the power of the written word subordinate to another power, a more glittering, a grosser power... something which tended to make my efforts obsolescent, as the chain stores have crippled the small merchant, an exterior force, unbeatable –[9]

Here the note of economic Darwinism is sounded with a fatalistic fury, muted only by the perfect past tense and a grudging awareness of which side of the bread is being buttered. It is a bitter despair given its fullest expression in Nathanael West's extraordinary *Day of the Locust*, and Theodor Adorno's and Max Horkheimer's 'Culture Industry' essay: contemporaneous jeremiads against the reign of the spectacle on behalf of the word. The 'direct attack' by cinema on the life of writers, of which Tolstoy had written so optimistically, had finally (in the heyday of Hollywood's triumph, 1938-41) come to a vanquishing, an elimination, or so it seemed, of an inferior and superseded species.

Or not quite. The Second World War makes an epoch, at which some kind of moral equalibrium is regained by writers under the shadow of Tinseltown. This was due in no small part to the enormous effect of Hollywood's product, and the U.S. Army it helped urge into action against Fascism, on the intelligentsia of a benighted Europe. The school of Bazin, on the pages of *Cahiers du cinéma*, recounted again and again the incontestable fact of 'the movies' as a bulwark against moribund classicism, called forever into disrepute thanks to its cooptation by totalitarianism. As the vanguard of a new consumerism of course American visual culture was corrupt, but the *Cahiers* school articulated what was felt generally by the vast majority of French intellectuals after the War (Sartre, Merleau-Ponty, Camus, Robbe-Grillet and Barthes to name but a few): the movies were, as William Carlos Williams first put it, 'a moral force'; and cinema's ablest practitioners, De Sica, Rossellini, Welles, Bergman and Mizoguchi, constituted the most palpable public conscience of a post-Fascist era. Robbe-Grillet and Duras wrote screenplays for Resnais; Godard, potentially one of the greatest literary talents of his generation, reinvented cinema instead; and Truffaut went to school in Hitchcock as though he were a living Shakespeare. This striking new accord between the literary intelligentsia and the cinema was echoed, across the Atlantic, by Frank O'Hara, who wrote, throwing all caution and cadence to the wind:

> Not you, lean quarterlies and swarthy periodicals
> with your studious incursions toward the pomposity of ants,
> nor you, experimental theatre in which Emotive Fruition
> is wedding Poetic Insight perpetually, nor you,
> promenading Grand Opera, obvious as an ear (though you
> are close to my heart), but you, Motion Picture Industry,
> it's you I love![10]

This exhilarated cry of relief, with its amoral imperative throbbing just beneath the surface ('Mothers of America/let your kids go to the movies!'[11]), shuffled off the Modernist coils of little magazines and terse poetic strictures. It is what we have been calling 'postmodernism' ever since. O'Hara's declaration of love rejoins Tolstoy's initial fervour of approbation, but after the fact of the Culture Industry, which it negates by sheer flamboyant audacity – just as the *nouvelle vague* would do. Henceforth literature, having learned its place in the new media ecology, is free to flourish in the topsoil of the spectacle.

By one account, the effect has been deleterious:

> Literalness, perhaps the dominant aspect of film, has come to occupy, largely because of film's popularity, a hegemonic place in all the arts. Its chief feature is the abandonment of subjectivity in the work. In place of interiority, which presupposed the individual who was distinguished from the objects outside of her- or himself by consciousness, even if socially determined or conditioned, literalism dissolves the subject-object split into object relations.[12]

The novel, overwhelmed by cinema's superficial visuality, apparently no longer plays that vital role assigned to it by generations of critics: the production of (good) subjectivity. It has 'abandoned' subjectivity, in anything other than a pastiched or parodic sense. And indeed, what could be more appropriate a literary 'symptom' in the collective desire to map our social and cultural present? If the structuralists and post-structuralists have been right to argue that what we call subjectivity has all along been an effect of various imbricated social, linguistic and psychological structurations, then where better than the postmodern, literalised, movie-conscious novel to look for a consciousness of *that*? While L=A=N=G=U=A=G=E poetry (Hejinian, Bernstein, etc.) playfully recycles the media's lamentable excuse for 'language', the postmodern novel – from Pynchon and DeLillo to Perec and Houellebecq – explores the 'post-subjective' landscapes of the media ecology with an eye to the elusive structures that govern and perpetuate it. The role of cinema in the twentieth-century's refashioning of not only art and literature, but of subjectivity, desire and the social itself, has been inestimable.

And if it has helped to refashion art and literature, cinema has also profoundly modified the critical languages through which these are apprehended. Fredric Jameson has written of the extent to which 'film has marked the life and work of writers in the twentieth century; and it is always worth remembering the degree to which going to the movies has been a very basic part of the weekly and even the daily life of modern intellectuals.'[13] It is an observation which encourages a reconsideration of critical discourse in the twentieth century in terms of this pervasive cinematographic experience. There has arguably been a 'colonisation' of traditional literary criticism by the terminology of film over the last century: visual and spatial metaphors, such as 'framing', 'close ups' and 'angles', along with the more basic categories of montage and focalization. Precisely because of its reifying tendencies (its objectifications of perception, its generic formulae, its apparatus and 'post-humanity', and so on) the cinema was the quintessential narrative and figurative medium of the twentieth century, embodying the technological and cultural logic of 'late capitalism' better than any other medium until television. It correspondingly enjoyed a 'privileged status' in the purview and language of the critical intelligentsia; and this has allowed for film criticism's 'gradual supersession of more traditional aesthetic languages'.[14] Thus, the very terms in which we have come to think of literature and the literary have been ineluctably shaped by the fact, the experience and the language of film and film criticism: the practice of literary education, in primary, secondary and tertiary institutions, is (as Colin MacCabe points out below) invariably 'augmented' by audio-visual, technological components; and the very act of reading seems almost impossible to rid of the temptation to play casting agent and director – designing the sets, arranging the arc lights and cameras, and coaching the performers. This always-already 'adaptedness' of *all* literature (even poetry, as Tony Harrison has repeatedly proven) to the medium of film haunts literary criticism in any number of ways; perhaps most symptomatically when it defensively insists on literature's textual purity. What seems undeniable is that, after cinema, literature has been opened up to a process of ceaseless 'secondary revision' in the light of the visual media, in something like the way that the dramatic text is opened up in the light of the theatre. André Bazin, whose reflections on 'Mixed Cinema' preside over this entire volume, grasped the truth of this media ecology in terms which still await their fullest reckoning:

> The truth is there is here no competition or substitution, rather the adding of a new dimension that the arts had gradually lost from the time of the Reformation on: namely a public.
>   Who will complain of that?[15]

As a mark of the methodological sweep of this book, we begin with two essays which confront the conceptual and institutional impact of visual technology in modern and contemporary 'literary' culture. Colin MacCabe combines theoretical, historical and material perspectives in a broad survey which seeks to demonstrate the absolute embeddedness of visual media in our general culture. MacCabe traces the 'dialectic' of film and literature through key points of interaction and contestation over the last century: Joyce's *Volta* cinematograph and its evident links with *Ulysses*; André Bazin's essay 'In Defence of Mixed Cinema', his declaration of the ongoing interrelation of film and literature, which this volume, and our introduction echoes; the apotheosis of this interrelation in magic realist prose; and the role and status of the visual media in education. According to MacCabe, the impact of the cinematic has been such that our cultural history, our literary forms, genres and institutions, cannot be considered in isolation from the visual media. Instead, their 'impurity' must be embraced, and a thorough integration of cinema studies with more established disciplines should be sought.

If Colin MacCabe is calling for a less ambivalent critical and institutional engagement with visual technology, Laura Marcus traces some of the origins of this cultural ambivalence in the critical reception of cinema in the early decades of the twentieth century. Marcus' essay examines the way in which film was at once acclaimed as an 'entirely new' art and entangled in an anxious preoccupation with history, memory and time. She follows this uncanny thread through a series of exemplary moments in Modernist culture and criticism, ranging from critiques and adaptations of H.G. Wells' futuristic fantasies; to the attempts of Jean Epstein, Béla Balázs and Elie Faure to theorize parallels between the new language of cinema and 'prelapsarian' pictographic languages; and to Dorothy Richardson's resistance to contemporary evolutionary models of technological and psychic development. Marcus elaborates and complicates the frequently asserted connections between cinema and modernity to reveal the complex interaction of the 'modern' and the 'primitive', of humanism and anti-humanism, in early cinematic discourse. Her analysis bears out the radical duality – stressed throughout this volume – of modern culture's response to visual technologies.

In keeping with the parameters set by the first essays in this volume, the extended section on modernist literature picks up on both the creative anxiety and fertility provoked by the 'mixing' of written and visual media. Where Michael North's essay highlights the profoundly paradoxical attitudes of the 'avant-garde' literati to the visual 'language' of cinema – simultaneously internationalist and elitist, transcultural and imperialist – Julian Murphet and Rachel Connor trace the heterodoxical synthesis of different strands of cinematic discourse in the work of specific modernist authors. Murphet argues that Gertrude Stein straddles the conflicting theories of Bergson and Münsterberg, and the technical evolution of cinema from chronophotography to standardized 35mm film, to create a 'cinematic' modernism which was at once American, materialist and avant-garde. Connor analyses the impact of the new visual culture on H.D.'s literary techniques, and sees in her 'narrative cinematics' an attempt to complicate notions of private and public spectatorship, personal and collective experience. The motivation for these formal innovations is thus social and political as well as aesthetic.

The multiplicity of formal responses to cinema within literary modernism testifies to not only to the 'shock' of the new medium in general terms, but the shock of different technical innovations within the filmic medium itself. Whether the introduction of sound, developments in film stock and methods, or early animation techniques, the capacity of these changes to intrude upon, distort, and mutate habitual literary forms cannot be overestimated. This is underscored by Keith Williams' chapter on Joyce's *Ulysses*, the monumental text in the modernist canon. His analysis of the 'Circe' episode in the novel finds striking parallelisms between the 'polymorphous plasticism' of Joyce's 'play for voices' and the surreal distortions and 'morphing' of objects created in contemporary cartoons and film animation. Where Briggs and Burkdall have identified the likely influence of the 'trick films' of Méliès and his French contemporaries, Williams' close analysis of the text reveals animated aspects which could not have been modelled on stop-motion dis/appearance. This suggests that we should expand our sense of the range of Joyce's democratic interest in the multiplicity of forms in contemporary visual media.

The second part of this volume reaches beyond the initial shocks of modernism's engagement with cinema into the ripples and reactions of later modernist and 'postmodernist' writers and commentators. Tim Armstrong's chapter, which analyses the creative collaboration of Len Lye and Laura Riding, is the first of the 'bridges' towards the later period. Armstrong parallels Lye's experiments in creating 'direct' films with Riding's poetry, and reads their joint projects as a reaction against representational notions of film, and thus as a testament to the 'impossibility' of combining film and literature. It thus runs counter to Bazin's idea of 'mixed cinema', and indeed, to the predominant theoretical thrust of this book. Conversely, Eric Robertson traces a whole lifetime of cross-fertilization between the two media, through the work of the avant-garde poet Blaise Cendrars. The essay spans Cendrars' early poetic fascination with cinematic visuality and movement, his collaboration on films such as *J'Accuse*, his creation of a hybrid form of 'cine-novel' and various auditory experiments in the 1950s. Robertson develops an intriguing thesis that Cendrars regarded film as a 'prosthetic' medium which held the power to extend the body's sensory capacity. In the last of our 'bridges', Elena Gualtieri provides a perspective on the still, rather than the moving image. However, her analysis of the impact of photography on constructions of time illuminates the complex adjustments provoked in modern narrative technologies by the visual. In *Camera Lucida*, Roland Barthes associates photography with the grammatical tense of the aorist, and with a linear temporality which collapses duration and memory. Gualtieri traces the different narrative mediations of photography in Robert Musil's *The Man Without Qualities* and Marcel Proust's *In Search of Lost Time*, and argues that while both authors are seeking to undo this linear chronology, they do not bear a purely antagonistic relation to photography: indeed their manipulation of the spatial dimensions of the medium enables them to suspend or open the modernist 'grammar of time'.

The after-life of the modern is traced in the final two essays of the book, where the web of cross-currents between different media, technologies and critical discourses bears witness to the permanent and complex legacy of the visual image in written culture. Both essays are indebted to Gilles Deleuze's theorization of modern cinema, but problematize the limits of his conceptual structure in relation to the heterogeneous forms of recent experiments in literature and film. Lydia Rainford questions Deleuze's readings of Samuel Beckett's television plays as attempts to exceed language and its memories, and aspire to the 'pure image'. She emphasizes the intertextual nature of these plays, and their foregrounding of the processes of technical recording, and argues that Beckett is creating an ironic and impure balance between visual and verbal media which serves to deconstruct classical notions of memorial 'inscription'. Arkady Plotnitsky and Paula Geyh employ deconstruction more directly in their analysis of Tom Phillips' 'artist's book', *A Humument*, and Peter Greenaway's postmodern 'textual' cinema. Both Phillips and Greenaway cross the boundaries of their respective art forms, and are characterized in particular by their incorporation of inscriptive elements and supplements into their visual creations. Reading these artistic practices as demonstrations of what Derrida called 'the end of the book and the beginning of writing', Plotnitsky and Geyh consider them as embodiments of a 'writing image' which supplants Deleuze's concepts of the 'movement-image' and 'time-image' in modern cinema. Thus they herald the formation of a specifically 'postmodern' cinema, and illuminate a further evolution in the relationship between newer visual media and older literary forms.

Notes

1   Quoted by Jay Leyda in 'A Conversation with Leo Tolstoy', in *Kino: A History of the Russian and Soviet Film* (London: Allen & Unwin, 1960), pp. 410-11.

2   Virginia Woolf, 'The Cinema', in *The Captain's Death Bed and other essays* (London: Hogarth Press, 1950), p. 171.

3   Woolf, 'Mr. Bennett and Mrs. Brown', *The Captain's Death Bed*, p. 109.

4   Ezra Pound, 'A Retrospect', in *Literary Essays of Ezra Pound*, ed. T. S. Eliot (London: Faber & Faber, 1954), pp. 11-12.

5   Gertrude Stein, 'Portraits and Repetition', in *Gertrude Stein: Writings 1934-1946* (New York: The Library of America, 1998), pp. 294-295.

6   Ernest Hemingway, *A Farewell to Arms* (London: Vintage, 1999), p. 165.

7   Marshall McLuhan, *Letters of Marshall McLuhan*, eds. Marie Molinaro, Corrine McLuhan and William Toye (Oxford: Oxford University Press, 1987), p. 193.

8   Woolf, 'The Cinema', p. 168.

9   F. Scott Fitzgerald, *The Crack-Up, with other Pieces and Stories* (London: Penguin, 1965), p. 49.

10   Frank O'Hara, 'To the Film Industry in Crisis', *Selected Poems*, ed. Donald Allen (London: Penguin, 1994), p. 99.

11   Ibid., 'Ave Maria', p. 179.

12   Stanley Aronowitz, *Dead Artists, Live Theories* (London: Routledge, 1994), p. 54.

13   Fredric Jameson, 'Introduction', in *Signatures of the Visible* (London: Routledge, 1992), p. 5.

14   Fredric Jameson, 'Allegorizing Hitchcock', in *Signatures of the Visible*, p. 126.

15   André Bazin, 'In Defence of Mixed Cinema', in *What is Cinema?* Vol. 1, trans. Hugh Gray (Berkeley: University of California Press, 1967), p. 75.

Parameters

1

On Impurity: the Dialectics of Cinema and Literature

Colin MacCabe[*]

When we consider the birth of film in 1895, we must recognise that it finds its principal significance for literature as threat and opposition. Whether we consider film from the point of view of the documentary record inaugurated by the Lumière brothers or the peep-show attraction with which Edison started, film very quickly reached audiences on a size and scale that literature could never dream of. As perhaps the most visible evidence of a new commercial mass culture, cinema became for many of the official representatives of literary culture the enemy. If one re-reads I. A. Richards' influential texts of the 1920s, *The Principles of Literary Criticism* (1924) and *Practical Criticism* (1929), one finds that the very justification of literary study is often framed in terms of an antidote to a mass culture of which cinema is the most obvious example. This deep-seated opposition is carried through to the present day. The biggest cheer that the late and unlamented Conservative education minister John Patten ever received at a Conservative Party conference was when he bellowed that he would insist that schoolchildren were taught Shakespeare and not soap-opera. Indeed, this opposition is not simply at work in discourses of cultural criticism or political opportunism. There is a literary sub-genre, the 'Hollywood novel', of which the two best examples are Nathanael West's *The Day of the Locust* (1939) and Evelyn Waugh's *The Loved One* (1948), that finds its fundamental opposition pitting the literary worker or artist against an uncreative industry which addresses a mass audience.[1]

I do not want to suggest that there is nothing whatever in this opposition of individual creativity and mass audience, but I do want to say that the merest

---

[*] I would like to thank Julian Murphet whose work on and contribution to this piece are much more considerable than the title of editor would suggest. In particular the final section which he wrote up from the most scanty of final written notes and verbal comments would more properly be attributed to him than to me although it makes the conclusion that I would wish to have written.

glance at the history of cinema and literature in the twentieth century should tell us that we will have understood nothing if we pit the two media in simple opposition. If cinema announces a death-sentence to 'Literature' – and one of my arguments will certainly suggest that it does – then I also want to advance the paradoxical argument that cinema only lives because of writing and that indeed one of the features of contemporary cinema is that the dominance of writing is becoming more and more marked. This can be read all the way from *Harry Potter* and *The Lord of the Rings* through what Plotnitsky and Geyh in this volume call the 'writing-image' pioneered by Godard and Oshima (*Dear Summer Sister* [1972] would be a central text for any full development of this notion) to a 'writerly' cinema elsewhere exemplified by the elaborate literary textures of *Se7en* (1995) or the 'new adaptations' of Proust (Ruiz) and Wharton (Davies). Indeed if we expand our field to include the new digital technologies, it is becoming harder and harder to say where writing ends and the image begins.

Modernism

Let us start, however, with a brief consideration of the historical record and limit ourselves to cinema and literature. Here, I would want to advance the provocative thesis that it is impossible to give a serious account of any twentieth-century writer without reference to the cinema. This is true at the level of the crudest material history – what successful novelist or dramatist of the last century has not had his works adapted for the cinema? – while there are many from Faulkner to Pinter who have spent a great deal of their time screenwriting. But there is a much deeper level, a level which Jameson has described as the ecology of the media, where cinema has had a more pervasive effect.[2] Jameson's point is that at both the economic and aesthetic level new media are not simply added to an existing discrete set of technologies audiences and forms but that each new form of media reconfigures a tightly integrated cultural-economic ecosystem. Just as it is impossible to think of *Paradise Lost* and its development of the epic without reflecting on the poetic form that it borrowed from the despised theatre, or to think of Hollywood cinema of the fifties without its new rival, television, so the advent of cinema has repercussions across the whole range of aesthetic possibilities from poetry to painting, from dance to theatre. My theme here is literature, and I will focus on narrative fiction; but the net could be cast much wider. If we think only of the pre-eminent poet of the twentieth century, T. S. Eliot, whose comments about the cinema are all of the most patronising and dismissive, it is difficult to imagine *The Waste Land* (1922) without the development of editing and montage within the cinema.[3]

But if Eliot and poetry might be a limit case, Joyce and the novel is a central one. I can think of no moment as transforming of my view of literary history as

Bloomsday 1995, when Luke McKernan and Phil Crossley of the British Film Institute premièred their 'evening at the Volta'.[4] The conventional mix of programming, which combined a Lumière-style documentary of city life with the exotic spectacle of crocodile fishing in Malaya, a slapstick comedy with a historical or literary classic, never forgetting a primitive melodrama, was a revelation. I had long believed that Joyce's life-long engagement with the cinema was of much greater significance than had conventionally been assumed. Walter Benjamin remarks that by the end of the nineteenth century, the routine demands of city life had reached the stage where we were all trapped within the city and that it was the movie camera which, by allowing the possibility of slowing down time until the rigid and predetermined structures of the city were exploded, opened up the possibility of travelling adventurously through the newly spatialised city.[5] The voyage of *Ulysses* (1922) is one that is impossible to conceive without the movie camera.

What the reconstructed Volta programme taught me was that it was not simply in terms of style – one could point to the 'Wandering Rocks' episode as inconceivable without the formal editing of the cinema – but also in terms of subject matter and the mixing of genres that *Ulysses* was indebted to the cinema. And indebted above all to that moment of the cinema which owed least to literature. André Bazin, in 'In Defence of Mixed Cinema', an article to which I shall be returning, makes the telling remark that the history of the cinema and literature is the reverse of what one might expect. A conventional view might have a new art borrowing from the existing arts before it developed topics and styles of its own, but the history of the cinema presents us with the reverse pattern: an initial decade in which the cinema develops independently from the established arts, and then a period of increasing interdependence which has not ceased to grow since Bazin wrote.[6] The cinema that Joyce encountered in Trieste in the first decade of the twentieth century was both a cinema of great commercial vitality and one unbothered by its relation to the traditional arts. The appeal of such an art must have been strong for a Joyce who, unlike Eliot, knew the reality of colonial subjection and could not divorce literature from its political history. If Eliot was to consummate his cultural theories with the assumption of British citizenship, Joyce wished to develop an art which would break with all existing models of citizenship as unacceptable politically as sexually. And where was this hybrid internationalism better exemplified than on the screen of his own Irish cinema, where Italian, French and American films jostled for attention?

One of the delights of these essays on the theme of 'Literature and Visual Technologies' is that they decisively confirm the centrality of cinema to a reading of *Ulysses* and how that centrality involves an international, a global rather than a national context. The awful repressions involved in the construction of the national, analogous to and intensifying of the repressions of monotheism, are unmasked and rejected in 'Circe'. As late in the evening Stephen and Bloom enter the brothel, their faces merge in the mirror and what gazes forth is a paralysed Shakespeare crowned by the cuckold's horns. The temptations to follow the tradition of English literature or invent an alternative Irish literature (the project of those who surround Stephen in the library), must be resisted in an attempt to rewrite literature so that the buried repressions begin to speak – which they do in the Nighttown sequence, which is as much film script as it is expressionist play. In 'Circe', as in the Volta, the polymorphous and protean forms of an international political and sexual unconscious walk the streets like restless spectres: 'Is not this something more than fantasy?' (*Hamlet* I. I. 57) And that 'something more' is in part the international language of cartoons which Keith Williams' '*Ulysses* in Toontown' analyses brilliantly.[7]

There is, however, a deep contradiction within this moment of modernism which applies as much to Eliot's *The Waste Land* or Virginia Woolf's *Mrs Dalloway* (1925) – both written under the immediate influence of *Ulysses*. If the writing is determined to break with the literary language established and developed since the last decades of the sixteenth century; to open the text to a much greater range of registers; to let many more voices speak; and, at the same time, to abandon the notion of a unified authorial voice – then the texts perform these tasks in contexts which are exclusively literary. First in the patronage and small presses in which they first circulated, and then in the university departments of English which found so much of their justification in these texts' ceaseless explication.

Bazin and impurity

In asking ourselves about the relationship between literature and visual technologies, it seems evident that we must begin with Bazin, who not only remains for me the pre-eminent theorist and critic of cinema but whose pre-eminence is in large part due to his determination to understand cinema in relation to the other arts: literature, theatre, painting, etc. Bazin's immediate intellectual context was formed in large measure by the Catholic magazine *Esprit* and it was in *Esprit* in the 1930s that Roger Leenhardt wrote a series of introductory analyses of the cinema which were unusual not simply for their acuity, but also for the fact that, against almost all the dominant intellectual currents of the day, Leenhardt welcomed the advent of sound. For many intellectuals who had early been drawn to the possibilities of the cinema (especially those associated with the journal *Close Up*), the appeal had lain in terms of a new universal art and the purity of the image.[8] The advent of sound dismayed such purists and it was against these purists that Bazin was to write one of his prescient and still under-explored essays, 'In Defence of Mixed Cinema'. Focusing on the relation between cinema and literature, Bazin was to give equal stress to each side of this relationship in the moment of modernism, even if his preferred reference is not to Joyce but to what he calls the American novel, above all the writings of Dos Passos and Hemingway. But Bazin is concerned to repudiate that easy notion of influence, most evident in Dos Passos's explicit use of cinema as a narrative device, which would have literature simply borrowing from the cinema. Bazin's point is much more complicated. He writes:

> Actually, the American novel belongs not so much to the age of the cinema as to a certain vision of the world, a vision influenced doubtless by man's relation with a technical civilization, but whose influence upon the cinema, which is a fruit of this civilization, has been less than on the novel, in spite of the alibis that the film-maker can offer the novelist.[9]

Bazin's point is two-fold: first, that cinema and literature are linked less by any simplistic model of causality, than by a general horizon of technologization and mass production, which the novel expressed technically and formally more quickly than the cinema (expressing it directly in its apparatus); and second that, by and large, when the cinema came into contact with literature and left its beginnings in circus and music hall behind, it was not the contemporary literature of the twentieth century that it turned to for its models and inspiration, but to nineteenth-century forms of realism. To find cinema catching up with the moment of modernism – with the literature of Joyce and Hemingway – Bazin turns to his two great examples of 'mixed' cinema: Welles and Rossellini. In praising these cinematic masters in terms of realism, Bazin was not harking back to the terms of the nineteenth century novel. If his philosophical vocabulary served his thought poorly here, it is crystal clear that the realism to which he is appealing is not the unified master representations of George Eliot or Balzac. The key is in the way in which the representational apparatus of cinema can not be simply subordinated to a human consciousness but offers a genuinely new access to reality.[10] It is this new access which is one of the key elements within the development of modernism and one might imagine Bazin as proposing a moment at which the failure of literary modernism, condemned to its limited circulation, and early commercial cinema, condemned to antique literary models, might be jointly redeemed.

Before returning to the moment of *Citizen Kane* (Welles, 1941) and *Paisá* (Rossellini, 1946), however, we must consider the literary developments of the last fifty years and come to terms with the overlooked fact that literature has been affected by cinema in a much more profound way than the missed encounter of modernism. Much of the development of literary theory and criticism of the past forty years has been determined by that final flowering of late modernism in the

Theory of the Parisian 1960s. Whether we look at Foucault in relation to Beckett and Roussel, Barthes in relation to Brecht and Robbe-Grillet, Derrida in relation to Artaud, and Bataille or Lacan in relation to the Surrealists and Joyce himself, this body of work is unable to engage either with the cinema, which is largely absent from its reflections,[11] or more importantly with the development of the popular literary genres of this century: science fiction, horror, the thriller, which evolve in continuous dialogue with the cinema. Nowhere are these failures more evident than in the development of magic realism. It is no accident that Gabriel García Márquez, whose *Cien años de soledad* (*One Hundred Years of Solitude, 1967)* took developments within the Latin-American novel and delivered them to a global audience, is an eminent writer on and for the cinema. Márquez is himself an emblematic figure who engages with the whole series of forms outside and beyond the book which are provided by the technological, social and economic advances of capitalism in the last century-and-a-half: the newspaper, photography, radio, cinema, television, recorded music. It is in such overlapping institutional spaces, traversing the whole 'ecology of the media', that contemporary cultural production takes place.

It is true of course that many of these new forms were crucial to literary modernism. I have already said that it is impossible to imagine the form of either *Ulysses* or *The Waste Land* without the developments of film editing. Joyce's experiences at the Volta or Eliot's attempts in his most radical experiment, *Sweeney Agonistes* (1932), to tap into the energy of the jazz that he so admired, could both be cited in this context. But both experiments were forestalled by literary modernism's formal decision to return to the comfortable space between the covers of a book. Capitalist culture, however, made no such choice, and writing is now dispersed across a variety of forms, which are unimaginable as recently as the time of the Romantics. Comic book, video game, film script, rap video, cartoon, novelisation: the impure forms proliferate across the technologies, mixing text and image at ever faster velocities.

Early modernism was caught in a constitutive contradiction, attempting to dismantle many of the conventions of Literature while remaining securely within its institutions. It is possible to read that limit clearly in Eliot's failed experiment with *Sweeney Agonistes*, a failure which the later plays merely confirm. But it is much more evident in Joyce. It is an easy moralism to condemn Joyce for his dependence on patrons both direct and indirect, but the political conditions of his time meant that he was without a broad audience to whom he could appeal. The founding of the cinema in Dublin, the notorious dramatic career in Zürich, the almost ludicrous support for the Irish tenor Sullivan – all these gesture towards a very different version of *Finnegans Wake*. In reality, had Joyce stayed in Dublin I have no doubt that as Stephen Dedalus predicted 'the archons of Sinn Fein' would have provided him with a suitable 'noggin of hemlock',[12] and London only offered the insufferable condescensions of the English exemplified by the figure of Haines in *Ulysses*. So Paris and patronage it was. But I often fantasise what could have happened had the British Government stood up to the Unionists and the Curragh mutiny of 1914 and forced through the Fourth Home Rule Bill. It may be that *Finnegans Wake* would have become the multi-media production at the Abbey that I am convinced it might have been.

I want to consider for a moment, if only to reject, an argument which would see in the development of magic realism, and particularly in the writings of Salman Rushdie, a resolution to the contradictions of modernism. Rushdie has himself acknowledged his debt to cinema and the interpenetrations of cinema and literature in referring to *The Wizard of Oz* (1939) as his first literary influence; and his first ten years as a writer were spent working within the advertising industry where word and image enjoy the most immediate relationship (we need think only of the efforts of Leopold Bloom himself, of course). Over and above these biographical facts, *The Satanic Verses* (1988) finds perhaps its major structural opposition in Gibreel Farishta's existence as a voiceless image of Indian cinema and Saladin Chamcha's being as an imageless voice of British television. Indeed the whole of *The Satanic Verses* can be read as a prolonged meditation on the media, from the transition from an oral to a literate culture in seventh-century Arabia, to the differing regimes of sound and image in India and Britain. Indeed the relation of literature to the entire range of contemporary media is one of the constant themes of Rushdie's work: one can think of the centrality of radio to *Midnight's Children* (1981) or painting to *The Moor's Last Sigh* (1995).

A more recent book, *The Ground Beneath Her Feet* (1999) emphasises photojournalism and that great form of the late twentieth century, rock music. The narrator, Rai, a photographer, tells the epic story of his friends Vina and Ormus Cama – the biggest rock band of all time, who blast out of Bombay as VTO. When Vina dies in an earthquake both Ormus and Rai, who have been bound in a triangle of love with Vina, fall into a state of total collapse. And then miraculously Ormus finds Vina's reincarnation in a young woman called Mira, and they mount the greatest rock tour of all time in which the myth of Orpheus and Eurydice is replayed but with, on this occasion, Eurydice truly rescued from hell. The complexity of the book's construction, and particularly its astonishing use of rock lyrics and history, defy easy summary. Suffice to say that Rushdie most fully integrates the science fiction genre which he used for his first novel *Grimus* (1975) into his concerns about identity, place and media on a fully globalised planet. He also makes clearer than ever before his relation to metamorphosis which has been perhaps the central motif of his work. Metamorphosis is not to be understood as a process of a constant change of surfaces, but as the fundamental revelation of our deepest natures (a rather different conception from that of the various transformations in the 'Proteus' and 'Circe' sections of *Ulysses*).

Rushdie's whole body of work, then, and particularly *The Ground Beneath Her Feet*, might seem to achieve a certain resolution of the contradictions of early modernism. The constitutive influence of film, the determining influence of the popular genres of science fiction and the continuous mixing of ancient myth with popular culture might seem like a more successful replay of the experiments of the early twentieth century. Indeed in an almost uncanny replay of the might-have-beens of *Finnegans Wake*, there is even a 'song of the book' with lyrics by Rushdie, performed by the Irish band U2 ('The Ground Beneath Her Feet', 2000). It might be tempting to suggest that the economic and technological developments of capitalism, and its ever growing contradictions, now allow the huge ambitions of modernism to be realised in a properly 'multi-media' form, a true *Gesamtkunstwerk* straddling the full gamut of the media. If such an argument be allowed, it must be one that is fully aware that those contradictions grow ever more acute and that the promise of resolution is not one to which any time scale can be assigned, and not without profound political transformations. In the meantime, the resolution is only fitful and symbolic, a ruse of the system itself whose only function is to draw us into the abstract fold made by the media and commerce. Rushdie himself makes this very clear. The epigraph of the novel is from Rilke:

> Set up no stone to his memory.
> Just let the rose bloom each year for his sake.
> For it is Orpheus. His metamorphosis
> in this one and in this. We should not trouble
>
> about other names. Once and for all
> it's Orpheus when there's singing.[13]

Rilke draws on that part of the myth long after Eurydice has been left behind, when Orpheus is torn to pieces by Maenads – Orpheus's dismembered head floats down the river but continues to sing. The image has been used time and time again to assert the eternal value of poetry. But any temptation to take Rilke's modernist poem as the last word is destroyed by the final paragraph of Rushdie's novel. The narrator has returned to life not simply because of Mira's love but because of his love for Mira's child Tara, and its is she who has the last word.

> Tara's got hold of the zapper. I've never got used to having the tv on at breakfast, but this is an American kid, she's unstoppable. And today, by some fluke, wherever she travels in the cable multiverse she comes up with Ormus and Vina. Maybe it's some sort of VTO weekend and we didn't even know. I don't believe it, Tara says, zapping again and again. I don't buh-leeve it. Oh,

puh-leeze. Is this what's going to happen now, for ever and ever? I thought they were supposed to be dead, but in real life they're just going to go on singing.[14]

Rushdie holds back, at the last, from the confidence of Rilke. The new media, the new children always pose new questions: no consolations of art can be eternal. There is always a new effort of understanding.

The current situation

If we look at the culture, there is no doubt that the new media of the twentieth and twenty-first century and universal education have completely transformed the cultural ecology installed by Gütenberg and the Renaissance humanists. If there can be no truck, of any kind whatsoever, with those who idiotically talk of 'the death of the book', if in some ways the cultural prestige of literacy, and the power that flows from it, has never been more evident, nonetheless the book, in particular, and writing, in general, have been displaced from the position of unquestioned dominance which they enjoyed for four centuries in the West. But our educational system and our disciplines remain unaffected by these transformations.

The enmity between literature and visual technologies that I touched on at the beginning of this paper is embedded institutionally. In England, literature and literacy are the preserve of the Department for Education and Employment, film and media is largely the province of the Department of Culture, Media and Sport. And while a survey conducted by the BFI suggested that there is almost no teaching of pre-twentieth century literature in secondary schools which is not accompanied by audiovisual representations,[15] the fact is that this kind of media remains a kind of guilty secret addressed neither in teacher training nor examination syllabi. What might offer the opportunity for considering two different semiotic systems, and thus allowing children access to genres and language which they find increasingly foreign, is often offered as no more than a plot summary which spares the child the arduous task of reading the book. The continuing division between literature and film is thus rendered invisible in the substitution of one by the other. The ideology which simply opposes the moving image to literacy ignores the ways in which the moving image can be used to develop literacy – what little research has been done on this suggests very different ways of developing children's reading and writing but it falls between all the existing institutional stools.[16]

If it is possible to gloss I. A. Richards' concern with close reading of a text in such a way that it opens up on a whole range of texts beyond the literary, and if his democratic concerns and the drive for Basic English continue to have valuable and timely lessons for us, the curricular and disciplinary victory belongs to Leavis and Eliot, determined to defend the book and its limited audiences against any form of new cultural settlement. From this perspective the American domestication of Derrida and Foucault has been nothing short of disastrous, retaining unchallenged a canon which is not questioned in relation to literacy or technology but in abstract notions of deconstruction and power which are as conservative as they are vacuous. Feminism has a better record here and a book like Margaret Ferguson's *Dido's Daughters* which juxtaposes material from the high cultural canon with the history of education is a real example of the kind of thinking and research which is now necessary; but by and large feminism has supped with the academic devil using an extremely short spoon and has been rewarded with a meagre amount of university pork in exchange for espousing the narrowest conception of gender and renouncing all of its subversive disciplinary ambitions.

The other side of this failure has been the development of film studies. While it is easy to reconstruct the local situations which led to the setting up of separate departments of film, this impulse led exactly away from the reality of cultural mixture and towards a fundamentally misleading construction of film as autonomous. It is true that much valuable work has been done on the history of film but the most valuable of this work, of which Tom Gunning's is *primus inter pares*, has been on the very early history of film where this autonomy reflects a genuine cultural reality.[17]

It is all too easy to criticize the false paths taken within higher education but they find their deepest explanation in the rigorous divorce between university and school which unites the various Western educational systems. If one were genuinely to consider how best to reconfigure the study of text and image it would have to imagine a reconfiguration of film and literary studies which would involve an engagement with education departments which remain the most important political and ideological forces within the humanities and social sciences while receiving scant intellectual or academic valuation from those very humanities and social sciences.

Back to Bazin

Bazin's importance, as Richards before him, lies in the commitment to education; a commitment which in both cases comes out of an experience of war and its clear demonstration of the failures of existing educational systems. It is that commitment which lends such force to the concept of a 'mixed' or 'impure' cinema, valorising cinema not as a purely 'new' form but one which reconfigured the traditional arts of literature, theatre, painting, and any of the other arts by which he insisted cinema had been enriched. Too often, Bazin is reduced in the critical literature to a campaigner against montage, a naïve realist who would claim for the 'purity' of the cinematic image in a temporalised depth of field something like an ontological affinity with Being itself, an approximation of God in a godless age. Yet this easy caricature surely overlooks the very complicated history of formal development which Bazin charts for cinema through its incorporation and negotiation of the other media; a development striving towards the 'realism' he so venerated, to be sure, but a dynamic, contested and agonised development which questions ultimately the very notions of realism drawn from literature.

It needs to be said again that this ecological argument for cinema's impurity was made on behalf of, and because of, sound cinema's eventual transformation into a properly modernist medium. The moment of realization that film is an inherently 'mixed' medium, not a pure one, is also the moment of Welles and Rossellini. It is to these two cherished, emblematic figures that Bazin repeatedly turns both to celebrate the achievement of cinema's profoundest artistic resonance in the *mise en scène* of their best work, and to insist on the ultimately transformative power of modernist literature within the moving image – which has, we shall see, become nothing short of writing itself.

Prior to this moment of modernism, sound cinema, for all its apparent 'modernity' of technique and relatedness to everyday urban life, was in fact lagging well behind literature in the representation of what Bazin called 'the dialectic of appearances and the psychology of behaviour', the true subjects of modernism.[18] 'While it is true' he went on, 'that it relies entirely on the outside world for its objects it has a thousand ways of acting on the appearance of an object so as to eliminate any equivocation and to make of this outward sign one and only one inner reality. The truth is that the vast majority of images on the screen conform to the psychology of the theatre or to the novel of classical analysis.' Classic Hollywood and European sound cinema reverted to that simplistic representational universe of actions and reactions, *milieux* and modes of behaviour, objects and forces, which is the moral geography of realism. Meanwhile the novel, adapting its form to some of the capacities that critical reflection had exposed in the film, was 'fifty years' ahead of the film in its ability to register complex and ambiguous states of affairs, submerged psychological processes, and the real dynamics of the modern world of mass production.

The gap did not close until the 1940s. *Citizen Kane*, about which Bazin spilled more ink than any other film, occupies the place that it does in his value system because of its transcendence of the 'classical analysis' of standardized studio cinema. The great deep shot of Susan Alexander's attempted suicide, with its multilayering of visual and sonorous elements, achieves for Bazin exactly the same breakthrough in the language of the cinema as *Ulysses* did in the language of the novel. Bazin's conception of 'realism' is thus the reverse of what we might expect it to be. The shot in depth, unfragmented by the interventions of montage, does not increase the real's legibility; rather, it lays bare its opacity, its paradoxes, its immanent dialectics. He says,

> depth of focus reintroduced ambiguity into the structure of the image if not of necessity at least as a possibility. Hence it is no exaggeration to say that *Citizen Kane* is unthinkable in any other way but in depth. The uncertainty in which we find ourselves as to the spiritual key or the interpretation we should put on the film is built into the very design of the image.[19]

So it is that the modernist fetish of 'ambiguity' discovers its proper cinematic realization not in the synthetic conjunctions of dialectical montage, but in the film composed of deep sequence shots which yield, as it were, *too much* information for the short-cuts of classical realist analysis; 'a film form that would permit everything to be said without chopping the world up into little fragments, that would reveal the hidden meanings in people and things without disturbing the unity natural to them.'[20] Is this not another way of stating the aesthetic of *Ulysses*, that greatest of modernist novels which makes its artistic revolution by so intensifying and multiplying the strategies of Naturalism that they implode on themselves? In both cases, the demotion of the conjunctive narrative short-cut, the insistence on holding the frame open so that everything creeps in and becomes exposed, is also what allows for the discovery of authorial style, a writerly presence in the text or film that is the very grace note of modernism.

Welles (and Rossellini and Bresson) are thus figured as 'authors' in the strictest sense. The dialectic between film and literature leaves its most elegant trace in the modernism of a film form which has assimilated the lessons of a literary movement that has in turn internalised the lessons of film. Welles's way 'of "writing" a film is undeniably his own. ... the connection between *Citizen Kane* and the novels of Dos Passos is obvious. ... It is fitting that, after having decidedly or indirectly influenced the novel, the cinema should in turn be influenced by it.'[21] The point is that film had eventually earned the freedom to embrace its own impurity, to use its own constitutive pollution by other media, as the means of overcoming its pre-modernist conventions and becoming a generator of styles, signatures, ambiguities, depths. If Welles, according to Bazin, 'doesn't "reinvent filmmaking,"', at least he

> reinvents his own cinema, just as Malraux, Hemingway and Dos Passos reinvent language for their own purposes. Perhaps Welles's endeavor was fully possible only beyond the standardized, transparent cinema of the studio system, in an arena where no more resistance is offered to the artist's intention than to the novelist's pen.[22]

Finally, I don't believe it is possible to overstate the significance of Bazin's extraordinary statement:

> Today we can say that at last the director writes in film. The image – its plastic composition and the way it is set in time, because it is founded on a much higher degree of realism – has at its disposal more means of manipulating reality and of modifying it from within. The film-maker is no longer the competitor of the painter and the playwright, he is, at last, the equal of the novelist.[23]

It is not just that this formulation succinctly captures the very urge of modernism, and exposes its foundation in impurity; but perhaps too it points a way out of the sterile impasse of a postmodernism still trapped in disciplinary straitjackets and formalism. The early 1950s opened a critical space that has, with isolated examples such as Godard, since been summarily closed, a space more conducive to the analysis and evaluation of the postmodern than any number of asinine caricatures of Bazin could hope to deny. We live in impurity, up to our eyes and ears; the question is how to think it. And that thinking will have to mix its media, will have to be fundamentally educational, and will have at its centre the possibilities of film as the democratic art allowing the most complicated mix of a fundamental humanism and a no less fundamental modernism; a mix which can provide the criteria and the concepts to move back in a re-evaluation of the traditional arts.

Notes

1   For more on the Hollywood novel, see Nancy Brooker-Bowers, *The Hollywood Novel and Other Novels about Film, 1912-1982: an annotated bibliography* (London: Garland, 1985), and Anthony Slide, *The Hollywood Novel: a critical guide* (London: McFarland & Co, 1995).

2   For excellent descriptions of this 'ecology', see Fredric Jameson, *The Cultural Turn*, (London: Verso, 1998), pp. 109-113; *The Geopolitical Aestheic* (London: BFI, 1992), pp. 138-143; and *Postmodernism* (London: Verso, 1991), pp. 67-69, 275-77.

3   Ezra Pound's biographer, Noel Stock, makes the following remarks: 'In the process [of reviewing Jean Cocteau's *Poésies 1917-1920*] he [Pound] claimed that Cocteau wrote a poetry that belonged to the city intellect and he went on to air a view which may have had some effect on Eliot when later that year he began to write his long poem *The Waste Land*. "The life of a village is narrative," Pound wrote.... "In a city the visual impressions succeed each other, overlap, overcross, they are cinematographic." One of the distinguishing marks of *The Waste Land* is the succession of scenes and impressions, crossing and overlapping.' Noel Stock, *The Life of Ezra Pound* (Harmondsworth: Penguin, 1974), pp. 296-97.

4   This 'evening' was reprised for the 'Literature and Visual Technologies' conference, and re-screened on the 19th September, 2000 at the Phoenix Cinema, Oxford.

5   Walter Benjamin, 'The Work of Art in the Age of Mechanical Reproduction', in *Illuminations*, trans. Harry Zohn (New York: Schocken, 1968), pp. 236-37.

6   André Bazin, 'In Defence of Mixed Cinema', in *What is Cinema?*, Volume One, trans. Hugh Gray (Berkeley: University of California Press, 1967), pp. 60-62.

7   See the chapter by Keith Williams, 'Vision Animated to Bursting Point', in this volume.

8   See the chapter in this volume by Michael North, 'International Media, International Modernism and the Struggle with Sound', as well as Part 2, 'From Silence to Sound' in *Close Up 1927-1933: Cinema and Modernism*, edited by James Donald, Anne Friedberg and Laura Marcus (London: Cassell, 1998), pp. 79-95.

9   Bazin, op. cit., p. 63.

10   For full elaboration of this argument see 'Balzac and Barthes', in Colin MacCabe, *Theoretical Essays: Film Linguistics Literature* (Manchester University Press, 1985).

11   Roland Barthes' work on Eisenstein notwithstanding, the signal exception to the silence of the *soixante-huitards* towards cinema is of course the extraordinary work of Gilles Deleuze, in *Cinema 1* and *2* and other scattered reflections. The vital importance of this work is in direct ratio to the absence of cinema as a category from most other post-structuralist thought.

12   James Joyce, *Ulysses* (London: Penguin, 1992), p. 243.

13   Rilke, quoted in Salman Rushdie, *The Ground Beneath Her Feet* (London: Jonathan Cape, 1999), p. v.

14   Salman Rushdie, *The Ground Beneath Her Feet*, p. 575.

15   James Learmont and Mollie Sayer, *A Review of Good Practice in Media Education* (London: British Film Institute, 1996).

16   See David Parker, 'You've read the book, now make the film: moving image, print literacy and narrative.' *English in Education* 33 (1): 24-35.

17   Tom Gunning, *D.W. Griffith and the Origins of American Narrative Film: The Years at Biograph* (Urbana: University of Illinois Press, 1991).

18   Bazin, op. cit, p. 62.

19   Ibid., p. 36.

20   Ibid., p. 38.

21   *Bazin at Work: major essays and reviews from the forties and fifties*, trans. Alain Piette and Bert Cardullo (London: Routledge, p. 233)

22   Ibid., p. 237.

23   *What is Cinema?*, pp, 39-40.

2

How Newness Enters the World: the Birth of Cinema and the Origins of Man

Laura Marcus

Exploring the writings about film of the first decades of this century brings into prominence the significance of film's newness for its early commentators. As the film theorist and aesthetician Rudolf Arnheim wrote in 1931:

> For the first time in history a new art form is developing and we can say that we were there. All other arts are as old as humanity, and their origin is as dark as ours. There is no basic difference between pyramids and skyscrapers, between jungle drums and a modern orchestra. Film, however, is entirely new.[1]

In this essay I want to look at some of the ways in which, in the writings about film of the first three or so decades of this century, 'cinema history' overlapped with broader models of historical development and histories of consciousness. That modernist and modernized consciousness is inflected by, and perhaps inseparable from, cinematic consciousness is now a widely held view. I want to flesh out at least one of its aspects by looking more closely at the ways in which writers on the cinema negotiated questions of the 'emergence' of this new form of representation and perception, and at some of the models and fantasies of time, history and consciousness developed on the back of the very terms of 'newness', 'emergence', 'coming into being'. The following quotations from the director Abel Gance, written in 1912, can stand here for many such imaginings. Cinema is to be

> A sixth art where we can evoke in minutes all the great disasters of history and extract from them an immediate objective lesson [...] To plumb the depths of each civilization and construct the glorious scenario that sums it up, embracing all the cycles of all the epochs, finally to have [...] the cinematographic classic that will guide us into a new era – that is one of my highest dreams.[2]

Here the emergence of and entry into the new is predicated on the gathering up of all that has gone before.

In the next sections I look at some 'models' and 'moments' from early writings about film. In the final part of the essay I turn to models of 'emergence' and to history, memory and modernity in the film writings of Dorothy Richardson and to a different fantasy of origin in the writing of the film critic Robert Herring who, like Richardson, contributed to the film journal *Close Up* in the late 1920s and early 1930s.

Time machines

I want to start with an episode which relates in important ways to issues of cinema, time and history – and to film and literature. It can serve as something of a founding moment, although, appropriately, it is a foundation that was not in fact realized. In October 1895, the year of the Lumière brothers' first films, the British film pioneer Robert Paul initiated a patent application for a 'Time Machine' based on H.G. Wells's novel of that name. The patent was for an arrangement of mobile platforms on which the members of the audience would sit, and which would 'move toward and away from a screen onto which still and motion pictures were to be projected'[3]: these would appear to carry the audience into the past and the future. The venture was abandoned because of its cost, and writing over thirty years later Wells states that, until reading Terry Ramsaye's film history, published in 1926, he had forgotten his involvement with the design which, in his words, 'anticipated most of the stock methods and devices of the screen drama'.[4]

Paul clearly saw in Wells's novel *The Time Machine* powerful 'cinematic' elements that could be translated onto screen and into spectacle. These elements include both the fascination with the time-space continuum and with the 'fourth dimension', expressed in the novel as philosophical/ scientific discussion, as well as the Time-Traveller's journeys into the future. These journeys would have found simulated expression in Paul's 'time machine'. The speculations on time, space and motion form the broader cultural context in which not only film but the technology, philosophy and ontology of cinema developed. The significance of Wells's writings for film is contained in a complex nexus of philosophical abstraction, scientific and technological experiment and design, magic and illusionism, storytelling and narration, and futuristic fantasy. The cross-disciplinary and generic nature of Wells's scientific romances (as of so much of his work) has its corollary in the peculiar placing of film as a technology that becomes an 'art'; one not divorced from machine culture but dependent upon it.

Wells has a particular place in film history because for several decades he was seen as one of its most important prophets. In his Preface to L'Estrange Fawcett's *Films: Facts, and Forecasts* (1927), Charlie Chaplin wrote:

it has been from the film itself, a device offering constant provocation to the imagination and senses of rhythm and colour that the sheer strength and crude grandeur of the motion picture industry have come. A giant of limitless powers has been reared, so huge that no one quite knows what to do with it. I, for one, am hopeful that Mr. Wells shall settle the question for us in his next novel.[5]

In 1930, the film theorist Paul Rotha commented:

Mr Wells has written that novel, but the question is no nearer being answered. 'The King Who Was a King' [a discursive film scenario, which was never realized as a film] was full of a thousand ideas, gleaned from a scrutiny of the output of Germany and America, but there was precious little in the book that had direct bearing on the position of the film itself. I believe that Mr. Wells saw and realised the greatness of the film, but did not know quite what to do about it.[6]

Wells may thus have been something of a failed prophet of the cinema, but he retained a significant status in relation to this new art and technology, a status which was substantially based on the admixture in his work and thought of, firstly, experiments with time and secondly, histories of mankind. I now want to turn to such categories and histories, though in several rather different contexts. My first examples are largely drawn from the writings of Jean Epstein, the Polish born, naturalized French film director and theorist, one of a group of French avant-garde film critics and film-makers writing in the late 1910s and 20s, and from the work of the Hungarian Béla Balázs, writing in 1920s and 30s Austria and Germany.

One significant context for Jean Epstein's writing is the anti-narrative project of much French avant-garde film criticism, which resonates in important ways with the focus on cinematic temporalities. Another is Epstein's and his contemporaries' concern with, in Richard Abel's phrase, 'the avant-garde of cinema's creation', which inevitably entailed an occlusion of the histories of commercial cinema.[7]

In an influential article of 1924, 'On Certain Characteristics of *Photogénie*', Jean Epstein asked the following questions:

What aspects of the world are photogenic, then, these aspects to which the cinema must limit itself? I fear the only response I have to offer to so important a question is a premature one. We must not forget that where the theater trails some tens of thousands of centuries of existence behind it, the cinema is a mere twenty-five years old. It is a new enigma. Is it an art? Or less than that? A pictorial language, like the hieroglyphs of ancient Egypt, whose secrets we have scarcely penetrated yet, about which we do not know all that we do not know? Or an unexpected extension to our sense of sight, a sort of telepathy of the eye? Or a challenge to the logic of the universe, since the mechanism of cinema constructs movement by multiplying successive stoppages of celluloid exposed to a ray of light, thus creating mobility through immobility, decisively demonstrating how right was the false reasoning of Zeno of Elea.[8]

I want to think about the implications of Epstein's questions, in the spirit of his assertion that 'People are only barely beginning to realize that an unforeseen art has come into being. One that is absolutely new. We must understand what this represents' (Abel, p. 241).

Epstein's is, at least in part, an exploration of time in the cinema, taking up, as in the previous quotation, the paradoxical relationship between the immobile image and the mobility of the projected film in ways which strongly echo Henri Bergson's early accounts of cinematographic time and movement as models of consciousness, and of time-consciousness in particular. *Photogénie* (which, Epstein writes, escapes definition, though other theorists variously defined it as a form of defamiliarization, as a seeing of ordinary things as if for the first time, and as the power of the camera to transform image-objects) is itself a temporal category for Epstein, defined as 'a value on the order of the second') as a sublime instant, though what it flashes up also exists in an impossible or illusory time, that of the present. As Epstein writes:

> There is no real present [...] today is a yesterday, perhaps old, that brings in the back door a tomorrow, perhaps far-away. The present is an uneasy convention. In the midst of time, it is an exception to time. It escapes the chronometer. You look at your watch; the present strictly speaking is already no longer there, and strictly speaking it is there again, it will always be there from one midnight to the next. I think therefore I was. The future I bursts into past I; the present is only this instantaneous and incessant molt. The present is only a meeting. Cinema is the only art that can represent the present as it is.[9]

In another article – 'Magnification' (1921) – Epstein asserts that 'the photogenic is conjugated in the future and in the imperative. It does not allow for stasis'.[10] The 'moment' (allied to the concept of *photogénie*) is both central to modernist conceptions of time and value, while at the same time 'the moment' or 'the present' is also that which escapes the experiencing self.

What of the other models or questions Epstein poses? The image of the cinema as 'an unexpected extension to our sense of sight, a sort of telepathy of the eye?', is closely paralleled in Freud's assertion in his 'A note upon the mystic writing-pad', that 'all the forms of auxiliary apparatus which we have invented for the improvement or intensification of our sensory functions are built on the same model as the sense organs themselves or portions of them: for instance, spectacles, photographic cameras, trumpets'.[11] This claim provided the basis on which film theorists such as Jean-Louis Baudry and Christian Metz built their theoretical models of the machinery of the cinema, identifying the psychical apparatus with that of the cinematic apparatus.

In asking if cinema is a 'pictorial language, like the hieroglyphs of ancient Egypt, whose secrets we have scarcely penetrated yet, about which we do not know all that we do not know?', Epstein invokes the concept and dream of a 'universal language' which began to flourish in the seventeenth century, was revived in the latter part of the nineteenth century, fuelled by the discoveries and translations of Egyptologists, and subsequently became closely linked with the image of (silent) film as a form of hieroglyphics, a thinking in pictures rather than words.

The dream of recapturing a prelapsarian, universal, pictographic language fed directly into early film aesthetics. Its chief North American exponent was the poet and critic Vachel Lindsay, author of the first book of film theory, *The Art of the Moving Picture*, published in 1915. Here, as in his subsequent writings on cinema, *The Progress and Poetry of the Movies*, and in his poetry, Lindsay spelled out his vision of modern America (with its advertisements, bill-boards, newspaper photographs, sign-writings) as 'a hieroglyphic civilization far nearer to Egypt than to England'.[12] In *The Art of the Moving Picture*, in which he painstakingly analyses a set of Egyptian hieroglyphs, their Roman letter equivalents, and their equivalents in 'the moving-picture alphabet', Lindsay writes that 'It is sometimes out of the oldest dream that the youngest vision is born'.[13]

Epstein's concept of the 'unexpected extension of our sense of sight' suggests a similar notion of an extended visual realm and capacity which is both new – even futuristic – *and* archaic. For Epstein, 'the cinema creates a *particular system of consciousness limited to a single sense*',[14] a model of sensory particularity and evolution perceived more negatively by Virginia Woolf, who dramatized the increasingly troubled relationship between 'eye' and 'brain' in her essay 'The Cinema', and, in 'Walter Sickert: A Conversation', compared the viewers of Sickert's paintings to 'those insects, still said to be found in the primeval forests of South America, in whom the eye is so developed that they are all eye, the body a tuft of feather, serving merely to connect the two great chambers of vision'.[15] As for Woolf and Freud, visual thinking is inextricably linked for early film theorists with 'primitive' mentation.[16] In this sense, and as in the discussion of cinema's 'hieroglyphics', the 'new' art of the film is held to represent both a modernized and an archaic or primitive consciousness.[17] To quote Epstein again:

... cinema is a language, and like all languages it is animistic; it attributes, in other words, a semblance of life to the objects it defines. The more primitive a language, the more marked this animistic tendency. There is no need to stress the extent to which the language of cinema remains primitive in its terms and ideas; so it is hardly surprising that it should endow the objects it is called upon to depict with such intense life. The almost godlike importance assumed in close-ups by parts of the human body, or by the most frigid elements in nature, has often been noted. Through the cinema, a revolver in a drawer, a broken bottle on the ground, an eye isolated by an iris, are elevated to the status of characters in the drama. Being dramatic, they seem alive, as though involved in the evolution of an emotion.

I would even go so far as to say that the cinema is polytheistic and theogonic. Those lives it creates, by summoning objects out of the shadows of indifference into the light of dramatic concern, have little in common with human life. These lives are like the life in charms and amulets, the ominous, tabooed objects of certain primitive religions. If we wish to understand how an animal, a plant, or a stone can inspire respect, fear, or horror, those three most sacred sentiments, I think we must watch them on the screen, living their mysterious, silent lives, alien to the human sensibility.

To things and beings in their most frigid semblance, the cinema thus grants the greatest gift unto death: life. And it confers this life in its highest guise: personality.[18]

The passage opens up an aspect of cinema which was central to its very first commentators. It is also one which is returning to dominate the current critical field: the uncanniness of cinema, its seeming power of life over death, and its abilities to create a total (virtual) world in which, as Woolf wrote in 'The Cinema', 'we have no part'.[19] The return to early film theory and the attempt to recapture its conceptual 'newness' is also an attempt to defamiliarize and to recapture the strangeness, the otherness, of cinema, in the spirit of Freud's model of the unconscious as *'ein Anderer Schauplatz'* – 'another scene'.

Faces and things

The Epstein passage also opens up one of the central paradoxes of early film theory: its combination of humanism and anti-humanism. Cinema, it is claimed, extends the realms of the human into the inanimate world. Yet it also effects a reversal, by which, as many commentators note, the human becomes the inanimate, the inanimate the human. For the psychologist Hugo Münsterberg, whose study *The Film* was published in 1916, 'the central aim of the photoplay [...] must be to picture emotions'.[20] Exploring the representation of 'gestures, actions and facial play', Münsterberg writes that 'The enlargement by the close-up on the screen brings this emotional action of the face to sharpest relief. Or', he adds 'it may show us enlarged a play of the hands in which anger and rage or tender love or jealousy speak in unmistakeable language'.[21] There are clear echoes here of Darwin's *The Expression of the Emotions in Man and Animals* (the first scientific work to rely on photography): more generally, early writing about film contains marked anthropological and physiological dimensions.

The work of Béla Balázs provides the fullest account of the interrelationship between 'the face of man' and 'the face of things', a model in which film gives face to human and non-human entities alike. Balázs, a Hungarian writer and critic who lived and worked in Vienna and Berlin in the 1920s before leaving for the Soviet Union in the early 1930s, published what he called 'the first film dramaturgy',[22] *Der sichtbare mensch* [*The Visible Man*] in 1924, and *Der Geist des Films* in 1930; his *Theory of the Film*, which includes sections from his earlier texts, appeared some two decades later. The overarching thesis of Balázs' study is that:

> The evolution of the human capacity for understanding which was brought about by the art of the film, opened a new chapter in the history of human culture ... We were witnesses not only of the development of a new art but of the development of a new sensibility, a new understanding, a new culture in its public.[23]

Yet this 'new sensibility' is also a return, Balázs argued in *Der sichtbare mensch*, to a time before the coming of print culture, and a consciousness and expressiveness predicated on gesture, play of feature, and bodily movements rather than words. 'The discovery of printing', he writes, 'gradually rendered illegible the faces of men. So much could be read from paper that the method of conveying meaning by facial expression fell into desuetude'. With the coming of film, and, more specifically, the education in 'the rich and colourful language of gesture, movement and facial expression', and in the art of reading faces, which film provides, 'Man has again become visible'.[24]

For Balázs, the 'close-up' – rather than movement or montage – is the central and most significant device of the cinema. For Balázs, whose apprehension of cinematic modernity is often combined with an aesthetic anti-modernism, a critique of avant-gardism and of theories of montage as collision rather than continuity, the power of the close-up seems to lie in its anthropomorphism, its democratizing of being. Whereas on the theatrical stage human beings are far more significant than objects, in (silent) film, he argues, man and object become homogeneous, equally pictures projected onto a screen. 'In significance, intensity and value' he asserts, 'men and things were thus brought on to the same plane'.[25]

At other points, Balázs produces a strongly anthropocentric model of cinematic representation, or at least an oscillation between anthropocentrism and anthropomorphism. As he writes:

When the film close-up strips the veil of our imperceptiveness and insensitivity from the hidden little things and shows us the face of objects, it still shows us man, for what makes objects expressive are the human expressions projected on to them. The objects only reflect our own selves ... When we see the face of things, we do what the ancients did in creating *gods* in man's image and breathing a human soul into them. The close-ups of the film are the creative instruments of this mighty visual anthropomorphism.

What was more important, however, than the discovery of the physiognomy of things, was the discovery of the human face.[26]

As in the work of a number of early film theorists – including Epstein – Balázs makes a connection between 'face' and 'screen'. The face becomes the screen or surface on which emotions are played out. It also becomes the means by which distance, 'the permanent distance from the work of art' (which as, Balázs notes, was 'hitherto a part of the experience of art'), 'fades out of the consciousness of the spectator', and is replaced by identification. 'It is here', Balázs claims, 'that the film manifests its absolute artistic novelty' (rather than, as for other early commentators, its play with time and space).[27]

Jean Epstein's anthropomorphic model, by contrast with that of Balázs, at times appears as an anti-humanism in its insistence on the otherness with which cinema endows its objects. His account refers to a primitive animism, but it could also lead to a way of thinking along the lines with which Michel Foucault ended *The Order of Things*. The anthropocentrisms and anthropomorphisms of early film writing both extend 'man' – draw his face everywhere – and disperse or displace him by fragmenting 'face' in the close-up or by giving 'personality', in Epstein's phrase, to those 'mysterious, silent lives, alien to the human sensibility'.[28]

Origins

I now want to turn to some models of cinematic origin and their imagined relationship to the origins of humanity. Balázs writes that 'the new theme which the new means of expression of film art revealed was not a hurricane at sea or the eruption of a volcano: it was perhaps a solitary tear slowly welling up in the corner of a human eye'.[29] If, for Balázs, the origin and essence of cinema are to be found in the birth of a tear, echoing Jean Epstein's focus on 'the evolution of an emotion', for the art historian and film theorist Elie Faure and for Virginia Woolf, cinema's birth is imaged precisely by the 'eruption of a volcano'.

Faure's *The Art of Cineplastics* (1920/23) suggests a model of *photogénie* as shock or 'commotion' and as recognition, 'in a flash', as he describes the moment in which he saw through or beyond the plot and melodrama of the film he was watching and achieved pure visual awareness: 'The revelation of what the cinema of the future can be came to me one day: I retain an exact memory of it, of the commotion that I experience when I observed, in a flash, the magnificence there was in the relationship of a piece of black clothing to the grey wall of an inn'.[30] Faure also defines film as a 'plastic' art in the terms of the Kantian sublime: film sets the mind in motion through an alternation between construction and negation. Referring to the 'new plastic impressions' that he received at the cinema, Faure writes:

> Their elements, their complexity which varies and winds in a continuous movement, the constantly unexpected things imposed on the work by its mobile composition, ceaselessly renewed, ceaselessly broken and remade, fading away and reviving and breaking down, monumental for one flashing instant, impressionistic the second following – all this constitutes a phenomenon too radically new for us to even dream of classing it with painting, or with sculpture, or with the dance, least of all with the modern theatre. It is an unknown art that is beginning, one that to-day is as far perhaps from what it will be a century hence, as the Negro orchestra, composed of a tom-tom, a bugle, a string across a calabash, and a whistle, is from a symphony composed and conducted by Beethoven.[31]

Faure's temporalities serve to equate and synchronize modernity and 'the primitive', as the now and the new of cinema's beginnings are imagined, from the vantage-point of a projected future, in the terms of 'the Negro orchestra', represented as the 'savage' origin of musical creation. The ambivalences of modernist primitivism are revealed, as Faure both seeks to put a distance between cinema's birth and its promise, and celebrates, as does Vachel Lindsay, an image of America as both modern and primitive:

> The American film is a new art, full of immense perspectives, full of the promise of a great future.... For the Americans are primitive and at the same time barbarous, which accounts for the strength and vitality which they infuse into the cinema.[32]

Exploring the time-space dimensions of cinematic representation, and the possibilities of a form of conceptual time-travel, Faure writes that 'we may easily imagine an expanded cineplastic art which shall be no more than an architecture of the idea'. Faure presents the analogy of 'the great eruption of Vesuvius' to illustrate his notion of a 'symbolic form of that grandiose art of which in the cinema we now perceive the germ ... namely: a great moving construction ceaselessly reborn of itself under our eyes by virtue of its inner forces alone'.[33] Here he strikingly echoes Virginia Woolf's 'The Cinema', from her focus on new relations of time and space, to the image of thoughts and emotions made visible 'as smoke can be seen pouring from Vesuvius'.[34]

Elsewhere in Faure's passage on cineplastics, cinema history (a history beginning to unfold) is imagined as a progression from the writing on the wall/screen as (thin) inscription, to the thickness of gesture ('a series of successive movements'), and finally to the future creation of a visual symphony understood as the projection – a throwing out or forth – of a whole being, a 'whole nature'. This trajectory is intertwined with Faure's invocation of a shift from an introspective, individualistic, and, perhaps, 'decadent' literary culture to the 'mass' and 'monumental' arts of sculpture, drama, architecture – and film.[35] Those beings who will project themselves forth are, perhaps, to be understood as the *Ubermenschen* of a future society.

Faure's aesthetics of synthesis, and his uses of the orchestral or symphonic analogy, which he shares with a number of writers on film at this time, draw on the Wagnerian concept of the *Gesamtkunstwerk* (total work of art). Faure's model of 'cineplastics' (cinema as the representation of forms either in repose or in movement), also marks the shift from a focus on *photogénie* in French film criticism of the 1920s as, in Richard Abel's words, 'the singularly transformative nature of the film image', to '*cinégraphie*' as 'the rhythmic principles governing the placement of film images', often analogized as orchestral accompaniment.[36] The 'musical analogy' in avant-garde French film criticism, which seems to have become particularly charged in the period immediately before the coming of sound film, has been explored by David Bordwell: its importance lies in part for him in its move towards semiotic and structural principles in film discourse.[37] The musical analogy is also clearly linked to modernist aesthetic principles, in which all art is held to aspire to the condition of music.

I would like to suggest a further link and to think of the orchestral metaphor as something of a founding image for cinema. It is there in one of the very first discursive works on film by the 'founders' of cinema: W.K.L. and Antonia Dickson's *History of the Kinetograph, Kinetoscope and Kinetophonograph* of 1895, with a preface by Thomas Edison. In his preface, Edison writes of his vision of a future cinema in which 'grand opera can be given at the Metropolitan Opera House at New York without any material change from the original, and with artists and musicians long since dead'. The Dicksons' model of 'the shadowy histrionics of the near future' culminates in a total symphony, all of whose effects of sight and sound will be embraced in the kinetoscopic drama, and yet of that living, breathing, moving throng, not one will be encased in a material frame. 'A company of ghosts, playing to spectral music.'[38] For Edison and Dickson, the plenitude of cinema – analogized or literalized as orchestral performance – co-exists with its spectrality, and its uncanny powers to bring the dead to life. The motif, perhaps, continues to haunt the later model of 'cinegraphie' as an orchestration of rhythmic components.

The novelist Dorothy Richardson's embedded history of cinematic emergence begins, by contrast with that of Elie Faure, not with the volcanic eruption but with the tide or wave. In her very first 'Continuous Performance' article for *Close Up*, Richardson describes a visit to a North London picture palace:

> It was a Monday and therefore a new picture. But it was also washday, and yet the scattered audience was composed almost entirely of mothers [...] It was a new audience, born within the last few months [...]. Watching these I took comfort. At last the world of entertainment had provided for a few pence, tea thrown in, a sanctuary for mothers, an escape from the everlasting qui vive into eternity on a Monday afternoon.[39]

'The first scene', Richardson continues, 'was a tide, frothing in over the small beach of a sandy cove, and for some time we were allowed to watch the coming and going of those foamy waves, to the sound of a slow waltz, without the disturbance of incident'.

The wave breaking on the shore was a highly significant image for early cinema. We know from contemporary descriptions that it was the subject of early Vitascope performances in the mid 1890s:

> Next came a picture of a tumbling surf on the Jersey shore. The waves were high and boisterous as they dashed one after the other in their rush for the sandy beach over which they ebbed and flowed. The white crests of the waves and the huge volume of water were true to life. Only the roar of the surf was needed to make the illusion perfect.[40]

For the first film-makers, the wave breaking on the shore became a way, perhaps, of figuring both the static or repetitive and the dynamic aspects of the cinematic medium. Richardson deploys the image of the wave – a moving threshold, the edge that never stops – primarily when she is figuring transitions in the filmic medium: from spectacle to narrative film in the passage quoted above, and from silent to sound film in a later article. Whereas the commentator on the Vitascope film of waves breaking on the shore suggests that sound – 'the roar of the surf' – would make the illusion perfect, Richardson writes that:

> Life's 'great moments' are silent. Related to them, the soundful moments may be compared to the falling of the crest of a wave that has stood poised in light, translucent, for its great moment before the crash and dispersal. To this

peculiar intensity of being, to each man's individual intensity of being, the silent film, with musical accompaniment, can translate him.[41]

Richardson's film writing thus deploys the film image to figure a kind of cinema history: one particularly attentive to transitions, while also seeking to complicate linear narrative, to break up sequence, and to make memory – in which film now plays a crucial role – a central aspect of historicity. Adopting the position of one both observing and participating in the emergence of a new form of consciousness, she also produces a complex model of development in which cognition is also recognition. In discussing, for example, the use of 'slow motion', she writes that:

> we may take courage to assume that from the first, behind the laughter, recognition was there and has grown. If now it is present, it was there from the first, for without its work there would be no second seeing. Each seeing would have been a first and the laughter would have continued.[42]

This complication of the question of origins re-emerges in her discussions of the question of the silent to sound 'transition', in which the silent film is presented as the gift of the move to sound, brought into (new) being by what succeeds it.

One of the elements of Richardson's 'cinema theory' is an embedded, continuously retranscribed model of film history which both produces and resists accounts of the entry of newness into the world, and which seeks to construct a history of consciousness neither wholly determined by nor distinct from a history of technologies. If on the one hand, her film writings conjure up a community of spectators, often female, becoming educated for modernity by 'the movies' – 'The only thing and everything. And here we all are, as never before. What will it do with us?'[43] – on the other she resists evolutionary models of development and 'becoming'.

Writing after the coming of sound of the 'treasure laid up' of 'all the silent films we had seen, massed together in the manner of a single experience', she defines this strange 'memory' as 'at the least, past, present and future powerfully combined'.[44] Such a model of historical consciousness is redemptive, in that it entails, in ways similiar to those in which Miriam Hansen has described Walter Benjamin's temporalities, a utopian sense of a restoration of past, present; and, anachronistically, future.[45]

Epilogue

In 'A New Cinema, Magic and the Avant-Garde', Robert Herring – one of the central contributors to the journal *Close Up* – explores the question of the 'magic' of the cinema as a relation to 'reality' – in particular, the realities of light and movement. He is critical of a self-proclaimed 'avant-garde' cinema whose experiments in distortion and abstraction disregard the abstract nature of all cinematic representations. The most conventional of narrative films is also, Herring suggests, a patterning of light and shadow moving in time: 'and so there is a little magic everywhere you see a cinema'.[46]

For Herring, cinematic 'magic' inheres primarily in projection:

> There is the screen, and you know the projector is at the back of you. Overhead is the beam of light which links the two. Look up. See it spread out. It is wider and thinner. Its fingers twitch, they spread in blessing or they convulse in terror. They tap you lightly or they drag you in. Magic fingers writing on the wall, and able to become at will ... a sword or an acetylene drill, a plume or waterfall. But most of all they are an Aaron's rod flowering on the wall opposite, black glass and crystal flowers ... Only now and again the rod becomes a snake, and whose films are those we know.
>
> ... You need not be a chamber to be haunted, nor need you own the Roxy to let loose the spirit of cinema on yourself. You can hire or buy or get on the easy system, a projector. You then have, on the occasions on which it works, people walking on your own opposite wall. By moving your fingers before the beam, you interrupt them; by walking before it, your body absorbs them. You hold them, you can let them go.[47]

Herring's models of the destruction of the 'aura' (the distance between spectator and spectacle) and of the blurring of a body/world division as the spectator inserts him or herself into the spectacle are characteristic of modernized vision and its altered perceptions of subject/object relationships.

In the article, Herring moves from the passages quoted above to imagining a future for cinema, an 'avantgarde', in which images would be rendered visible without the mediation of the screen, bodies and beings becoming solid projections of themselves. There is 'no reason', Herring writes, 'why [man] should not create himself in motion and speech, moving in the patterns of his creation'. He reaches this by way of a discussion of recorded voice:

> Now. We know sound waves can be caught on wax. The human voice recorded. Up till now, it has only been possible to reproduce it. That is very thrilling of course, that the noise made by a person some time ago can be let out again later, it is doing things with time. But it remains reproduction. You can't get voice pure, but reproduced voice. But suppose there is a machine which really lets the living voice itself out into the room ... Could not the avant people, the real ones, do the same with the visual image? Can we not see

people as we shall soon hear them? At present there is the screen and gramophone. But the gramophone will soon cease to insist itself any more than the person's presence detracts from the voice. If the voice can leave this machine, as I know it can, and be itself, why should not the visual image leave the screen, why should we not do without screens? They are giving stereoscopy to the image, giving them depth and solidity. They will be able to be brought into the room, as the voice is. It is after all, absurd to be tied down to a screen.

First what [man] did can survive, now what he is. First the work of his hands, work of brain, the effects of his hands and brain. But all still and mute. Then his voice could be kept, and his image could be kept. Moving. Now they will have to be detached, and instead of him contenting himself with making dolls and statues and music he could only hear as it was being played, he will have these images in which sound and sight meet, detached so to speak from their owners. Man making man, of a kind. ... There is logically ... no reason why he should not ultimately create himself in motion and speech, moving in the patterns of his creation ...[48]

Herring's article thus moves from projection as the *inscription* of images, symbols and hieroglyphics by 'magic fingers writing on the wall' to projection as the *patterning of light* which creates cinematic reality, by means of a lamp allied to that of Aladdin and, finally, to *projection* as a throwing-forth of the self firstly, by way of the insertion of the spectator's body into the spectacle ('You hold them, you can let them go') and, finally, by the construction of three-dimensional moving-image-beings. I now want to situate these dimensions of Herring's article in two contexts: firstly, as part of a history of early film criticism and secondly, as the product of a distinct biographical and cultural moment.

One striking aspect of early film criticism and theory is the extent to which paradigms of and fantasies about the new art of the cinema emerging from very diverse contexts share very similar language and images. Herring's seemingly idiosyncratic model in his 'Magic' article interestingly echoes, for example, Faure's *The Art of Cineplastics* (discussed above), describing a similar conceptual trajectory. In Faure's account, I argued, cinema history is imagined as a progression from the writing on the wall/screen as (thin) inscription, to the thickness of gesture and finally to the future creation of a visual symphony understood as the projection – a throwing out or forth – of a whole being, a 'whole nature'. I asked whether those beings who would project themselves forth were to be understood as the *Übermenschen* of a future society. In *The Meaning of Meaning* C. K. Ogden (who is cited by Herring in an important letter to Bryher[49]) and I. A. Richards took as one of their many philosophical targets what they called Word-Magic: a 'primitive' 'instinctive attitude to words as natural containers of power'.[50] It is a nice irony that magic should return so vividly – at least in Herring's account – in the realms of sound and the power of virtual presence.

Herring's narrative (describing a visit to Ogden's house in the company of Paul Robeson) contains this passage:

> There were records and records and a cabinet of records ... Two odd square machines in opposite corners. Robeson was in a black suit and a black hat and a shirt of perfectly Spanish whiteness. He is 9 feet high: and the room was low and white. There were stacks of gramophone records in albums and some in envelopes. Ogden played a machine. It was the voice in the room. It was *not* a reproduction, but a release. Robeson was in the room; Robeson's voice was in the room. Robeson stood and listened.

This is an echo of an earlier technological fantasy: Villiers de L'Isle Adam's novel *L'Eve future* (1880), in which a Lord Ewald meets the female automaton/Android Hadaly, invented by a fictionalized Thomas Edison (the inventor of the phonograph) in her subterranean chambers. The link is the way in which new technologies bring forward Frankensteinian fantasies of origins and of newly created, automatic or virtual beings; the difference lies in the fact that the New Woman, and the representation of technology as an (artificial) female, has given way to the New Man – 9 feet high in the low white room. Robeson, a study in black and white, like a film, is doubly present, not least because his voice *is* his presence, and thus Herring is able to imagine newly created visible beings added to sonorous/aural presence. Here sight is added to sound, rather than sound to sight. The inversion (which is also a 'true' history, in that the phonograph precedes the kinetoscope and leads from thence to the cinema) reminds us that this is a critical period in the transition from silent to sound cinema, taking place a year before the *Close Up* group made its silent film *Borderline* – in which Herring acted the part of a pianist and Robeson appeared as Pete (a Negro), shot as if he were indeed nine feet high but, of course, voiceless. Representations of 'the Negro' in *Borderline* as both the New Man of the cinema and the primitive Other of modernism also reveal the profound imbrication of fantasies, and fears, of origins and of the future with modernity's relationship to the technologies which both shape and are shaped by it.

Notes

1   Rudolf Arnheim, *Film Essays and Criticism*, trans. Brenda Benthien (Madison: University of Wisconsin Press, 1997), p. 13.

2   Abel Gance, 'A Sixth Art' (1912), in Richard Abel, *French Film Theory and Criticism*, Volume 1: 1907-1929 (Princeton, NJ: Princeton University Press, 1988), p. 67.

3   Raymond Fielding, 'Hale's Tours: Ultrarealism in the Pre-1910 Motion Picture', in John L. Fell (ed.), *Film Before Griffith* (Berkeley and Los Angeles: University of California Press, 1983), pp. 116-7.

4   H.G.Wells, *The King who was a King: the book of a film* (London: Benn, 1929), p. 10.

5   Charlie Chaplin, 'Foreword', in L'Estrange Fawcett, *Films: Facts and Forecasts* (London: Geoffrey Bles, 1927), pp. v-vi.

6   Paul Rotha, *The Film Till Now* (London: Cape, 1930), p. 57.

7   In Richard Abel, *French Cinema: The First Wave, 1915-1929* (Princeton NJ: Princeton University Press, 1984), p. 241.

8   In Abel, *French Film Theory and Criticism*, Vol. 1, p. 315.

9   Jean Epstein, *Écrits sur le cinéma, 1921-1953* (Paris: Seghers, 1974), pp. 179-80. Quoted by Leo Charney, in *Empty Moments: Cinema, Modernity and Drift* (Durham: Duke University Press, 1998), p. 155.

10   In Abel, *French Film Theory and Criticism*, 1, p. 236.

11   *Standard Edition of the Complete Psychological Works of Sigmund Freud*, Vol. 19 (London: The Hogarth Press and the Institute of Psychoanalysis, 1958), p. 228.

12   Vachel Lindsay, *The Art of the Moving Picture* (New York: Liveright, 1970), p. 22.

13   Ibid., p. 288.

14   Epstein, 'Magnification', in Abel, *French Film Theory and Criticism* Vol. 1, p. 240.

15   Virginia Woolf, 'Walter Sickert', in *The Captain's Death Bed and Other Essays* (London: The Hogarth Press, 1981), p. 173.

16   In *The Interpretation of Dreams*, for example, Freud explores the 'regression' into visuality effected by the dream-work. He also argues that language systems evolve from 'primitive' concrete images to the words which replace them. See my discussion of this aspect of Freudian theory, in Laura Marcus (ed.), *Sigmund Freud's The Interpretation of Dreams: New Interdisciplinary Essays* (Manchester: Manchester University Press, 1999), p. 23.

17   See Rachel Moore's excellent discussion of the fascination with the magical and the primitive in early film theory in *Savage Theory: Cinema as Modern Magic* (Durham: Duke University Press, 2000). Although my discussion overlaps at points with Moore's, her book was in fact published after this article was written.

18   Epstein, in Abel, *French Film Theory and Criticism*, 1, pp. 316-7.

19   Virginia Woolf, 'The Cinema' (1926), *The Captain's Death Bed*, p. 167.

20   Hugo Münsterberg, *The Film: A psychological study* (New York: Dover, 1970), p. 48.

21   Ibid, p. 48.

22   Béla Balázs, quoted in Sabine Hake, *The Cinema's Third Machine* (Lincoln: University of Nebraska Press, 1993), p. 222.

23   Béla Balázs, *Theory of the Film*, trans. Edith Bone (London: Dobson, 1952), p. 34.

24 Ibid., p. 41.

25 Ibid., p. 58.

26 Ibid., p. 60.

27 Ibid., p. 48.

28 There are clearly gendered questions here – Balázs plays out his concept of 'microphysiognomy' on the faces of Asta Nielson and Lilian Gish – but the universalistic discourse also demands the generic 'man'.

29 Balázs, *Theory of the Film*, p. 31.

30 Elie Faure, *The Art of Cineplastics*, trans. Walter Pach (Boston: The Four Seas Company, 1923), p. 25.

31 Ibid., p. 27.

32 Ibid., p. 32.

33 Ibid., pp. 39-41.

34 Woolf, *The Captain's Death Bed*, p. 171.

35 Faure, *The Art of Cineplastics*, pp. 40-42.

36 Abel, *French Film Theory and Criticism*, Vol. 1, p. 215.

37 David Bordwell, 'The Musical Analogy', *Yale French Studies* 60, 1980, pp. 141-56.

38 W.K.L. Dickson and Antonia Dickson, *History of the Kinetograph, Kinetoscope and Kinetophonograph* (Twickenham, Middlesex, 1895), p. 50.

39 Dorothy Richardson, 'Continuous Performance', *Close Up* Vol. 1, no. 1, July 1927, reprinted in *Close Up 1927-33: Cinema and Modernism*, eds. James Donald, Anne Friedberg and Laura Marcus (London: Cassell, 1998), pp. 160-1.

40 *New York Herald*, April 24th, 1896, quoted in E.W and M. M. Robson, *The Film Answers Back* (London: Bodley Head, 1939), pp. 27-8.

41 Richardson, 'A Tear for Lycidas', *Close Up 1927-33: Cinema and Modernism*, p. 200.

42 Richardson, 'Slow Motion', *Close Up 1927-33: Cinema and Modernism*, p. 182.

43 Richardson, 'The Increasing Congregation', *Close Up 1927-33: Cinema and Modernism*, p. 171.

44 Richardson, 'A Tear for Lycidas', *Close Up 1927-33: Cinema and Modernism*, p. 196.

45 See Miriam Hansen, 'Kracauer's Early Writings on Film and Mass Culture', *New German Critique* 54, Fall 1991, p. 53.

46 Robert Herring, 'A New Cinema, Magic and the Avant-Garde', *Close Up 1927-33: Cinema and Modernism*, p. 51.

47 Ibid., p. 54.

48 Ibid., pp. 55-6.

49 Beinecke Library, Yale University, New Haven CT. Herring, Robert – Correspondence with Bryher. Gen Mss 97, Box 18.

50 C.K.Ogden and I.A.Richards, *The Meaning of Meaning* (London: Kegan Paul, 1930), p. 225.

Modernisms

3

International Media, International Modernism, and the Struggle with Sound

Michael North

I

An early episode in the history of globalization took place in the fall of 1927 with the première of what was commonly referred to at the time as 'the most important picture in the history of the movies.'[1] The picture in question was F. W. Murnau's *Sunrise*, and one source of its contemporary prestige was the fact that it could be billed as the 'first international' film production.[2] It's a little hard at this remove to see what right *Sunrise* had to such a claim, for though it was Murnau's first American film, other German directors had been working in Hollywood for some time. But Murnau brought to Hollywood a film technique that was so conspicuously different from that of most American studios that it was received as if it were another language.[3] Low-key lighting, 'free' camera movement, and a complete avoidance of inter-titles had made Murnau's final German production, *Der letze Mann* (1924), a sensation, not just in Hollywood but also among amateur film makers and the aesthetic avant-garde.[4] By bringing German expressionism to Hollywood, therefore, Murnau was also bringing one of the most conspicuous of avant-garde film techniques to a big-budget, mass market production. One of the borders crossed by *Sunrise* on its way to becoming the 'first international' film was that between the avant-garde and modern mass culture.[5]

Whatever claim *Sunrise* may have had as 'the most important picture in the history of the movies' was probably based, however, on the crossing of a different border, for it was the first original feature to appear with Fox's Movietone sound system. At this point in the evolution of the Movietone system, Fox had not incorporated speech into any of its films, but *Sunrise* was notable because it came equipped with a recorded, synchronized, professionally arranged orchestral score that was actually crafted at one or two key points to take the place of speech.[6] To show that the Movietone system was capable of rendering speech itself, Fox added to the premiere of *Sunrise* a newsreel that featured Benito Mussolini delivering a 'message of friendship' to the American film audience in both Italian and English.[7]

The première of *Sunrise* thus seems a richly ambiguous episode in the history of international modernism, in part because the internationalism it defines is of so many different kinds. First is the American cultural hegemony exemplified by the reach of Hollywood, which assumed even in 1927 that anyone of artistic consequence would end up sooner or later in Los Angeles. If Murnau's removal to Hollywood exemplifies the inevitability with which film came to serve the cultural presumptions of the United States, however, the films he made at this time also illustrate a very different kind of internationalism. The complete removal of the inter-titles from *Der letze Mann* seemed to many a thrilling fulfillment of film's promise as an international art language, 'the only universal, common world language understood by all,' as Béla Balázs put it in 1923.[8] In this analysis, film took part in the search for a universal language of visual forms, a search so much a part of international modernism that the paintings, designs, and buildings inspired by it still seem the highest expressions of 'high modernism.'

These two very different international movements collide with a third in 1927 with the arrival of sound. An important part of the inevitable social progress promised by science was the final annihilation of distance, as every corner of the globe could be equipped to see and hear virtually anything happening in any other corner. The final convergence of visual and aural technologies, heretofore separated into the distinct realms of telephone, gramophone, and moving pictures, also seemed inevitably to entail the collapse of time and space, which humankind had finally made irrelevant.[9] This internationalism, for all its utopian promise, begins to converge on the fourth in evidence at the première of Murnau's *Sunrise*, the totalitarianism of Mussolini and his fascists. Mussolini was so entranced by film that he started his own production company, which at least planned a feature based on the *Divine Comedy*. For political addresses, he is said to have preferred film to live appearance because it cut down on the risks of assassination, but just in case he also taped a 900-foot Fox Movietone statement to be shown throughout Italy in the event of his death.[10] In this case, the annihilation of time and space seems to coincide with the annihilation of human freedom, as film gives Mussolini a kind of ubiquity only dreamed of by earlier tyrants.

The cultural imperialism of the American mass media, international modernism, the scientific industrialization of the senses, and modern totalitarianism, all touch and overlap at many other points than the première of one film in 1927, and yet they are in conflict as well, particularly where sound is concerned. For sound was not by any means an unambiguous addition to the technological sensorium. While it seemed the last important step in constructing a fully represented, fully recorded humanity, and thus was publicized as finally making ubiquitous communication possible, it also brought cultural specificity, in the form of language, back into film and thus into the visual art that meant so much to modernism. This is a revealing, if heretofore obscure, moment in the history of aesthetic modernism, for the arrival of sound illuminates the way in which modernism framed its own internationalism in relation to that so recently announced by the new media.

II

The addition of sound to American film was not by any means the instantaneous conversion experience that appears in Hollywood mythologies of the time. Sound arrived slowly, gradually, and in a number of different forms, aesthetic and technological, and for a number of years silent films continued to be made alongside talkies. There was a good deal of opposition, even within the studios, to what Stanley Cavell has called 'the loss of silence.'[11] Directors such as Sam Taylor, Herbert Brenon, and Fred Niblo, stars such as Lilian Gish, Lon Chaney, and Charlie Chaplin, and even studio executives, including Joseph Schenck of United Artists and Monta Bell of Paramount, expressed strong conservative distrust of the film voice.[12] As late as the première of Chaplin's *City Lights* in 1931 there was some nostalgic hope in Hollywood that the silent film might be revived.[13]

For such film industry die-hards, one of the strongest practical arguments against sound was offered by what was commonly called the 'foreign problem,' a whole set of difficulties brought about by the fact that language was now to be integrated into a film in spoken form, not added on later in written form.[14] The 'foreign problem' had at least two distinct aspects: with the integration of English dialogue, American films were suddenly much more difficult to export, not just because of audience incomprehension but also because of governmental opposition in many countries to the invasion of English;[15] and, on the other hand, it was also more difficult to follow the time-honored Hollywood practice of importing European film talent, which often spoke English, if at all, with accents the American public found objectionable or comic.[16] In the late 20s and early 30s Hollywood experimented with a number of different solutions to these problems. For a few years, most studios actually made, either here or in Europe, multiple versions of most feature films, sometimes in as many as five different languages. Props, costumes, and scenery would be reused, with translated dialogue delivered by native-speaking actors, some of whom established brief careers standing in for established Hollywood stars.[17] Outside the industry other, more utopian, solutions were suggested, not the least impractical of which, by any means, was the suggestion that Esperanto sub-titles might be added to all films, with short lessons in Esperanto to be given after the newsreel.[18] One enterprising aesthete suggested that films might achieve international intelligibility by speaking in the Esperanto currently being invented by James Joyce in his *Work in Progress*, which ultimately became *Finnegans Wake*.[19] But the most utopian of all solutions was suggested by Rudolf Arnheim in 1930, when he predicted that movie-goers in all countries would begin to learn other languages in order to understand the films they loved: 'To speak several languages will become just as usual as reading and writing; and in consequence the various languages will soon grow to have a great deal in common. An important advance will thereby have been made towards universal peace.'[20]

What actually happened, of course, was a good deal messier and less utopian. After a brief reverse, Hollywood ultimately reasserted its domination of the world film market, partly by sub-titles, partly by dubbing, partly by using stars whose voices attracted a world-wide audience whether they were intelligible or not, and ultimately by helping to spread English as a second language. Film industries in many other countries survived and became self-sufficient, though there were complicated disputes about the rights to sound technology, which U.S. companies tried to restrict. Most European film stars managed to make themselves heard in English, but European films were more or less banished from general distribution in the U.S.[21] The same fate befell amateur film-makers in the United States and Great Britain, few of whom had the money or the expertise to convert to sound.[22] The result was a general stratification, at least of the U.S. film world, with the foreign and the avant-garde banished together to the commercial periphery and fewer opportunities for the general audience to see movies that did not conform to the classical Hollywood model.[23]

For this reason, among others, sound was greeted with great disdain by those in the literary world who followed film. As Donald Crafton puts it, 'sound came just when critics were elevating the silent cinema to "art," and it was difficult for them to conceive how talking was conducive to the kind of filmmaking they revered....[24] The talkies, according to one such critic, Francis Ambrière, writing in the little magazine *Tambour* in 1930, are 'the negation of cinematic art' and a violation of 'the spirit of our times.'[25] Of course, this put certain writers in the paradoxical position of opposing the word, of objecting that the introduction of language to film would rob it of all its intelligence and its wit. But this is just what was asserted by John Gould Fletcher, charter member of the Imagist movement, who ringingly insisted in 1929 that 'A complete boycott of "talking films" should be the first duty of anyone who has ever achieved a moment's pleasure from the contemplation of any film.'[26] In 1930, James Sibley Watson, who was an aspiring amateur film-maker as well as part owner of *The Dial*, denounced the new trend by making a sound-film spoof that included all the idiocies that critics ascribed to sound: poorly synchronized dialogue, egregious sound effects, stilted and poorly delivered speeches.[27] Watson's former managing editor at *The Dial*, Gilbert

Seldes, who probably wrote more thoughtful articles on the coming of sound than anyone else at this time, took only very slight exception to the trend when he said, of the silent film, 'the aesthetes are weeping over its demise as the populace turns to the talking picture.'[28]

III

The most consistent and the most complex resistance to sound came from what Seldes called 'the fascinating inter-national magazine of the cinema-aesthetes,'[29] a magazine published from 1927 to 1933 under the name of *Close Up*. Describing itself as 'the first review to approach films from the angles of art, experiment and possibility,'[30] *Close Up* had at its core the editorial team of Kenneth Macpherson and Bryher, who produced, with the more or less constant assistance of H.D., a monthly from 1927 to 1930 and a quarterly from then to 1933. Any claim that *Close Up* might have had to speak for the 'aesthetes' on the subject of film was based primarily on the presence of H.D., but also on the very considerable contributions of Dorothy Richardson, as well as occasional pieces by other writers such as Gertrude Stein and Marianne Moore. Because the magazine was published in Switzerland, it was well situated to report on European films, which it covered almost to the exclusion of the commercial American product. The pronounced internationalism of the magazine therefore sometimes took the form of a pan-Europeanism designed to offset the gigantic influence of Hollywood.[31] Mainly because of this European orientation, *Close Up* looked at the developments exemplified by Murnau's *Sunrise*, which premièred the year it began publication, with a highly critical eye.

The general position of *Close Up* could probably be summarized by Bryher's later reference to silent film as 'the art that died.' One contributor, Ernest Betts, called the acceptance of sound 'the most spectacular act of self destruction that has yet come out of Hollywood.'[32] Macpherson in particular was bitterly hostile to what he sarcastically called 'Noises with films,'[33] at least in part because the coming of sound made film-viewing in Switzerland far more difficult than it had been when *Close Up* started. By 1930, films simply weren't being distributed as freely across borders as they had been even a few years before, so that Switzerland, which had once been 'an open market for the world,' was now limited to French and German films, and even those were in the process of being divided up between French and German-speaking areas.[34] *Close Up*, in other words, was suffering from its own version of the 'foreign problem,' and the arguments it mounted as it struggled with the various aspects of the problem tell a lot about the complicated relationship of international modernism to the other internationalisms implicated with it at this time.

On the surface, at least, internationalism meant variety in the pages of *Close Up*, and opposition to sound meant opposition to the industrial monolingualism that sound was bringing to film. Sound was frequently criticized in these years as 'mechanical,' which meant in part that the reproduction quality was so low that voices sounded unnatural, but the term also betrayed a marked resentment that what many considered an art form should be subordinated to a mere invention. Resentment of the 'mechanical apparatus'[35] also meant resentment of the industrial system behind it and of the American companies that exemplified that system. Thus *Close Up* followed like a watch dog Hollywood's attempts to solve its 'foreign problem,' attempts that it interpreted as part of a concerted plan to 'dominate the entire foreign market in talking films.'[36] At this level, opposition to sound meant opposition to the further industrialization, centralization, and standardization of film, to what Macpherson denounced as 'the militant imperialism of the screen.'[37]

This opposition to American cultural imperialism did have a disconcerting tendency to shift over into fear of the American public. Thus there is among the *Close Up* principals a great deal of frankly elitist opposition to 'popular appeal,' which is consistently opposed to intelligence or ideas.[38] Bryher confidently informs her readers in 1931 that even in America the 'middle classes' do not go to the movies but leave them to 'children and the unskilled, whose parents probably could not speak English.'[39] Thus it is no surprise that sound films are puerile, since they are, according to another contributor, 'made by half wits for half wits.'[40] All this despite the fact that the addition of sound was perceived in the U.S. industry as calling for more intelligent performers, who could no longer simply mug their way through a film but would actually have to enunciate whole sentences, and for more attentive audiences, who often complained of the 'added strain' of listening to spoken dialogue. Sound, it was commonly thought within the industry, would force Hollywood to 'go in for brains.'[41]

Close Up also argued against sound for more purely aesthetic reasons, which were related in complex and sometimes contradictory ways to the implicit politics of the journal. Film theorists from the time of Hugo Münsterberg had argued for the intrinsic visuality of film, for a 'visual purity' that could only be violated by the spoken word.[42] These arguments were dusted off by Hollywood conservatives who opposed the introduction of sound, by European film-makers in France, Germany, and Russia, and by public intellectuals like Seldes in the U.S.[43] They appear rather liberally in *Close Up* as well, voiced even by Dorothy Richardson, who declared in one issue that 'cinematography is a visual art reaching the mind through the eyes alone,' and warned that 'concentrated listening is fatal to cinematography.'[44] These arguments are partly psychological, for they depend on the rather counter-intuitive notion that human beings cannot watch and listen at the same time, partly aesthetic, based on distributions of artistic labour going back to classical times, and partly semiotic, since they argue that visual images offer a fully functional, wholly motivated sign system that can only be polluted by the conventionality of spoken language. By this argument, every language is foreign to film, which is already complete, intelligible, and without need of supplement.

The 'foreign problem' faced by *Close Up* was therefore much more complex than that faced by Hollywood, for the writers at this magazine were arguing not just that the addition of language to film made particular films unintelligible to those who did not speak the particular languages in which they were recorded, but also that any language tended to make any film less eloquent for all viewers. Film, in this analysis, is already a universal language, the 'universal interpreter,' as Ambrière put it, to which the addition of sound means incomprehension and linguistic division.[45] The editors of *Close Up* clearly had a vested interest in this argument, since the very existence of their publication as an international film magazine depended on access to examples from all over the world. Thus in one of Macpherson's first comments on sound, he maintains that 'it will impose the restriction of language on films, whereas now their language is universal.'[46] The same argument is made in *Close Up*'s first year of publication by Dorothy Richardson, who also claimed a bit more intricately a year later that 'the film, with its freedom from the restrictions of language, is more nearly universal than the book and can incorporate . . . the originality of each race unhampered by the veil of translation.'[47] Exactly how film is able to preserve the 'originality of each race' while remaining universal is a mystery, but other writers for *Close Up* rather frequently asserted something like this, not just that film was *a* language but also that it was *all* languages: 'for the film, being silent,' as Rudolf Schwartzkopf put it, 'speaks all languages of the world.'[48] Film, in this analysis, depends on a visual alphabet, the characters of which are intelligible to all, from which particular film-makers might choose in particular ways to express individual or national idioms. The basic unit of this system cannot be anything so conventional as a letter, of course, but is usually compared to, or even called, a hieroglyph or ideogram. This analogy, as Laura Marcus so ably shows, was especially congenial to H.D., whose writings on the hieroglyph, though brief, provide an intriguing link between the dream interpretation of Freud and the film theory of Eisenstein.[49]

Behind this analogy, and behind the whole universal language argument that it serves, is the ancient European dream of a universal script that Derrida has traced in *Of Grammatology*.[50] The promise to fulfill this dream, to provide what was often called a modern Rosetta Stone, plays a crucial role in establishing the authority of the new media. Photography was promoted as a universal visual language as early as 1841.[51] Both Bell and Edison used the hieroglyph metaphor in relation to phonography, despite the fact that the prestige of the hieroglyph was directly related to its apparent difference from phonetic alphabets.[52] In regard to film, the metaphor was most widely popularized by Vachel Lindsay, who came out against sound in 1915.[53] Lindsay's chapter on 'Hieroglyphics' in *The Art of the Moving Picture* seems to have had widespread influence among film-makers and writers, and its traces can be found, as Marcus suggests, in the work of H.D., in Eisenstein, and, as Miriam Hansen has shown, in the films and writings of D. W. Griffith.[54] In fact, the notion that film depended on some sort of universal script was so popular by the time it appeared in *Close Up* that it also featured prominently in the publicity sheets of the lowliest studio hacks.

In Hollywood, the coming of sound had little impact on this line of reasoning, so that the very argument *Close Up* was mounting against sound was frequently used in studio propaganda for sound films. In a little book appropriately titled *See and Hear*, published in 1929, Will Hays confidently proclaims that 'The motion picture knows no barriers of distance nor of speech. It is the one universal language.'[55] Though this may simply have been Hays's way of blustering his industry past its 'foreign problem,' the universal language argument was used at least a few times in relation to recorded or transmitted speech. The phonograph, of course, was originally praised for registering speech and making it retrievable without the aid of writing, or for writing sound directly as its name implies, and this was often seen as a way to circumvent alphabets, if not language itself. But even the radio, which did not itself inscribe or store, was sometimes spoken of as if it could somehow universalize the language it transmitted. Thus Edward Van Zile proclaims, along with movies and the Esperanto of the Eye, 'the coming of the wireless and the Esperanto of the Tongue,' as if the mere act of distant transmission could make a language universally intelligible.[56]

The very ease with which the universal language argument moves from technology to technology helps to isolate the crucial element on which it depends. What photography, phonography, the telephone, film, and radio all have in common is the automatic and therefore ostensibly indiscriminate registering of sense data possible only for machines. As Kenneth Macpherson puts it, speaking of the movie camera in an early volume of *Close Up*, 'One turn of the handle and a complete series of pictures is made, no matter who turns that handle.'[57] This is to repeat, in regard to film, the claim originally made for photography by Fox Talbot at its very birth when he called these new works 'self representations.' The same claim was made in the very name given in the 1850s to the precursor of all aural recording devices, which was called the *phonautographe*.[58] The name suggests what Talbot also asserts of the photograph, that these are media in which phenomena inscribe themselves, without the messy intervention of human senses or sign systems. Thus for Jean Epstein, writing in 1925, the camera 'is an eye without prejudices, without morality, free of influences; and it sees in the face and in human movement traits which we, weighted down by likings and dislikings, by habits and considerations, can no longer perceive.'[59]

This is actually a rather curious notion, especially when it leads to the corollary idea that only machine inscription can yield a natural language. As W. J. T. Mitchell has suggested, it is somewhat incoherent to call natural only that which can be produced by a machine.[60] And it is hard to see how our machines can be neutral and unprejudiced if we can't be. The appeal of mechanical inscription, however, at least in this analysis, is not so much that it removes the prejudices of any individual observer as that it avoids the prejudices and habits of thought congealed within conventional languages. Recording devices seem to remove the layer of mediation that inscription and preservation had heretofore required. Not only might reality be perceived directly, and therefore uniformly, but it could also be preserved in perfect memory without recourse to the selectivity and condensation of conventional languages. The universality of recording technologies begins with the fact that they sense and preserve universally; that is to say, they take in everything.

Unfortunately, this is where the whole concept of a universal language breaks down, in the oxymoronic relationship between the adjective and the noun. There is an implicit conflict between universality and the linguistic, which appears precisely in the notion that recording technologies can communicate universally because they inscribe indiscriminately. The technologies themselves express this contradiction as the competition between signal and noise. The more faithfully a recording preserves every sense impression within its scope the less legible is the result, information drowned out by insignificant noise. The more indiscriminate a recording is, then, the less it can carry the burden of information, emotion, or expression that would make it like a language. According to James Lastra's expert discussion of this issue in regard to early sound technology, this is also what acoustic engineers discovered as they tried to adapt sound recording to film: fidelity, which tended to register every sound created during a take, favored noise and reduced legibility, whereas to achieve legible sound, the fidelity of the recording had to be limited in various ways, by damping, by particular microphone placement, and finally by skillful editing.[61] This is the truth behind the curious argument that the addition of sound somehow made film less eloquent, for in the early days film sound was, both literally and theoretically, mere noise, and the addition of it to the developed language of silent film introduced an incoherence that felt to many early audiences like gibberish and which many film critics of the time treated with the sort of xenophobic prejudice usually reserved for foreign languages.

Opposition to sound thus reveals within the internationalism of *Close Up* a complex and conflicted resistance to the foreign. This contradiction appears most neatly in the very term *Close Up* adopted to epitomize itself. In one sense, the journal was appropriately named, for the close up was considered, in Jean Epstein's words, 'the soul of the cinema.'[62] Once disdained as distorting and unnatural, the close up had come to be particularly associated with the experimental European cinema of which *Close Up* was the chief English exponent. It was also in the form of the close up that film most nearly approached the hieroglyphic. As Béla Balázs puts it in a frequently cited discussion, the close up 'reveals the most hidden parts in our polyphonous life, and teaches us to see the intricate visual details of life as one reads an orchestral score.'[63] In this analysis, film makes the visual world legible by directing attention to carefully circumscribed parts of it: the close up, in Epstein's words 'limits and directs attention.'[64]

The term taken for the title of this magazine was also meant, however, to designate its international scope. As Marcus says, *Close Up* promised to bring its readers news of farflung places, to make 'the distant proximate.'[65] But this impulse toward geographical extension and inclusion does conflict with the technique of the close up, insofar as it works, as Epstein suggests, by limiting and directing attention. In other words, there is a conflict in the very title of *Close Up* between film language, the legibility of which is achieved by blocking out noise, and the international scope the magazine hoped to achieve by extending its attention to every part of Europe and beyond. Some of the conceptual strain caused by this conflict is evident in a very strange column written by Macpherson in 1929, ostensibly reporting on a stereoscopic demonstration given by R.C.A. The new system, complete, of course, with sound, also seems to have allowed for extended telescopic shots, which provoked Macpherson to worry that 'the close up will vanish and the far-off will take its place.' As it turns out, the 'far-off' is a metonym for everything that Macpherson fears in the new technology, and the column ends with what must be one of the first diatribes against TV: 'An expedition through Nicaragua will necessitate no greater hazard than a ride round the suburbs or a rostrum on the roof. We shall be able to sit at our desks and photograph Titicaca and the fauna of Popocatapetl.'[66] What precisely is wrong with photographing Titicaca from afar is never made entirely clear, but the column explains a lot nonetheless by pitting the close up, and perhaps therefore *Close Up* itself, against the 'far off.' The indiscriminate way in which images from all over the world could come together in a single space caused Macpherson the same sort of cultural vertigo that it currently inspires in critics of TV. That aspect of the new media, the international aspect, turned out to be not only subordinate to the legibility offered by the close up but even inimical to it.

This conflict between the close up and the far off appears more frequently in the magazine's illustrations, which were mostly stills from German or Russian films unavailable to the English-speaking audience. From time to time, however, the editors also published publicity stills for their own films. The very first issue, for example, included two stills from *Wing Beat*, a short film starring Macpherson and H.D., made in 1927. In one case, the caption asserts, 'The feeling of "something about to happen" pervades the whole, reaching a climax at the point from which this "still" is taken.' The picture itself, of Macpherson staring rather dyspeptically off into one corner, seems to portray ennui rather than climax, but the pose does seem to match, in its tense inwardness, a conflict in the caption, which is apparently trying to be both vague and revelatory at the same time. The caption wants to celebrate the photograph, to demonstrate its eloquence, but it remains tongue-tied by the guilty knowledge that the picture should be able to speak for itself.

The situation is even more complex in the other still, which features H.D. slightly raising her hands. The caption says nothing about the dramatic situation at all, but it does insist of the actress that 'The same clear genius is in her acting that sets her so high among contemporary poets and authors.' The picture is apparently meant to portray this clarity, in and of itself, which is to be found in the rather severe profile shot and the spare elegance of H.D.'s pose, clothing, and hair style. The connection between this clarity and a certain kind of Imagist aesthetics hardly needs to be made, though the caption insists on it. In her acting as in her poetry, H.D. epitomizes an aesthetic of the close up, an image whose utter legibility depends on a severe excision of extraneous detail. But the caption, in its eagerness to praise, reveals how much this supposed clarity depends on a prior familiarity: the appearance of H.D.'s 'clear genius' here in the film still depends on the 'same clear genius' well-known from her writings. Without this push from the caption, it's entirely possible that one might read the still as signifying confusion or indecision. In fact, an anonymous reviewer for *Hound and Horn* found the picture 'quite . . . funny,' though it is just as hard at this remove to find the humor in it as it is to sense the profundity announced in the caption.[67] In the very gesture with which it celebrates the sufficiency of the picture, the caption betrays how much this visual legibility depends on written language outside the frame.

At the same time, these stills help excavate another layer in the culture of the close up, which has such a contradictory relation to the far off. Immediately after the photographs of Macpherson and H.D. are two stills from Marc Allégret's documentary of Gide's *Voyage to the Congo*. Standard ethnographic photographs, these full figure shots show two groups of naked Africans, identified only in geographical terms. There is no celebration of clarity here, but rather a printed directive, actually quite uncommon in the pages of *Close Up*, which did not tend to use these stills as mere illustrations, to an accompanying article by Jean Prévost. It is little wonder, though, that these film images require an entire article's worth of explanation, for, as Prévost says in that article, the visual language of Africa takes a European great labor to understand:

The everyday happenings so commonplace to those who do not understand their significance are set here in their essential picturesqueness. The disappointed fiancé who rubs her belly to express and soothe her grief, the caresses of her small sister, are here no mere native custom nor the language of a savage; one had to know what they meant, and now for the first time an exotic film explains this to us without being pedantic.[68]

Thus in the very first issue of *Close Up*, the universal language argument receives its fullest disconfirmation, for if the language of gestures and images must be learned then it is just as particular and as culturally specific as written language, on which it turns out in any case to depend. What is most telling, however, is not the disconfirmation itself, but rather the fact that it does not appear until the visual attention of the close up passes from Europe to Africa.

What is revealed in these stills is not, therefore, just the familiar truism that visual language is ultimately no less culturally specific than verbal, but that the designation of the visual as a language at all depends on excluding from it the extraneous, the irrelevant, the foreign, which in a European context ultimately means the racial. As Miriam Hansen suggests, Griffith began to assert the universality of the language of film after widespread criticism of the racism of *Birth of a Nation*.[69] In fact, *Birth of a Nation* itself had seemed a perfect example of the universal language of film to Thomas Dixon, author of *The Clansman*, on which the film was based.[70]

This is not to say that *Close Up* can be charged with the frank racism of Griffith and Dixon, though Macpherson did dislike sound enough to lose his balance at least once. In one of his many public attempts to reconcile himself to the inevitable arrival of the talkies, Macpherson finally blurts out, 'The one thing that is awful is the thought that [sound] may become a vehicle for those polite, not even dimly Creole "negro" rhythms of the East Side Jew composers for impeccable though androgynic rendering by Argentines and Dagoes.'[71] Within the generally romantic approach to race visible in Macpherson's film *Borderline*, there may lurk this sort of all-inclusive prejudice, brought out in this case by the association of sound with everything Macpherson can think of as deviant. The denunciation of sound as Jewish, homosexual, ethnically repellant and racially suspect shows how much must be excluded to make film into a 'universal' language and how much the close up has apparently to fear from the invasion of the far off. In this sense, at least, the internationalism of modernism's universal form languages seems in utter contradiction to the social and cultural internationalism ostensibly promoted by *Close Up*.

IV

Of course, arguing that film is a universal language open to one and all was always a fairly contradictory thing for a magazine to do. For most proponents, particularly for Griffith, the argument was merely a kind of boosterism, designed to cry off critics and frustrate potential censors, and this was also a considerable part of the effort to which *Close Up* dedicated itself. But *Close Up* also intended to explain film to its audience, even to educate an audience for audacious and innovative films, and it is a little hard to see why this should have been necessary if film was already, as H.D. once claimed, 'a universal art open alike to the pleb and the initiate.'[72] If it is part of film's universality that it does not require any particular kind of literacy, then why did *Close Up* put so much effort into the development of what James Donald calls 'skilled spectatorship'? There seems to be a real conflict between two of the most cherished aims of this publication: to defend the visual sufficiency of silent film and to develop a skilled audience capable of receiving difficult and unfamiliar works.

Thus the writers at *Close Up* also promoted a very different argument against sound, a variant quite at odds with the main line, to the effect that sound threatened the 'picture sense' developed by the experience of attending silent films.[73] Film-goers would become lazy, in other words, and lose a visual acuity built up when pictures carried almost the entire burden of the film. If sound is inevitably to come, Macpherson suggests, at least we are fortunate 'to have had the silent film first, for without it our eye would not have been trained to see.'[74] The idea that the eye needs to be 'trained to see' is actually rather a common theme in *Close Up*. As Zygmunt Tonecky puts it in an article heavily indebted to Balázs: 'The film has refined and trained our sight; we have learned to perceive fugitive situations; we perceive at once the tiniest details and understand in a moment the symbolic significance of the pictures; we know how to "think optically," to create associations of ideas and optical metaphors.'[75]

The *Close Up* contributor who was the most attentive to the actual experience of watching a film, Dorothy Richardson, was also the one most aware of the dependence of 'picture sense' on 'ideas and optical metaphors.' Though she follows the dogma that film is essentially visual and therefore should not be sullied with sound, she also calls film images and their inter-titles 'Siamese twins [that] . . . have never yet been separated.'[76] She is also aware that the implication of language in the visual imagery of film means that film is never universal. This, in fact, is one of its chief virtues for Richardson, for whom the development of a skilled spectatorship is dependent on 'the insensibly learned awareness of alien people and alien ways.'[77] The film sense thus developed is not universal but rather transnational, as Laura Marks maintains all film is, 'in that its audiences will not be able to decode its images perfectly, insofar as they originate from other places and times.'[78] In quite a few of the essays she published in *Close Up*, Richardson finds this transnational quality, which she calls 'the breath of otherness,' even in domestic films, and her notion of skilled spectatorship is one in which film-goers 'become for a while citizens of a world whose every face is that of a stranger.'[79] In this analysis, film internationalizes even the familiar by translating it into an unknown language, not by making visual experience transparent but rather by requiring that even the apparently transparent be read.

Thus *Close Up* registers the crisis of sound in two diametrically different ways, and the distance between these measures the space in which international modernism comes to terms with the social and cultural implications of the new media. The arrival of sound provoked such strong and varied responses because, as Stanley Cavell says, it 'broke the spell of immediate intelligibility.'[80] Anguished complaints about the violation of the universal language of film suggest that this crisis is both accidental and unnecessary, but what they ignore is that the legibility of film had to be achieved in the first place. At first, the purely reproductive powers of any recording medium always turn out to be more or less useless to human beings, whose perceptions are never quite as raw as those of a machine, which ultimately have to be subjected to the same processes of selective attention that make our own sense impressions useful to us. The new media don't make the world somehow more artificial, more fraught with representation; instead they force on us, through conflicts like the crisis over sound, an awareness of the representational quality of ordinary perception, which is why they challenge us much as a foreign language does.

There may be something appropriate, then, in the fact that the 'first international film' was also one of the first to incorporate sound. The sort of internationalism that brought Murnau to Hollywood, of course, is that provided by American cultural imperialism, by the centralization, standardization, and industrialization of global experience that American aesthetic might made such a feature of the 20th century. The controversy over sound suggests, however, that there is always something inherently transnational even within this sort of internationalism, even perhaps that the transnational disturbance of experience that Hollywood called its 'foreign problem' is a dialectical effect of that other internationalism. The new media may promise to bring everything close up, but the very means they use to do so have the distressing tendency to make it seem far off again.

It was this kind of 'far off' that Macpherson and his colleagues at *Close Up* finally found the most difficult to accept. The internationalism of this magazine often depended on a film aesthetic that denied the transnational by insisting on the immediacy and transparency of the visual image. In this, they represent a very general tendency in international modernism, where a universal form language, with its promise of a universal utopian future, somehow results in the sort of totalitarian architecture that gave post-modernism its reason for being. At the same time, however, even in its haughtier and more elitist moments, *Close Up* registers an awareness in modernism of the strangeness opened up within ordinary experience by the new media, which, instead of establishing a new universal language, had exposed the inherent unfamiliarity of languages long in use.

Notes

1   Scott Eyman, *The Speed of Sound: Hollywood and the Talkie Revolution 1926-1930* (New York: Simon & Schuster, 1997), p. 150.

2   James Morrison, *Passport to Hollywood: Hollywood Films, European Directors* (Albany: State University of New York Press, 1998), p. 31.

3   For a definition and a discussion of the 'German influence' on Hollywood film production, see David Bordwell, Janet Staiger, and Kristin Thompson, *The Classical Hollywood Cinema: Film Style and Mode of Production to 1960* (New York: Columbia University Press, 1985), p. 73.

4   The film without inter-titles was an important ideal for much of the European film avant-garde. See P. Adams Sitney, *Modernist Montage: The Obscurity of Vision in Cinema and Literature* (New York: Columbia University Press, 1990), p. 21.

5   Morrison, p. 58.

6   Donald Crafton, *The Talkies: American Cinema's Transition to Sound, 1926-1931* (Berkeley: University of California Press, 1997), p. 94.

7   Crafton, p. 96.

8   Bela Balazs, *Theory of the Film* trans., Edith Bone (1952; New York: Arno Press, 1972), p. 45. Chapter 5 of this volume is a series of quotations from Balázs' *Der sichtbare Mensch*, published in 1923.

9   Crafton, pp. 72-73. Even some relatively contemporary observers have been caught up in the promise of this technology. In his collection *Sound and the Cinema: The Coming of Sound to American Film* (Pleasantville, NY: Redgrave Publishing, 1980), Evan William Cameron declares the coming of sound 'the sole cataclysmic event in the history of art,' after which 'created and natural events' are no longer 'perceptually distinct.' See pp. xii and xiv.

10   Crafton, pp. 96, 567 n. 41.

11   Stanley Cavell, *The World Viewed: Reflections on the Ontology of Film* (New York: Viking, 1971), p. 147. It has become something of a credo among scholars of early film that 'the silents were not silent,' since there were so many different ways in which audio accompaniment could be added during the showing of a film. For a number of relevant discussions, see *The Sounds of Early Cinema*, ed. Richard Abel and Rick Altman (Bloomington: Indiana University Press, 2001).

12   Crafton, pp. 166-67, 172. For Chaplin, see pp. 296, 348, and 374.

13   Crafton, p. 378.

14   For an unattributed use of the term, see Crafton, p. 151.

15   Crafton, p. 439.

16   Crafton, pp. 290, 461-63.

17   Crafton, pp. 424-30; Nataša Ďurovičová, 'Translating America: The Hollywood Multilinguals 1929-1933,' in *Sound Theory Sound Practice*, ed. Rick Altman (New York: Routledge, 1992), pp. 138-53.

18   R. d'E.B., 'A Thought,' *Close Up* 3.5 (November 1928): 68.

19   O. B. [Oswell Blakeston], 'Anthology,' *Close Up* 7.1 (July 1930): 76.

20   Rudolf Arnheim, *Film* trans., L. M. Sieveking and Ian F. D. Morrow (1930; London: Faber & Faber, 1933), p. 280.

21   Crafton, p. 544.

22   Patricia R. Zimmermann, 'Startling Angles: Amateur Film and the Early Avant-Garde,' in *Lovers of Cinema: The First American Film Avant-Garde 1919-1945*, ed. Jan-Christopher Horak (Madison: University of Wisconsin Press, 1995), p. 146.

23   Alan Williams, 'Historical and Theoretical Issues in the Coming of Recorded Sound to the Cinema,' in *Sound Theory Sound Practice*, p. 136.

24   Crafton, p. 448.

25   Francis Ambrière, 'Variations sur le Cinéma,' *PMLA* 115: 1024. See also Crafton, p. 448.

26   John Gould Fletcher, *The Crisis of the Film* (np: University of Washington, 1929), p. 28.

27   Lisa Cartwright, 'U.S. Modernism and the Emergence of 'The Right Wing of Film Art': The Films of James Sibley Watson, Jr., and Melville Webber,' in *Lovers of Cinema*, p. 168.

28   Gilbert Seldes, *An Hour with the Movies and the Talkies* (Philadelphia: J. P. Lippincott, 1929), p. 124.

29   Seldes, p. 116.

30   Pool advertisement, *Transition* 6 (September 1927): front.

31   See, for example, Kenneth Macpherson, 'As Is,' *Close Up* 1.6 (December 1927): 14 and 'As Is,' *Close Up* 2.1 (January 1928): 11.

32   Ernest Betts, *Heraclitus or The Future of the Films* (London: Kegan Paul, Trench, Trubner, 1928), erratum slip at p. 88. This slip was inserted to signify that Betts' hopes during the composition of his book that sound could be stopped had been frustrated.

33   Kenneth Macpherson, 'As Is,' *Close Up* 1.5 (November 1927): 5.

34   Kenneth Macpherson, 'As Is,' *Close Up* 7.6: 367-68.

35   Wilbur Needham, 'The Photography of Sound,' *Close Up* 3.2 (August 1928): 31.

36   C. H. [Clifford Howard], 'Hollywood Notes,' *Close Up* 6.6 (June 1930): 529.

37   Kenneth Macpherson, 'As Is,' *Close Up* 5.1 (July 1929): 6.

38   Kenneth Macpherson, 'As Is,' *Close Up* 7.6 (December 1930): 369.

39   Bryher, 'The Hollywood Code,' *Close Up* 8.4 (December 1931): 281.

40   A.W., 'All Talkie!,' *Close Up* 5.1 (July 1929): 58.

41   Crafton, p. 450. See also pp. 449, 485-88.

42 See the discussion in Friedrich A. Kittler, *Gramophone, Film, Typewriter*, tr. Geoffrey Winthrop-Young and Michael Wutz (Stanford: Stanford University Press,1999), p. 172.

43 Crafton, pp. 167, 379. Seldes, pp. 145, 149.

44 Dorothy Richardson, 'Dialogue in Dixie,' *Close Up* 5.3 (September 1929): 215.

45 Ambrière, p. 1024.

46 Kenneth Macpherson, 'As Is,' *Close Up* 1.5 (November 1927): 8.

47 Dorothy Richardson, 'Films for Children,' *Close Up* 3.2 (August 1928): 24.

48 Rudolf Schwartzkopf, 'Volksverband fur Filmkunst,' *Close Up* 2.5 (May 1928): 28.

49 Laura Marcus, 'Introduction to Part 3,' in *Close Up 1927-1933: Cinema and Modernism* ed., James Donald, Anne Friedberg, and Laura Marcus (Princeton: Princeton University Press, 1998), p. 96-104.

50 Jacques Derrida, *Of Grammatology* trans.,Gayatri Chakravorty Spivak (1967; Baltimore: Johns Hopkins University Press, 1976), p. 76.

51 Allan Sekula, *Photography Against the Grain: Essays and Photo Works 1973-1983* (Halifax: Press of the Nova Scotia College of Art and Design, 1984), p. 82.

52 James Lastra, *Sound Technology and the American Cinema: Perception, Representation, Modernity* (New York: Columbia University Press, 2000), p. 28-31.

53 Vachel Lindsay, *The Art of the Moving Picture* (1915; New York: Modern Library, 2000), pp. 10, 110.

54 Miriam Hansen, *Babel to Babylon: Spectatorship in American Silent Film* (Cambridge: Harvard University Press, 1991), p. 184-85.

55 Hays, p. 36.

56 Edward S. Van Zile, *That Marvel—The Movie: A Glance at its Reckless Past, Its Promising Present, and Its Significant Future* (New York: Putnam's, 1923), p. 198.

57 Kenneth Macpherson, 'As Is,' *Close Up* 2.2 (February 1928): 13.

58 Lastra, p. 47.

59 Quoted in Sitney, p. 35.

60 W. J. T. Mitchell, *Iconology: Image, Text, Ideology* (Chicago: University of Chicago Press, 1986), p. 37.

61 Lastra, pp. 49-50.

62 Jean Epstein, 'Magnification,' in *French Film theory and Criticism: A History/Anthology 1907-1939*, ed. Richard Abel (Princeton: Princeton University Press, 1988), p. 235. Quoted in *Close Up 1927-1933*, p. 1.

63 Balazs, p. 55.

64 Epstein, p. 239. Quoted in *Close Up 1927-1933*, p. 1.

65 Close Up 1927-1933, p. 243.

66 Kenneth Macpherson, 'As Is,' *Close Up* 5.1 (July 1929): 10.

67 [Anonymous], 'Periodical Review,' *Hound and Horn* 1 (September 1927): 66.

68 Jean Prevost, 'Andre Gide and Marc Allegret's Voyage to the Congo,' *Close Up* 1.1 (July 1927): 40.

69   Hansen, pp. 164-165.

70   Lary May, *Screening Out the Past: The Birth of Mass Culture and the Motion Picture Industry* (New York: Oxford University Press, 1980), p. 82.

71   Kenneth Macpherson, 'As Is,' *Close Up* 7.2 (August 1930): 89.

72   H.D., 'Conrad Veidt: The Student of Prague,' *Close Up* 1.3 (September 1927): 44.

73   'Robert Herring Gives Four Points about Hearts in Dixie,' *Close Up* 5.2 (August 1929): 162.

74   Kenneth Macpherson, 'As Is,' *Close Up* 5.6 (December 1929): 449.

75   Zygmunt Tonecky, 'The Preliminary of Film-Art,' *Close Up* 8.3 (September 1931): 193.

76   Dorothy Richardson, 'Continuous Performance: Captions,' *Close Up* 1.3 (September 1927): 55.

77   Dorothy Richardson, 'Continuous Performance: This Spoon-Fed Generation?,' *Close Up* 8.4 (December 1931): 307.

78   Laura U. Marks, *The Skin of the Film: Intercultural Cinema, Embodiment, and the Senses* (Durham: Duke University Press, 2000), p. 94.

79   Dorothy Richardson, 'Continuous Performance: The Cinema in Arcady,' *Close Up* 3.1 (July 1928): 55-56.

80   Cavell, p. 150.

Fig. 1. Kenneth MacPherson in a publicity still for *Wing Beat*, published in *Close-Up* 1.1 (July, 1927).

Fig. 2. H.D. in a publicity still for *Wing Beat*, published in *Close-Up* 1.1 (July, 1927).

Fig. 3. Voyage to the Congo, published in *Close-Up* 1.1 (July, 1927).

4

Gertrude Stein's Machinery of Perception

Julian Murphet

The emergence of cinema can be shown to have been heralded – in France as nowhere else – as the salvation of a literature which, according to Georg Lukács, was 'based on *ad hoc* observation' and 'must perforce be superficial'.[1] If Naturalism was the misguided attempt 'to make literature scientific, to transform it into an applied natural science, into sociology' (p. 140), then cinema, belonging technically to that 'scientific' paradigm, might relieve literature of its 'paltry and schematic' descriptive vocation, and liberate its humanistic potentials once more. Certainly for André Gide, the newer recording media prompted a radical reconsideration of the novel's properties:

> Just as photography in the past freed painting from its concern for a certain sort of accuracy, so the phonograph will eventually no doubt rid the novel of the kind of dialogue which is drawn from the life and which realists take so much pride in. Outward events, accidents, traumatisms, belong to the cinema. The novel should leave them to it. Even the description of the characters does not seem to me properly to belong to the genre. No; this does not seem to me the business of the *pure* novel (and in art, as in everything else, purity is the only thing I care about).[2]

On this account, which has since been rearticulated by many others (not least André Bazin and Jean-François Lyotard[3]), the superficial descriptivism of Naturalism might simply be transferred to the media that 'described' automatically, allowing the novel to purify itself of all those 'outward elements' and contingencies of mere reality – luxuriating rather in the inward, abstract, and formal properties of aestheticism and psychologism. Thus the new machines were assumed to enjoy representational sway over the perceptual forms of the external world, while literary art, promoted once more as a handicraft, dwelt in a more relativistic and affective realm.

This critical commonplace, which I will call the hypothesis of *technical privation*, runs throughout theorizations of modernism, and has a telling echo in the vitalist philosophy of Henri Bergson. It is not so much that Bergson, like Gide, recognises the aesthetic purification invited by the cinema, but that he seizes on the cinema as an apt metaphor for attacking what the 'Naturalist', 'scientific', materialist worldview has done to consciousness in the first place. That worldview, he states, has inculcated a positive indifference to actual becoming: 'Instead of attaching ourselves to the inner becoming of things, we place ourselves outside them in order to recompose their becoming artificially.'[4] This is virtually a paraphrase of Lukács' critique of Naturalism, and it segues immediately into his famous cinematographic metaphor:

> We take snapshots, as it were, of the passing reality, and, as these are characteristic of the reality, we have only to string them on a becoming, abstract, uniform and invisible, situated at the back of the apparatus of knowledge, in order to imitate what there is that is characteristic in this becoming itself. Perception, intellection, language so proceed in general. Whether we would think becoming, or express it, or even perceive it, we hardly do anything else than set going a kind of cinematograph inside us. We may therefore sum up what we have been saying in the conclusion that the *mechanism of our ordinary knowledge is of a cinematographical kind.*
>
> (Bergson, p. 306)

The vitalist dualism, which counterposes this artificial and cinematographical 'mechanism' of analytic rationality to consciousness or *'need of creation'*,[5] rejects the apparatus of cinema as just one more trick of the 'divisible and repetitive' logic of intellection.

Lukács, of course, developed a social and economic name for what Bergson repudiates as a 'scientific' corruption of our vital intuitions. Lukács's analysis of Naturalism, and his disdain for the 'scientific' subsumption of art, derive from his larger theory of *reification*, with which it would be advantageous to relate Bergson's 'cinematographical' model of consciousness in a more extended manner, if space permitted. Lukács's fundamental point is that the reduction of complex, organic unities of 'becoming' into static and reified 'snapshots' is precisely the logic of consciousness under capitalism. 'Just as the capitalist system continuously produces and reproduces itself economically on higher and higher levels, the structure of reification progressively sinks more deeply, more fatefully and more definitively into the consciousness of man':[6]

> [...] we can see a continuous trend towards greater rationalisation, the progressive elimination of the qualitative, human and individual attributes of

the worker. On the one hand, the process of labour is progressively broken down into abstract, rational, specialised operations so that the worker loses contact with the finished product and his work is reduced to the mechanical repetition of a specialised set of actions. On the other hand, the period of time necessary for the work to be accomplished (which forms the basis of rational calculation) is converted [...] to an objectively calculable work-stint that confronts the worker as a fixed and established reality. With the modern 'psychological' analysis of the work-process (in Taylorism) the rational mechanisation extends right into the worker's 'soul'....

(Lukács, *History*, p. 88)

There can be no question that this analytic reification of a vital process (human labour) has profound affinities with Bergson's account of a perception that 'manages to solidify into discontinuous images the fluid continuity of the real'.[7] What has yet to be properly formulated is the degree to which the cinema itself intimately collaborated with this fateful process of spiritual 'restructuring'. If Bergson is right, the cinematic apparatus is the ideal synecdoche of this process, an invisible machine within us, 'situated at the back of the apparatus of knowledge', reifying our worldly perceptions into frozen and inert fragments that are only 'artificially' reanimated by the apparatus.

Fredric Jameson has commented further on the decisive role cinema played in this regard, insisting that 'the human perceptual machine is constructed on the basis of its own mechanical products at any given moment', and so demanding a 'genealogical perspective in which the medium ... is grasped less as a source of innovation in its own right, than rather as the material reinforcement of an on-going tendency in social life as a whole.'

This is Lukács' concept of 'reification' in its broadest sense of a gradual fragmentation and division of labour within the psyche, as the latter is retrained and reprogrammed by the reorganization of the traditional labour processes and human activities by [...] capital. The sharp structural differentiation of active and passive *within* a single mental function – such as this 'new' one of filmic perception – would then be seen as a historic intensification of the reification process, and one which could then go a certain distance in accounting for the privileged status of the new medium, for its gradual supersession of more traditional aesthetic languages.[8]

We will note that Bergson's model makes this sharp distinction between 'passive' and 'active' moments in the mental functions of intellection and perception, by distinguishing between a passive 'taking' of snapshots, and an active 'setting go' of the mental cinematograph: singular evidence of precisely the intensification of reification that Jameson is describing.

Bergson produced his remarkable thoughts on the cinema in Paris in 1907, a year during which an American woman in the same city was mid-way through the composition of a long novel written under the influence of a comparable 'cinematographical mechanism'; a mechanism that she had adopted at Harvard some ten years previously. Reflecting in the 1930s on the method of her thousand-page performance, Gertrude Stein unwittingly reverted to precisely the analogy that Bergson had used to discredit the scientific anaylsis of the *élan vital*:

> ... in the *Making of Americans*, I was doing what the cinema was doing, I was making a continuous succession of the statement of what that person was until I had not many things but one thing. ...
>
> I of course did not think of it in terms of the cinema, in fact I doubt whether at that time I had ever seen a cinema but, and I cannot repeat this too often any one is of one's period and this our period was undoubtedly the period of the cinema and series production. And each of us in our own way are bound to express what the world in which we are living is doing.
>
> ... In a cinema picture no two pictures are exactly alike each one is just that much different than the one before, and so ... there was ... no repetition. Each time that I said the somebody whose portrait I was writing was something that something was just that much different from what I had just said that somebody was and little by little in this way a whole portrait came into being, a portrait that was not description and that was made by each time, and I did a great many times, say it, that somebody was something, each time there was a difference just a difference enough so that it could go on and be a present something.[9]

From Harvard to Paris (via Detroit)

Stein entered the Harvard Annex (later, Radcliffe College) in 1893, and gravitated swiftly to the psychology department under William James, who had recently hired Hugo Münsterberg of Freiburg to run the psychology labs. Münsterberg had studied directly under Wilhelm Wundt, the founder of positivist experimental psychology, and it was Münsterberg who directed and taught Stein in the labs, where he famously called her his 'ideal student'. The acknowledgement of Münsterberg's influence on Stein, rather than James's, is critical.[10] 'Münsterberg [unlike James, whose drift towards Bergsonism is declared in *A Pluralistic Universe*] remained true to the consciousness as an entity in the tradition of Kant and Wundt,'[11] and Stein took away from Harvard his classical positivist intellectualism, more than she did the increasingly pragmatist and vitalist preoccupations of James. Indeed, her period at Radcliffe coincided exactly with James's great intellectual crisis, and there is little if any indication that this crisis registered with her.

When the full history of social reification comes to be written, an honourable place in the chapter on its intellectual development will be reserved for the uniquely positivist atmosphere of Münsterberg's laboratory, the stated aim of which was 'no longer to speculate about the soul, but to find the psychical elements and the constant laws which control their connections'.[12] Here Stein was to produce her work on 'Motor Automatism', and from here she ultimately derived the singular aesthetic of *The Making of Americans*. Münsterberg himself went on to become the high priest of the new science of 'psychotechnics', a resolute effort to make the lessons of the laboratory available for social use, to extend reification programmatically into the lifeworld. In 1912, he published *Psychology and Industrial Efficiency*, the most substantial essay in psychotechnics. The book argued consistently for a rationalization of labouring subjects in 'the service of commerce and industry'. 'We ask [he wrote] how we can find the men whose mental qualities make them best fitted for the work which they have to do; secondly, under what psychological conditions we can secure the greatest and most satisfactory output of work from every man; and finally, how we can produce most completely the influence on human minds which are desired in the interests of business.'[13] Rationalization here amounts to the standardization of the 'human mind' itself, reduced to the simplest functions and habits, just as Georg Lukács was to lament of the full psychological effects of Taylorism. Münsterberg was the first significant psychologist to effect this 'extension' of reification into the 'soul' of the modern worker, ramifying the lessons of Fordism and Taylorism at the level of consciousness itself, conceived as a set of innate predispositions and learned reflexes.

Meanwhile, F. W. Taylor, in *The Principles of Scientific Management* (1911, the same year that Stein completed *The Making of Americans*), insisted that management should control a monopoly of technical knowledge-power, while workers were progressively reduced to the level of machines. Pioneering the use of time-and-motion studies, and breaking down complex tasks by means of chronophotography to the simplest gestures, Taylor believed he had 'scientifically' adapted the entire culture of work to the rigours of Fordism. And Fordism *was* Americanism, admired the world over, by Right and Left (think only of Lenin and Gramsci), for its accent on efficiency. 'In effect', writes Peter Wollen, 'Fordism turned the factory into a kind of super-machine in its own right, with both human and mechanical parts'.[14] And if the workers and machine tools were functional and interchangeable, then so too were the cars themselves, the Model Ts of which Ford famously said: 'Any customer can have a car painted any color that he wants as long as it is black'. Stripped of decoration and ornament, aggressively utilitarian, blandly generic, the Model T was the primordial modern object. With it was born the acutely Steinian problematic of 'series production' – objects and subjects haunted by their own infinite repetitions.

Stein's admiration for the tenacity and speed of the Ford automobile was underscored by her awareness of its industrial origin in a mass-production, assembly-line process. The realities of mass production, especially the Münsterbergian reification of its psychological component, had only confirmed Stein's positivist theory of the human personality as this had been formed in the Harvard labs. Indeed, since her time under Münsterberg, his lessons and their application had spread to cover the very industrial coordinates of the present. When Stein wrote about the 'making of Americans', she was self-consciously employing concepts and techniques learned from her mentor; the reification of human psychology and movement was intellectual property that she had long since assimilated. It was this theory that she gave such extensive treatment in *The Making of Americans*. As Janet Hobhouse remarks, '*The Making of Americans* was in Gertrude's mind to some extent a scientific work. It was to set forth a theory of behaviour'.[15] In *The Making of Americans*, Lisa Ruddick observes, 'Stein seems interested not so much in her characters' conscious interactions as in their ways of impinging on one another, rather as physical objects impinge on one another. People are not primarily centers of subjectivity but forces or motions, encountering other person-motions, which they either repel, besiege, or submit to'.[16] What is more, as we are about to see, the more significant subject-matter of the narrator is not this relative eclipse of interiority itself, but the specter of *repetition*, both within subjects and between them – the *series production* of humanity itself.

It is worth mentioning first, however, the importance of the Fordist axiomatic for Stein in general, not just as a set of psychological and physiological laws for economic, 'productive' behavior, but moreover as a model for conceiving of both her nationality and the very art of the novel itself. Above all speed, the very basis of the Taylorized approach to efficiency, serves as a dynamic idea fusing human subjects with their mass-produced vehicles – and Stein's aesthetics. At the outset of her lecture on 'Portraits and Repetition', Stein used the following analogy to underscore her interest in a peculiarly American velocity, which she was committed to capturing in her prose:

A motor goes inside of an automobile and the car goes. In short this generation has conceived an intensity of movement so great that it has not to be seen against something else to be known, and therefore, this generation does not connect itself with anything, that is what makes this generation what it is and that is why it is American....[17]

Americanness is thus conceived, not unusually, as 'intensity of movement'. The notion is mediated by a very industrial image: that of the combustion engine which, when inserted into the body of the automobile, propels it beyond all known organic speeds. According to Stein, this intensity of movement obliterates background itself. We no longer require the leisurely scenery or genealogy of Europe to measure such velocity. It is a value in itself which, like the generation it consumes, 'does not connect itself with anything'. It is free, unbounded, abstract: American.

Elsewhere the assembled automobile served her as an apt figure for contemporary being. 'Stein suggested that what distinguished twentieth-century experience as such might be summed up as the difference between "conceiv[ing] an automobile as a whole ... and then creat[ing] it," much as the twentieth century had, or first "see[ing] the parts" and only afterwards "work[ing] towards the automobile through them," as the nineteenth century would have done'.[18] Modern production techniques and sensibilities, and artistic labours, work from the model to the parts, and not the other way. Furthermore, as she wrote of her own technique: 'The assembling of a thing to make a whole thing and each one of these whole things is one of a series, but beside this there is the important thing and the very American thing that everybody knows who is an American just how many seconds minutes or hours it is going to take to do a whole thing'.[19] From this it would appear that psychotechnics and the scientific efficiency of time-and-motion studies undergird the productivity of *every* American, even the artist-genius herself; and every product is but 'one of a series'. Stein thus arrived at a virtual homology between being American and the Fordist assembly line. Hers was, as she said, an age of series production; and her great novel, *The Making of Americans*, was effectively being presented as the first significant artistic response to Fordism.

It only remains to re-emphasise what role cinema itself was playing in this general dissemination of a new practical theory of being, apart from the obvious fact that industrial production techniques were increasingly applied to the new medium. Once again, it is Münsterberg who serves as the critical mediating link, since his work, *The Photoplay: a psychological study* (1916) took up where his work in psychotechnics left off, and celebrated the colonisation of middle-class and working-class consciousness by a new machine-art that perfectly complemented the reifications of workplace discipline. Realizing that the greatest interest for the psychologist lay in cinema's inherent analysis of movement, Münsterberg notably surpassed Bergson in his description of a latent psychological mechanism that transcended the synthetic illusion of frame-by-frame projection: 'the perception of movement is an independent experience which cannot be reduced to a simple seeing of a series of different positions. A characteristic content of consciousness must be added to such a series of visual impressions.'[20] We will see the full relevance of this later, in Stein's insistence on the new freedoms and speeds paradoxically brought about by reification; but it is crucial to realise the importance of what Münsterberg was doing with the cinema in terms of the extension of reification into the fibres and neurons of the brain itself. He hailed the cinema as a social laboratory for psychotechnicians everywhere: 'The screen ought to offer a unique opportunity to interest wide circles in psychological experiments and mental tests and in this way to spread the knowledge of their importance for vocational guidance and the practical affairs of life.'[21] Münsterberg's enthusiasm for the new medium revolved around the fact that it did our thinking and apperception for us: *'the photoplay tells us the human story by overcoming the forms of the outer world, namely, space, time, and causality, and by adjusting the events to the forms of the inner world, namely, attention, memory, imagination, and emotions.'*[22] Cinema adapted reality to consciousness, and consciousness to reality, programming both in the service of commerce. Gertrude Stein's great novel attempted to patch these reifications of the machinery of perception onto the high art of fictional narrative.

Making Americans

To begin with, Stein's narrator insists that one only gets to know others through their manifestations, either gestural or verbal; and these are invariably repetitious:

> The nature in every one is always coming out of them from their beginning to their ending by the repeating always in them, by the repeating always coming out from each one. Sometimes, often, one looking at someone forgets about that one many things one knows in that one, always soon then such a one brings it back to remember it about that one the things one is not then thinking by the repeating that is always in each one. ...[23]

'Each one' is, in this much repeated theory, nothing other than his or her ceaseless repetition of a 'nature' that is 'in them'. To be is to repeat; or, 'I repeat therefore I am'.

This deadening sense of internal repetition is next related to its extrinsic counterpart: *resemblance*, which threatens to serialize character from without as repetition had standardized it from within.

> There are many ways of being a man, there are many millions of each kind of them, more and more in ones living they are there repeating themselves around one, every one of them in his own way being the kind of man he has in him, and there are always many millions made just like each one of them.
>
> (p.115)

And just like the Model T, the vertiginous opening up of authorial discourse onto the vast horizon of 'many millions' is characteristic of Stein's strategy of destabilizing subjectivity from the point of view of seriality. Again:

> Sometimes in living one sees so many repeating, so many who seem when one knows them to be so individual there can never be any one anything like them, a pair of them with so individual a relation made up of two who are so singular in their being that it never seems that there can be others just like them. Always then one sees another pair of them and sometimes it is almost dizzying, it gives to each one of the pairs of them an unreal being, and then it comes again that one understands then that repeating is the whole of living.
>
> (p. 221)

What emerges from the 'repeating' of human types in this conception are two intimately linked responses: first, the 'dizzying' and 'unreal being' articulated in that last passage, an existential nausea; and second, an incipient excitement about the possibility of a scientific treatise, a new knowledge *à la* Taylor and Münsterberg, about this new 'American' seriality of human being:

> This is then a beginning of learning to make kinds of men and women. Slowly then all the resemblances between one and all the others that have something, different things in common with that one, all these fall into an ordered system sometime then that one is a whole one, sometimes that one is very different to what was in the beginning the important resemblance in that one but always everything, all resemblances in that one must be counted in, nothing must ever be thrown out, everything in each one must be included to know that one and then sometime that one is to some one a whole on and that is then very satisfying.
>
> (p.340)

What begins by being baffling and dizzying, can ultimately yield the greatest epistemological satisfactions, provided 'one' has amassed sufficient data to sort and quantify all the various 'pieces' through which men and women resemble each other into an 'ordered system'. What one must do, as Stein's narrator says, is to *make kinds of men and women*, to construct models and typologies for everyone – to *make Americans*. The 'making of Americans' of the book's title refers not to any frontier narrative of hardy survival in the face of adversity, but to the lab-work of the narrator herself who constructs Americans from models down to interchangeable 'pieces', pieces which are objectively calculable and invariant: snapshots, gestures, habits, 'bottom natures'. In the most profound radicalization of the aesthetics of Naturalism in the history of the novel, the static reifications of typology take the place of narrative variation and transition. The birth of American modernism takes place in this sterilized experimental space.

Or, not quite. What we have to return to, of course, is the question of cinema and how, in the 1930s, Stein saw that medium as the perfect analogy for her modernism in *The Making of Americans*. The answer hinges on the nature of movement and speed. Movement, as she would have studied it in her classes on zoology at Harvard, was a subject of intensive speculation and increasingly scientific quantification at the end of the nineteenth century. The work of Bergson's colleague Étienne-Jules Marey on animal and human movement, which by the 1890s was drawing technical inspiration from the great American-based chronophotographer Eadweard Muybridge, meticulously analysed animal and human movement down to its tiniest detail. It was this kind of work on movement which Taylor was to apply directly to his time-and-motion studies.

The key was the standardization of the unit of time, expressed in the interval between exposures on a plate through a rapidly rotating shutter. Whether the interval between each image is 1/10 or 1/500 of a second, it no longer matters where or when you begin in the analysis of movement; what matters is the quantification of spatial change from instant to instant.[24] By projecting this rationalized conception of movement on to photographic plates, Marey installed a logic of equidistant instants in place of the residual Aristotelian conception of mutating substances.[25] Gertrude Stein was fully aware of this breakthrough in the understanding and representation of movement. Consider the following passage in the novel which challenges the apparent repetition through an insistence on minute variations:

> Always, one having loving repeating to getting completed understanding must have in them an open feeling, a sense for all the slightest variations in repeating, must never lose themselves so in the solid steadiness of all repeating that they do not hear the slightest variation. If they get deadened by the steady pounding of repeating they will not learn from each one even though each one always is repeating the whole of them they will not learn the completed history of them, they will not know the being really in them.
>
> (p. 294)

The ubiquity of repetitions in modernity forces upon the intellect a compensatory sensitivity to difference that is always on the verge of being extinguished by the 'steady pounding' of industrial production. Individuality is now immanent in apparent seriality. 'There is [Stein states] always then repeating in all the millions of each kind of men and women, there is repeating then in all of them of each kind of them but in every one of each kind of them the repeating is a little changing. ... repeating with a little changing just enough to make of each one an individual being, to make of each repeating an individual thing that gives to such a one a feeling of themselves inside them'. (p. 191)

The aesthetic capture of these minute variations required a revolution in technique. Stein's sentences, according to the logic she embraced, *begin again*, over and over again. They are committed to a logic of repetition with 'a little changing', for only such an approach can capture the true nature of the space of time she wants to map. Stein's art is thus a virtual chronophotography of the human soul. Or, in her own later words, her prose has become a *cinema* of the personality. Each sentence is an arbitrary point of entry into an ongoing psychological process. The revolving shutter mechanism of Stein's sentence-form exposes minute syntactical and phrasal variations. These delineate a movement. On the final page of the work, we find the passage on 'family living':

> Family living can be existing and every one can come to be a dead one and not any one then is remembering any such thing. Family living can be existing and every one can come to be a dead one and some are remembering some such thing. Family living can be existing and every one can come to be a dead one and every one is then a dead one and there are then not any more being living.
>
> (p. 925)

As a major statement on the demise of the Victorian bourgeois family, the passage only gains strength from the apparently mechanical repetition, which in fact subtly varies the content in a devolutionary direction. As she argued later: 'It is not repetition if it is that which you are actually doing because naturally each time the emphasis is different just as the cinema has each time a slightly different thing to make it all be moving. And each one of us has to do that, otherwise there is no existing.'[26]

Toward the rhythm of the visible world

The obvious aesthetic question to ask is whether or not the 'intensity of movement' she wanted to capture and reproduce in her syntactical 'cinema' is in fact evident there at all. And the answer must surely be *no*, since no text in literary history seems quite so bereft of momentum as this one, whose laborious rotation of near-identical sentences congeals on the reading mind like a scab, rather than conveys that effect of movement which it was the cinema's genius to have perfected. Whatever her retrospective identification with motion pictures, the fact that she 'never saw a cinema' is quite evident from this leaden rhythm. Gilles Deleuze marks a decisive break between the chronophotography of Muybridge and Marey and cinema proper, between : (i) instantaneous images, static sections of movement; and (ii) movement-images, mobile sections of duration in the early cinema. '[T]he essence of the cinematographic movement-image lies in extracting from vehicles or moving bodies the movement which is their common substance, or extracting from movements the mobility which is their essence.'[27] Whereas the essence of chronophotography is a spatial division of instantaneous, immobile parts. It is just this crucial distinction that Bergson also failed to appreciate, collapsing as he did the revolutionary impact of cinema back into the static reifications of chronophotography. Stein, for all her technical audacity and evident immersion in the logic of repetition and seriality, was not yet capable of making the transition from static sections of movement to mobile ones: a leap she happily made with her next, most important text, *Tender Buttons* (1914). Before that, in her enormous novel, the sentences themselves look the way individual film frames look on a flatbed in the editor's booth, prior to projection: each one almost identical to the last, but containing sufficient variations to distinguish it from all the others; and yet still denied the miracle of movement: the speed, the abstract lines of flight of the cinema and the Model T, and of America itself.

In conclusion, then, I want to suggest that *Tender Buttons* and the portraits which immediately predated it, make the aesthetic break into cinematic 'movement-images' for which the paragraphs of *The Making of Americans* served as chronophotographic prototypes. Of course, such analogies must always beg more questions than they answer; but it is at least clear from her own testimony that, whether or not she 'knew' a cinema at the time, her preoccupation with rendering American velocities and mobile images of 'personality' was profoundly cinematic – that is to say, quasi-scientific, mechanistic, repetitious, and yet striving from within this reified system towards art.

The transcendence of narrative form in *The Making of Americans* was ultimately, in this sense, a greater breakthrough than its typologies and paragraph formations. 'A thing you all know', Stein insisted in a lecture, 'is that in the three things written in this generation, there is, in none of them a story. There is none in Proust in *The Making of Americans* or in *Ulysses*. ... the important things written in this generation do not tell a story. You can see that it is natural enough.'[28] Making a bridge from this statement on high literary art to popular culture in general, she went on to say, 'Instinctively as I say you all agree with me because really in these days you all like crime stories or if you have not you should have and at any rate you do like newspapers or radio or funny papers, and in all these it is the moment to moment emphasis in what is happening that is interesting, the succeeding and failing is really not the thing that is interesting.'[29] This is the critical point. The 'moment to moment emphasis' in the course of events and its representation was what had eluded the sentences of *The Making of Americans*, which tended to stretch events out over intolerable periods. In her task of rendering the vitality of movement in America, Stein wanted to capture the kind of decentering of attention that makes each instant irrevocable and alive with intensity. She failed through the detail and heaviness of her own psychotechnic attention.

In *Tender Buttons*, Stein brought her crucial observation about narrative down from the larger structural business of plot construction to the molecular level of syntax itself. The uncanny and nonsensical style of this work is best explained as an adamant refusal to allow the sentence-form to relax into any convenient or familiar structure. Here at last are sentences which frustrate the memory's habitual task of retrieving from each of them a single, coherent thought. If the book is in some sense a series of descriptions of everyday articles and spaces, what animates these descriptions is that the 'moment to moment emphasis' of attention shifts radically within the frame of each sentence. 'A kind in glass and a cousin, a spectacle and nothing strange a single hurt color and an arrangement in a system to pointing.'[30] Grammatically, the elements are held together in what appears to be a regular sentence (although, note the absence of any verb); but syntactically, the whirring spin of nouns and noun phrases around the repeated pivotal conjunction radically dislocates our attention. We are caught within a linguistically realized 'space of time'.[31] Lyn Hejinian has written: 'Stein's analysis, in this sense, is lateral; she does not trace things back to their origins, her investigation is not etymological. That would reduce things to nouns, and Stein's concern was to get away from the stasis ... of the name'.[32] The stasis that had fatally afflicted the great experiment of *The Making of Americans* had been surmounted.

It was in the face of the system of mass production, where each species of item consists of virtually identical series of products, that Gertrude Stein wanted to mount the challenge of what she called 'the rhythm of the visible world'.[33] Within this world were untold speeds and rhythms which 'series production' had both unleashed and then occluded through repetition. Accordingly, her syntax restores the dissimilarity of things to their description. But what 'visible world' is this? It is remarkable, of course, that the various objects and spaces she chooses to express in her unique way in *Tender Buttons* are *not* those of industrial mass production. Rather, we get carafes, handkerchiefs, roastbeef, cream and pastry – in a word, the entire domestic object-world of Victorian fiction, preserved as if in aspic from the serial repetitions of modern mass-manufacture. It is just that she has abstracted a certain stylistic rhythm from the dynamism of the modern world of speed and series production, and grafted it on to this older object-world of nineteenth-century provincial French domesticity: the world of Flaubert's *Madame Bovary*. Like us perhaps, Stein's Finnish servant found it 'difficult to understand why we [Stein and Toklas] are not more modern. Gertrude Stein says that if you are way ahead with your head you naturally are old fashioned and regular in your daily life'.[34] Stein's intellect grasped that the American intensity of movement necessitated a new and radical approach to syntax and form; but this quality is nevertheless appropriated from the newer commodities and used to intensify and deepen the fading phenomenological qualities of the 'old fashioned and regular' Flaubertian universe. Such is the amazingly unstable and contradictory significance of the prose style in *Tender Buttons*. And we need only conclude by remarking that such, also, was the paradoxical condition of the early American cinema, caught up in a constitutive contradiction between its own technical and formal novelty, and a thoroughly conventional and 'Victorian' set of contents. The 'rhythm of the visible world' was, in that sense, always a split rhythm, a waltz played as *musique concrète*.

Notes

1 Georg Lukacs, *Writer and Critic*, trans. Arthur Kahn (London: Merlin, 1978), p. 139.

2 André Gide, *The Counterfeiters*, trans. Dorothy Bussy (London: Penguin, 1990), pp. 70-71.

3 André Bazin, *What is Cinema?* Volume One, trans. Hugh Gray (Berkeley: University of California Press, 1967), p. 119; Jean-François Lyotard, *The Postmodern Condition: A Report of Knowledge*, trans. Geoff Bennington and Brian Massumi (Minneapolis: University of Minnesata Press, 1984), pp. 74-75

4 Henri Bergson, *Creative Evolution*, trans. Arthur Mitchell (New York: Dover, 1998), p. 306.

5 Ibid., p. 251.

6 Lukacs, *History and Class Consciousness*, trans. Rodney Livingstone (London: Merlin, 1971), p. 93.

7 Bergson, *Creative Evolution*, p. 302.

8 Fredric Jameson, 'Allegorizing Hitchcock', *Signatures of the Visible* (London: Routledge, 1992), pp. 125-26.

9 Gertrude Stein, 'Portraits and Repetition', in *Gertrude Stein: Writings 1934-1946*, (The Library of America: New York, 1998), pp. 294-295.

10 Tim Armstrong also makes this point, in *Modernism, Technology, and the Body* (Cambridge: Cambridge University Press, 1998), p. 197.

11 Donald Sutherland, *Gertrude Stein: A Biography of Her Work* (New Haven: Yale UP, 1951), p. 5.

12 Hugo Münsterberg, *Psychology and Industrial Efficiency* (Boston & New York: Houghton Mifflin, 1913), p. 5.

13 Ibid., pp. 23-24.

14 Peter Wollen, 'Modern Times', in *Raiding the Icebox* (London: Verso, 1993), p. 36.

15 Janet Hobhouse, *Everybody Who Was Anybody: A Biography of Gertrude Stein* (London: Weidenfeld & Nicholson, 1975), pp. 70-1.

16 Lisa Ruddick, *Reading Gertrude Stein: Body, Text, Gnosis* (Ithaca & London: Cornell University Press, 1990), p. 68.

17 'Portraits and Repetition', p. 287.

18   Steven Meyer, 'Introduction' to Gertrude Stein, *The Making of Americans* (Normal, Illinois: Dalkey Archive Press, 1995), p. xxxii.

19   Gertrude Stein, 'The Gradual Making of The Making of Americans' *in Gertrude Stein: Writings 1934-1946*, pp. 285-286.

20   Hugo Münsterberg, *The Film: A Psychological Study* (New York: Dover Publications, 1970 [c. 1916]), p. 26.

21   Ibid., p. 12.

22   Ibid, p. 74.

23   Stein, *Making of Americans*, p. 186. Further references in text.

24   See Mary Ann Doane, *The Emergence of Cinematic Time* (Cambridge MA: Harvard University Press, 2002).

25   See Étienne-Jules Marey, *Movement*, trans. E. Pritchard (London: W. Heinemann, 1895).

26   Stein, 'Portraits and Repetition', p. 295.

27   Gilles Deleuze, *Cinema 1: The Movement-Image*, trans. Hugh Tomlinson and Barbara Habberjam (London: Athlone, 1992), p. 23.

28   Stein, 'Portraits and Repetition', pp. 298-99.

29   Ibid., p. 306.

30   Stein, 'Tender Buttons', in *Selected Writings of Gertrude Stein*, ed. Carl Van Vechten (New York: Vintage, 1990), p. 461.

31   'An American can fill up a space in having his movement of time by adding unexpectedly anything and yet getting within the included space everything he had intended getting'. Stein, 'Poetry and Grammar', *Writings 1932-1946*, p. 323.

32   Lyn Hejinian, *The Language of Inquiry* (Berkeley: University of California Press, 2000), p. 101.

33   '... it was there [in Granada] and at that time that Gertrude Stein's style gradually changed. She says hitherto she had been interested only in the insides of people, their character and what went on inside them, it was during that summer that she first felt a desire to express the rhythm of the visible world'. Stein, *The Autobiography of Alice B. Toklas* (London: Penguin, 1966), p. 130.

34   Stein, *Autobiography*, p. 266.

5

H.D.'s *The Gift*: an 'endless store room of film'[1]

Rachel Connor

As a 'heterodoxical modernist', H.D.'s aesthetic vision extends beyond the imagist poetry with which she first made her name.[2] Yet, although there has been sustained interest in her writing since the early 1980s, her involvement in avant-garde film in the late 1920s and her contribution to the film journal *Close Up* (1927-33) have only recently begun to attract critical attention.[3] Cinema precipitated a natural shift in H.D.'s conceptualisation of the image. Just as imagist poetry responded to what were considered to be outmoded Victorian poetic forms, cinema – with its new technology – came to be identified with 'the modern'. 'We had to get away from the nineteenth century if we were to survive' states Bryher in her memoir, *The Heart To Artemis*, and film was the medium which seemed to best represent this escape.[4] In what follows, I argue that H.D.'s discursive construction of the visual is intimately bound up with the paradigmatic cultural shift precipitated by early cinema. As such, her work is located at the very intersection of literary and visual cultures and needs to be given primary attention in discussions of modernity and visual technology. As we shall see, H.D.'s engagement with the emergent discourse of film is twofold. It is evident, firstly, in her formulation of what I term a 'narrative cinematics': the use of techniques such as close-up, superimposition, flashback and 'voice over' that are also deployed in film. Secondly, despite the fact that her involvement with film-making and film criticism ceased with the demise of the silent film in the 1930s, her awareness of the social implications of cinema extends well into the 1940s and beyond.

In order to comprehend fully H.D.'s conceptualisation of cinematic spectatorship, we need to consider the development of her spiritual vision, a vision formulated by the doctrine of the Christian Moravianism that shaped the early years of her childhood. H.D. grew up in the Moravian community in Bethlehem, Pennsylvania and her maternal family was directly descended from the first settlers, known as the Unity of the Brethren, or *Unitas Fratrum*. Founded on Christmas Eve 1741 by German migrants, Bethlehem had been one of the first

Moravian settlements in the United States.[5] Developing a doctrine of purity and grace, the early Moravians practised love and tolerance, amongst each other and towards other religious sects. The emphasis on equality and community was paramount: the congregation was arranged into communal living groups known as 'choirs', which placed together those of the same age, gender and marital status. While the community was centred around the *Gemeinhaus*, which housed the kitchens, dining room and chapel, each choir – widowers, widows, single men, single women, older and younger boys and girls – had their own residence, where members lived and worked together. To the original Moravian settlers, therefore, the traditional concept of the family did not exist: the entire community was considered one family and all Moravians worked for the community which, in turn, housed, fed, clothed and supported them. By the time H.D. was born in 1886, the community had evolved and undergone reorganization, but the communal values and the importance of the extended family remained. Raised in a tightly-knit community, in a house adjoining that of her grandparents, H.D. would have grown up with a sense of alternative social organization from that of the traditional patriarchal, nuclear family.[6] It is perhaps this aspect of her early spiritual life that allowed her to embrace the democratic values of Moravianism, while at the same time remaining equivocal about the tenets of organized religion.

The observation of ritual was an important aspect of Moravian worship: ceremonial practices like the 'kiss of peace' and the 'lovefeast' not only acknowledged Moravian history, customs and tradition but celebrated the connections that bound them together as a community. The love feast – the sharing of unconsecrated food and drink, in a ritual based on the early Christian gatherings occurring after the Pentecost – was an important symbol of union and equality. As a central part of social and religious occasions, it was an inclusive celebration of friendship and connection. And since the love feast could be shared by all alike – including children and members of other denominations – it was an outward sign of the Moravian doctrine of equality and religious tolerance. H.D.'s understanding of vision and spectatorship is directly connected to this sense of ritual and community: in *Trilogy*, for example, the central spiritual experience or vision of the narrator is represented as collective:

> The Presence was spectrum-blue,
> ultimate blue ray,
>
>
> rare as radium, healing;
> my old self, wrapped round me,

was shroud (I speak of myself individually
but I was surrounded by companions

in this mystery).[7]

Significantly, this blue ray – the illumination that ensures the salvation of the 'seer' – has close parallels with the manifestation of faith in the Moravian doctrine, which is experienced as 'a direct and supernatural illumination from God'.[8] As Barbara Guest points out, in the Moravian creed, 'there is no morality, piety, or orthodoxy existent, unless it has been touched by this "sufficient, sovereign, saving grace,"' passed on and witnessed by other members of the community (Guest, p. 9).

Despite H.D.'s ambivalent relationship with orthodox religion, her notion of visionary 'seeing' was shaped by the illuminations or spiritual manifestations she experienced throughout her lifetime. On a visit to the Scilly Isles with Bryher in 1919, for instance, H.D. had a sensation – a spiritual vision manifesting itself through the body – which she later called her 'jellyfish experience':

> We were in the little room that Bryher had taken for our study when I felt this impulse to "let go" into a sort of balloon, or diving-bell as I have explained it, that seemed to hover over me [...] There was, I explained to Bryher, a second globe or bell-jar rising as if it were from my feet...I felt the double globe come and go and I could have dismissed it at once and probably would have if I had been alone...It was being with Bryher that projected the fantasy.[9]

Bryher's collaboration in H.D.'s 'projection' of the image, here, is significant: for it recurs in her later 'writing-on-the-wall' episode, the revelatory vision recorded in *Tribute To Freud* that she experienced in Corfu in 1920. Like the projected moving images of the cinema, the 'writing-on-the-wall' vision is represented as 'a series of shadows or of light pictures'.[10] And, as in the 'jellyfish' experience, Bryher's presence is crucial to H.D.'s projection of the vision: 'I can turn now to [Bryher] though I do not budge an inch or break the sustained crystal-gazing stare at the wall before me. I say to Bryher [...] "Shall I stop? Shall I go on?" .Bryher says without hesitation, "Go on"' (H.D., *Tribute*, p. 70). Acknowledging Bryher's emotional support in the act of 'seeing' the images, H.D. states: 'I knew this experience, this writing-on-the-wall before me [...] could not be shared with anyone except the girl who stood so bravely there beside me' (H.D., *Tribute*, p. 72). The image of the two women in a semi-darkened room, looking together at the projected images on the wall or "screen" is crucial, for it becomes a key trope in H.D.'s representations of her spiritual manifestations or visions as cinematic. As in *Trilogy*, where H.D. defines herself as a member of an audience that is collective, her role as "seer" depends on her inclusion within a community of spectators who support and sustain her vision.[11]

In H.D.'s work, and especially in her film criticism, the visual is underpinned by an acute awareness of the interconnections between the political and the spiritual. In 'The Mask and the Movietone' (1927) she defines cinematic spectatorship as a collective – and a religious – experience:

> We sank into light, into darkness, the cinema palace [...] became a sort of temple. We sank into this warmth and were recreated. The cinema has become to us what the church was to our ancestors. We sang, so to speak, hymns, we were redeemed by light literally.[12]

This notion of the film spectator being recreated through the viewing process has resonances, of course, with the notion of the 'creating spectator' propounded by the Soviet film director, Sergei Eisenstein. His theory of 'intellectual montage' – brought to life in such classics as *The Battleship Potemkin* (1925) and *October* (1927) – aimed to construct a national Soviet cinema that would rouse the spectator to political action in the Russian socialist revolution. Like H.D., Eisenstein draws on the terminology of the Old and New Testaments, describing the cinematic image as 'the flesh of the flesh of the spectator's risen image'.[13] Given the atheistic leaning of socialist and communist theory, the use of such religious vocabulary might seem contradictory, evoking what – to a Marxist – would be the repressive and totalising regime of Christianity. Yet, for the time in which Eisenstein was writing, it is a vocabulary that is highly appropriate. To the growing number of cinema-goers in the increasingly secular climate of early twentieth-century Europe, the visit to the picture palace was fast replacing the weekly ritual of church-going. Eisenstein's identification of the cinema with religious worship shares similarities with that of H.D., as well as with Dorothy Richardson who describes the cinema audience as a 'congregation' and film itself as 'a eucharistic form of bread'.[14] The suggestion of moral redemption through the viewing of film in the writing of these modernists suggests a belief that the cinema was a collective visual experience, in which it was possible for 'a community of spectators' to become 'educated for modernity'.[15]

The Gift: 'stores in the darkroom of memory'

Written during the Second World War in London – between 1941 and 1944 – *The Gift* is H.D.'s attempt to reconstruct her early years in Bethlehem.[16] Indeed, critics often read *The Gift* as H.D.'s attempt to recapture the maternal heritage of her mother's Moravian faith and the ideals of community that are fundamental to its organisation.[17] This reconstruction of a spiritual ancestry in *The Gift* is often regarded as a political strategy on the part of H.D., a means of asserting her pacifist ideals. Thus, Susan Stanford Friedman argues, the text itself becomes '[H.D.'s] gift to bring the message of peace to a world perpetually at war'.[18] Expanding upon these critical readings, I want to explore how we might gain further insights into *The Gift*'s notion of 'community' by considering the intersection of the literary and the visual in the text. For H.D., as for Bryher and the other *Close Up* contributors, silent film offered the possibility of 'a single language across Europe', of moving beyond the demarcations of national identity (Bryher, *Artemis*, p. 246). This desire for synthesis is also a fundamental aspect of *The Gift*, in which, through the processes of memory, H.D. reconstructs the 'lost' community of the Moravian Protestant church. But in order to understand fully the complex and contradictory nature of H.D.'s representation of community, and its connection to the visual, it is vital to take into account the context of the cinematic culture of the 1940s.

The Second World War, as Sarah Street argues, had a huge impact on the birth of a national British cinema. Film-makers set out to produce films which would stress the need for unity so that film itself became a tool of propaganda.[19] Thus, in the British cinema of the mid-1940s, the war generated an impulse 'to produce images which would create a sense of national collectivity' through the activity of spectatorship itself as a public and collective experience (Street, p. 50). While such 'collectivity' is directly translated to the literary construction of the visual in *The Gift*, this political impulse towards social unity in H.D.'s work is neither straightforward nor unproblematic, since there are inherent tensions in her notions of spectatorship between the public and the private. As we shall see, the notion of community in H.D.'s writing not only relates to collective social organisation, but extends to incorporate the private 'community' of her partnership with Bryher and with Kenneth Macpherson, who was both Bryher's husband and H.D.'s lover.[20]

Before moving on to examine the narrative strategies of *The Gift*, it may be useful to outline the background and context of the memoir itself. In the dual time scheme of *The Gift*, H.D. mediates between her childhood past in the Moravian community – which is related through the voice of the young narrator, Hilda – and the narrative present of wartime London. Crucial to the text are the reflections of Mamalie, H.D.'s maternal grandmother, who, through the powers of 'psychic recall' describes an encounter between the newly-arrived Moravian settlers and the native Americans at 'Wunden Eiland' in 1741.[21] This meeting is represented as a defining moment in the text, since it marks the founding of 'a secret powerful community that would bring the ancient secrets of Europe and the ancient secrets of America into a single union of power and spirit, a united brotherhood, a *Unitas Fratrum* of the whole world' (H.D., *Gift*, p. 214). Transcribed onto a 'scroll of flexible deerskin', the account of the meeting at Wunden Eiland between the

Moravian settlers and the native Americans, is discovered almost a hundred years later by Mamalie's first husband, Christian (H.D., *Gift*, p. 168). Christian achieves his 'guided' reading of these unknown languages by piecing together fragments from the deerskin scroll. This knowledge is manifested as spiritual vision, a 'gift' which originated at Wunden Eiland and was passed down through ensuing generations. Through Christian's spiritual and creative enlightenment, the legacy of the gift is revived. Thus, the text itself becomes a journey towards the realisation of a forgotten or buried inheritance and a spiritual power. This legacy of the gift is crucial to *The Gift*'s representation of community, as it was to the early Moravians. Through H.D.'s reconstruction of the memories of the child Hilda, this gift is passed on to the reader who collaborates in the creation of its meaning, so that the gift operates both as Hilda's/H.D.'s realisation of her maternal ancestry and as a passing on of knowledge to the reader.

The Gift's constant mediation between past and present is achieved, in part, through the narrative device of analepsis. In filmic terms, analepsis – or flashback – is a means of returning to an earlier, clearly marked 'subjective moment' in a character's life.[22] Susan Hayward points out that, as a 'representation of memory and of history', cinematic flashback dates back to 'the beginnings of film history [...] thus coinciding with the birth and burgeoning of psychoanalysis' (Hayward, p. 122).[23] It is the concept of cinematic flashback, therefore – rather than literary analepsis – which informs my reading of *The Gift*, since there it enacts a similar retrieval of personal history through a process of memory that is rooted in the visual. The link between memory and the technical apparatus of film is apparent in the description of the 'long strips of continuous photographs' which are 'stored in the darkroom of memory' (H.D., *Gift*, p. 50). Such descriptions also extend to the writing of *Majic Ring*, which was composed in parallel with *The Gift* between 1943 and 1944. For H.D. writes: 'these [memories] may have been random projections from that great store-house where we are told all the past is rolled and neatly filed and edited, like the endless store-room of film, waiting for the suitable moment to be projected and re-projected' (H.D., *Majic*, p. 201).

Friedman interprets the direct association between film and memory in *The Gift* in the light of H.D.'s engagement with psychoanalysis.[24] In Friedman's analysis it is H.D.'s own psyche – as the adult narrator in *The Gift* – which constructs memories as visual images and then projects them as though running a film:

> The mind – and the text as the representation of the mind – is a darkroom in which memories are developed into photographic images that flow like film into a projector. In this 'camera obscura' [...] 'these flashes of flash-backs' are 'film [that] unrolls in my head' [...] The montage of this 'film' parallels the 'dark room' of cinematic creation with the 'dark room' of Freudian analysis.
>
> (Friedman, *Penelope*, p. 332-3)

While Friedman's reading of the deployment of cinematic devices in *The Gift* is a valid one, it overlooks H.D.'s attempt to construct an audience for the fragments or flashes of film which constitute the text. The composition of *The Gift* is itself equated with the process of watching a film. Thus, the act of reading H.D.'s literary text is transformed into a process of viewing, an effect which is achieved, as we shall see, through the use of visual close-up and the suggestion of 'voice-over'. This technique again evokes comparisons with Eisenstein's notion of the 'creating spectator', an intrinsic part of his theory of intellectual montage. H.D.'s memoir seeks, through its discursive construction of the visual, a way to bind the audience together through the collaborative experience of spectatorship.

How, then, do the political implications of cinema illuminate the spiritual notions of community underpinning H.D.'s *The Gift*? This question is answered when examining the journal *Close Up*, produced in the late 1920s and early 1930s amidst the increasing tension in Europe that culminated in the Second World War. On the whole, as Jane Marek points out, the editors of *Close Up* took a critical view of 'the problem of the mass coercion used to promote war'.[25] Bryher's voice, above all, is resoundingly pacifist, especially in the essay 'What Shall You Do In the War?':

> Let us decide what we will have. If peace, let us fight for it. And fight for it especially with cinema. By refusing to see films that are merely propaganda for any unjust system [...] above all, in the choice of films to see, remember the many directors, actors and film architects who have been driven out of the German studios and scattered across Europe because they believed in peace and intellectual liberty.[26]

Two key issues emerge from this passage. Firstly, if we accept the view that avant-garde culture is usually more preoccupied with form rather than content – and with aesthetics, rather than politics – Bryher's piece demonstrates an unusually close engagement with the current political climate. Secondly, her reference to the artists who are 'driven out of Germany' and 'scattered across Europe' anticipates the enforced exodus of the Holocaust. Implicitly, there is a desire to include these expelled film artists in a community of intellectuals across Europe who believe in 'peace and intellectual liberty'.[27] More significantly, Bryher's words resonate with those of H.D. in *The Gift* when she speaks of her gift of a 'vision of [...] peace' enabling her to see into the past as a means of reconstructing the future (H.D., *Gift*, p. 214).

Street argues that despite the 'vanguard rhetoric' of *Close Up*, the journal was 'primarily interested in aesthetic rather than political aspects of film' (Street, p. 153). Yet, while *Close Up* is often seen as a mouthpiece for the liberal avant-garde, the journal took seriously issues of national identity. It was founded on a real urgency to construct itself as 'transnational' and to advocate 'a transnational cinema'.[28] Since *Close Up* had correspondents in Moscow, Berlin, Paris, Geneva, London, New York and Los Angeles, it played a significant role, as Anne Friedberg notes, 'in a growing community without borders' (Friedberg, 'Reading', p. 10). In considering *The Gift*, it is vital to take into account H.D.'s stake in *Close Up* and her understanding of the ideological implications of film: for the internationalist ethos at the heart of the journal was inscribed directly into the narrative of her memoir. This is borne out through *The Gift*'s social and political concerns, in the attempt to reconstruct a lost community and to create a sense of cohesion in the midst of war. But it also emerges in H.D.'s textual practice, through her use of analepsis, outlined above, and through her deployment of voice.

The discursive style of many of H.D.'s film reviews suggests that her interest in film lay not so much in the analysis of individual images but in the process of spectatorship itself. In 'Conrad Veidt: The Student of Prague' (1927), for instance, H.D. does not provide the reader with a retrospective analysis of the film but conveys her immediate reactions to its narrative:

> The music ought, it is evident, be making my heart spring but I don't like student songs and these Heidelbergish melodies especially leave me frigid. There's something wrong and I have seen those horses making that idiotic turn on the short grass at least eight times. What is it? I won't stay any longer.[29]

As Laura Marcus argues, this 'performative running commentary on the processes of spectating' is a common feature of H.D.'s film reviews.[30] It assumes a form of '"inner speech," acting as a screen onto which the film images can be projected' (Marcus, p. 101). However, this 'commentary' is not limited to H.D.'s essays alone: it is also employed in *The Gift* where narrative voice and visual image are closely intertwined.[31] In an early scene of the memoir, the image of Hilda and her two brothers sitting on a sofa combines with a direct address from the narrator that is intended to guide the reader's 'viewing':

> You yourself may wonder at the mystery in this house, the hush in this room; you may glance at the row of children on the horsehair sofa and at the plaque of mounted butterflies [...] the children can not tell you for no one has been able to answer that question for them. (H.D., *Gift*, p. 85)

Like H.D.'s autobiographical prose fiction, which utilises close-up as a means of involving the reader in the active process of viewing, *The Gift* contains moments of intense focus on the characters' surroundings. In one instance towards the end of the text, where the adult narrator is recalling her conversation with

Mamalie, the actions and observations of childhood are remembered in vivid and precise detail across the distance of time:

> Now it seems, while I pour out water from the pitcher into the glass, that I am Hilda pouring out water from a washstand jug that has roses and a band of dark blue that looks like a painted ribbon round the top. The tooth-mug matches the pitcher. There is a soap dish with a little china plate, with holes in it, that is separate so that the water from the soap will drip through. The basin has the same roses. (H.D., *Gift*, p. 174)

Here the narrator's senses are heightened by the solemnity of the occasion of learning the forgotten 'secrets' of Moravian history from her grandmother. Paradoxically, despite the clear visual detail through which H.D. invites the reader to share the moment, the narrative evokes a sense of detachment. The 'adult' narrative voice, relating the image of her childhood self, operates here almost like a cinematic 'voice over', where the direct intervention of the narrator from a distance across a period of time is signalled by the gap between the image on the screen and the soundtrack.

Hayward argues that the device of voice-over in film 'bridges the gap between the past and the present [in which] the present is speaking about the past' (Hayward, p. 127).[32] As such 'the voice-over represents a subjectivity that is a controlling of the past' (p. 127). While the first-person narrative voice in this extract from *The Gift* relates to the narrative present, the image to which it corresponds is rooted in the past. In addition to accentuating the temporal split in the narrative, this technique simultaneously represents two distinct 'selves', implying a split in the narrator's subjectivity. The text appears, on the one hand, as H.D.'s invitation to share her visions, to 'connect us into her community' (Morris, p. 66). On the other hand, the division between image and voice renders this process more complex through the suggestion of a divided identity. This division establishes a tension between the public and private aspects of spectatorship, suggesting that, in the end, while H.D. embraces the ideal of a spiritual vision as a way of reinforcing social connections, the political effectiveness of that ideal is limited.

Film: 'a privatized form of reception'

The contradictions between 'public' and 'private' aspects of spectatorship are underscored in the correspondence between H.D. and Bryher in the late 1920s. Written in the code language the two women reserved for their letter-writing, H.D. ('Cat') conveys to Bryher ('Fido') her delight at the prospect of an evening alone watching the magic lantern she purchased as a gift for her daughter, Perdita ('Pup'):

> The magic lantern is that so tonight I can slip in little bits of film. I have already peeled and prepared the films for the private show I give one CAT tonight. The lantern is pup's Christmas present [...] so does a wise cat salve its cat-conscience [...] The Cat believes with all its nine cat hearts and souls and brains in the film, in we us as opposed to them there monkeys who say "our big producers". Even if we are never shown anywhere, cat loves and believes in us. (30 July 1928)

H.D.'s letter establishes an opposition between the more widely-shown mainstream productions of the commercial film industry, run, she suggests by 'monkeys' and the private reels shot by 'we us' – herself, Bryher and Macpherson. Despite H.D.'s fascination and pleasure with these home-made reels of film, the implication is that they are too obscure or too experimental to be shown in public, and that they are intended for private viewing. The fact that this is conveyed in the coded language used exclusively within H.D.'s circle intensifies the notion of a 'private' aesthetic still further.

Such contradictions reveal the inherent complexities in H.D.'s awareness of the political implications of the cinema. Spectatorship is at once private and public for H.D.: it mediates between the realm of the personal and that of the social or collective, always carrying with it political implications. This dual perspective is translated into the literary narrative of *The Gift*. For, like the poetry and prose H.D. produced earlier in her career, the memoir reinforces her connection with the reader through its invitation to collaborate in the text's construction. In this respect, as a modernist narrative that troubles nineteenth-century realism and the existence of an omniscient narrator, *The Gift* works, like film itself, to rouse what Watt terms the spectator's 'collaborating creative consciousness' (p. 77). Like film, which – for H.D. – had the potential to foster international relations, the text reinforces social connections through its visual dynamic. Conversely, *The Gift* also functions as H.D.'s *personal* journey through the labyrinths of her memory and as a means of reinforcing a private community with Bryher. Thus, she is able to explore a mode of spectatorship which is collective but which is also, as Friedberg points out, 'a *privatized* form of reception'.[33]

By valorising silent, European art film above more commercial, mainstream productions, H.D. appears to uphold the privileging of aesthetic form that informs canonical literary modernism. Indeed, in the criticism and reviews that she wrote for *Close Up*, film is consistently figured as a work of art or as autonomous 'artefact'. Like the other contributors to the journal, H.D. professes an opposition to mainsteam cinema, a position that appears to underscore a modernist avant gardism.[34] If, as Jill Forbes and Sarah Street suggest, the making of a modernist film is 'more like writing a private diary than manufacturing a car', then the experimental cinema produced by H.D. and her circle could be seen as a type of aestheticised, highbrow 'home movie'.[35] At odds with this view – and what is apparent from H.D.'s correspondence – is the notion that, for her, film also functions as an object of exchange, a currency that reinforces her sexual and emotional connection with Bryher and Macpherson. Paradoxically, in considering the 'narrative cinematics' of *The Gift* – and by taking into account H.D.'s legacy of visionary and spiritual experience – we see her literary-visual text operating within a kind of 'gift economy' that exists in opposition to the norms of capital exchange.[36]

The complex matrix of ideologies inscribed into *The Gift* – spiritual and economic, aesthetic and political – illuminates the contradictions in H.D.'s engagement with the visual and their representation in her texts. These contradictions, I argue, can only be fully brought into view by reading the memoir in the context of a 1940s national British cinema. On the one hand, H.D.'s invitation to the reader of *The Gift* to share her private vision of the past is a means of countering the destruction of war. On the other, the aims of British cinema to boost the nation's flagging morale – and to foster patriotism in its promotion of the war effort – operate in complete opposition to *The Gift*'s expression of pacifism. As Donald, Friedberg and Marcus argue in their preface to the *Close Up* anthology, considering the aesthetics of early cinema is essential to a re-evaluation of *literary* history. Read in this context, H.D.'s involvement in film production and the inscription of cinematic techniques into her textual practice complicates the boundaries of literary modernism. But if *The Gift* challenges literary historiography, then the representation of film in H.D.'s essays and letters complicates the binary – between the aesthetic and the political – intrinsic to cinematic modernism. A consideration of H.D.'s conceptualisation of cinematic spectatorship, then, offers a fresh approach to the reading of her literary texts. This is especially true in the case of *The Gift*, which, until now, has largely been read in the light of H.D.'s Moravian heritage. For, ultimately, *The Gift*'s central premise of 'a single powerful community' (H.D., *Gift*, p. 214) was also shaped by H.D.'s awareness of the emergent visual technology of the modern age.

Notes

1   The quotation in the title is taken from H.D.'s unpublished typescript of *Majic Ring*, composed between 1943 and 1944, at around the same time as she was writing *The Gift*.

2   Dianne Chisholm, 'H.D.'s Autobiography', in Harriet Devine-Jump (ed.), *Twentieth Century Women Writers in English* (London: Harvester, 1991), p. 62.

3   Charlotte Mandel, Anne Friedberg and Susan Edmunds were the first to address the relationship between H.D.'s work on film and her literary texts. For more recent discussions of H.D.'s involvement in film and film-making, and particularly her involvement in *Close Up*, see James Donald, Anne Friedberg and Laura Marcus (eds.), *Close Up 1927-1933: Cinema and Modernism*, (London: Cassell, 1998).

4   Bryher, *The Heart to Artemis: A Writer's Memoirs* (New York: Harcourt and Brace, 1962), p. 246. Bryher (Winifred Ellerman) became H.D.'s lover and lifelong partner in 1918. However, H.D.'s relationship with her was part of a more complex series of bisexual identifications, which included affairs with both Bryher's husbands, Robert McAlmon and Kenneth Macpherson. Bryher herself is an important figure who has been overlooked in discussions of early twentieth-century literary and visual culture. She was the heiress to the Ellerman shipping fortune, a wealthy woman who was a patron of the arts and who subsidised the work of several modernist writers, including Dorothy Richardson.

5   Persecuted in their native Moravia by Catholics and Lutherans, the Moravians had originally taken refuge in Saxony in the early eighteenth century, under the protection of Count Nikolaus von Zinzendorf, on whose land they built a settlement called 'Herrnhut' ('watched over by the Lord'). In 1951 H.D. wrote 'The Mystery', a detailed historical novel about Zinzendorf and her Moravian ancestors. While it remains unpublished, it offers important insights into the connection H.D. makes between her Moravian roots and what she regarded as her 'visionary' abilities.

6   Adalaide Morris, 'A Relay of Power and of Peace: H.D. and the Spirit of the Gift', in Susan Stanford Friedman (ed.), *Signets: Reading H.D.* (Wisconsin: University of Wisconsin Press, 1990), p. 61.

7   H.D., *Trilogy*, in *Collected Poems 1912-1944*, ed. Loius L. Martz (New York: New Directions, 1986), p. 520.

8   Barbara Guest, *Herself Defined: The Poet H.D. and her World* (New York: Doubleday, 1984), p. 9. Guest defines 'supernatural' in this context as 'above the natural order of things' (p. 9).

9   H.D., 'Advent', cited in Kathleen Crown, 'H.D.'s Jellyfish Manifesto and the Visible Body of Modernism', *Sagetrieb* 14. 1-2 (1995), p. 223.

10   H.D., *Tribute to Freud* (New York: Pantheon, 1956), p. 61.

11   Towards the end of *The Gift*, too, Bryher's presence is crucial to H.D.'s ability to envisage past memories and the memories of her Moravian ancestors. It could be argued that there is a lesbian erotic at work here: in the act of looking together, the women share an identification which is based on proximity and therefore undercuts the dominant, phallocentric power of the scopic economy.

12   H.D., 'The Cinema and the Classics III: The Mask and the Movietone', in *Close Up* 1. 5 (1927), p. 23.

13   Sergei Eisenstein, 'Montage I 1938'. Rpt. 'Word and Image', in Jay Leyda (ed. and trans.), *The Film Sense* (New York and London: Harcourt and Brace, 1975), p. 33.

14   Carol Watts, *Dorothy Richardson* (Plymouth: Northcote House, 1995), p. 78.

15   Laura Marcus, 'Continuous Performance: Dorothy Richardson', in Donald, Friedberg and Marcus (eds.) , *Close Up*, p. 152.

16   H.D., *The* Gift, ed. Jane Augustine (Florida: University Press of Florida, 1998). First published in 1969, the New Directions version of the text was abridged and heavily truncated. The recently-published version is edited by Jane Augustine and is complete and unabridged. All references to *The Gift* in this essay are taken from Augustine's version.

17   See, for instance, Morris and Friedman.

18   Susan Stanford Friedman, *Penelope's Web: Gender, Modernity, H.D.'s Fiction,* (Cambridge: Cambridge University Press), p. 330.

19   Sarah Street, *British National Cinema* (London and New York: Routledge, 1997), p. 50.

20   Although Macpherson is solely credited with directing *Borderline* (1930) – which featured Paul Robeson as well as H.D. herself – in reality the conception, direction and editing of the film was a collaborative venture between Macpherson, Bryher and H.D.

21   Perdita Schaffner, 'Unless a Bomb Falls'. Introduction to H.D.'s *The Gift* (New York: New Directions, 1982), p. xiii Since the text fails to acknowledge the colonising project at the heart of this encounter, H.D.'s vision of the fusion of the two cultures could, of course, be read as a romanticisation of native American spirituality. From their arrival in north America, the first Moravian settlers were involved in a missionary enterprise which sought to convert the 'Indians' in the area.

22   Susan Hayward, *Key Concepts in Cinema Studies* (London and New York: Routledge, 1996), p. 122.

23   Hayward locates the origins of the flashback technique to 'at least 1901' to Ferdinand Zecca's *Histoire d'un Crime*.

24   Both H.D. and Bryher had a keen interest in psychoanalysis and Bryher paid for H.D. to undergo a period of analysis with Freud in 1933.

25   Jane Marek, 'Bryher and *Close Up*, 1927-1933', *H.D. Newsletter*, 3.2 (1990), 30.

26   Bryher, 'What Shall You Do in the War?', Rpt. In Donald, Friedberg and Marcus (eds.) *Close Up*, p. 309.

27   It should perhaps be pointed out that this 'community' constituted a privileged minority of intellectuals, made up of an 'internationally disperse [sic] group of patriots dedicated to developing the potential of the film as an art'; Anne Friedberg, 'Reading Close Up', in Donald, Friedberg and Marcus (eds.), *Close Up*, p. 10.

28   Anne Friedberg, 'Reading Close Up', in Donald, Friedberg and Marcus (eds.), *Close Up*, p. 12.

29   H.D., 'Conrad Veidt: The Student of Prague'. Rpt. in Donald, Friedberg and Marcus (eds.), Close Up, p. 120.

30   Laura Marcus, 'The Contribution of H.D.', in Donald, Friedberg and Marcus (eds.), *Close Up*, p. 101.

31 An instance of this 'performative running commentary' also occurs in *Bid Me To Live* when the protagonist, Julia, is part of a cinema audience full of soldiers. As Trudi Tate argues, 'the narrative interweaves images from the film with Julia's vision of the crowd of doomed men' (Trudi Tate, 'H.D.'s War Neurotics', in Suzanne Raitt and Trudi Tate [eds.], *Women's Fiction and the Great* War [Oxford: Clarendon Press, 1997], p. 256) and this operates as a series of questions and snippets from popular wartime songs. Again, this suggests that H.D.'s vision of peace may well be informed by her experience of visual culture, especially cinematic culture.

32 Hayward further points out how the techniques of flashback and voice-over in film noir – in Billy Wilder's *Double Indemnity* (1944) and John Brahms' *Mildred Pierce* (1946), for instance – serve to underscore the masculinity of the male protagonist. For a discussion of how voice-over and synchronisation serve to reinscribe gender representation, see Kaja Silverman, 'Dis-Embodying the Female Voice', in Patricia Erens (ed.), *Issues in Feminist Film Criticism* (Bloomington and Indianapolis: Indiana University Press, 1990), pp. 309-27.

33 Anne Fiedberg, 'On H.D., Woman, History, Recognition', *Wide Angle: A Film Quarterly of Theory, Criticism and Practice*, 5 (1982), 29.

34 Paradoxically, although H.D. eschewed mainstream cinema, her private papers at Yale contain numerous newspaper clippings, film reviews and photographs of contemporary film stars such as Greta Garbo and Marlene Dietrich. This implies a further contradiction between the realms of the public and private in H.D.'s attitude to film spectatorship.

35 Jill Forbes and Sarah Street, *European Cinema: An Introduction* (London: Palgrave, 2000), p. 38.

36 There are close resonances between H.D.'s representation of the 'gift' in her memoir and Marcel Mauss' anthropological notion of the 'gift economy'. Although there is no specific evidence of H.D.'s familiarity with Mauss' work, her library contained 'tomes on the history of religion and mythology, archaelogical investigations, and explorations of archaic society', all of which suggests a similarity in their interests (Morris, p. 59).

6

Ulysses in Toontown: 'vision animated to bursting point' in Joyce's 'Circe'

Keith Williams

Not only did James Joyce become professionally involved with early film in his ill-starred venture to set up Ireland's first regular cinema in 1909-10, but his own formative movie-going took place when the industry was still all but shunned as vulgar catchpenny entertainment of scant aesthetic worth, by most 'serious' writers and cultural pundits.[1] In this sense, Joyce was prescient, as well as democratic, in embracing this popular medium for the groundbreaking possibilities it helped fertilise in his work. Indeed, what seems most remarkable about the manifold parallels with early movies in Joyce's texts is the sheer catholicity of his taste. The paradox is that Joyce was just as interested in the medium, for its 'lowbrow' appeal, as for its avant-garde potentials, and his work was all the more innovative, formally and philosophically, for that.

In its broadest sense, intertextuality with film is, arguably, one of the most energising drives in his Modernist project. In effect, the influences and analogies to be found in the 'polyvisual' content and style of his writing are as pluralistic and unprejudging as the typically 'mixed programmes' he exhibited at the Volta in Dublin. Such receptiveness is admirably implied in Pat Murphy's recent biopic about Joyce's partner *Nora* (2000). The most self-reflexive and cinematically insightful moments take place when Nora whiles away dull Triestine afternoons by watching sentimental Italian melodramas, or when he is shown reacting to their erotic correspondence in the Volta's projection room, against the background of a comic 'trickfilm'. Such scenes suggest not just the intimate and historically-situated nature of the Joyces' cinema-going, but also the deep creative ferment it set off in his writing, in all the creative indirection of its workings.

The extent of the inadvertently modernist potentials Joyce might have seized on in early film's primitive populism is illustrated by a selection of surviving one-reelers shown by Joyce in Dublin (some of which Murphy excerpts). These were exhibited by the British Film Institute from its National Film and Television Archive, under the title of 'An Evening at the Volta', at the 'Literature and Visual

Technologies Conference' (St John's College, Oxford 18-19 September 2000)). This eminently 'mixed programme' testifies mutely but eloquently to the sheer openness of Joyce's precocious 'film-mindedness'. This ranged through early documentaries and travelogues, to Biblical spectaculars and from Film d'Arte tragedies, to slapstick comedy and trickfilms. We can, of course, only speculate about actual links between particular films and specifically Joycean themes and techniques. However, the undeniably striking effect of watching them now is as a tantalising cornucopia of possible thematic imprintings and formal cross-fertilisations.

The comedies must have been particularly stimulating to Joyce's anarchic and eminently trans-generic imagination. But perhaps most importantly two early trickfilms indicate Joyce's awareness of the medium's ambiguous potential for being what Joseph Conrad (underlining the equally cinematic tendency of H.G. Wells's early writings) called the 'Realist of the Fantastic',[2] for presenting the actual and the impossible simultaneously and with apparently equal verisimilitude. The first of these, Percy Stow's *Beware of Goat's Milk* (GB, 1909), depicts a respectable gent's metamorphosis into demonic satyr. With wonderful, vernacular proto-surrealism, he chases and butts over people, trees, buildings and even, climactically, an omnibus. Leering facial close-ups suggest rampant eroticism, as well as his glee at creating a miniature, one-man 'mockalypse', as it were, anticipating Joyce's full-blown one in the 'Circe' chapter of *Ulysses* (1922). Moreover, the transformation effect, in which horns magically grow out of his head (by inflating 'prosthetics'), seems to anticipate not only Bloom's cuckolding and metamorphoses in the same chapter, but Stephen's distinctly monochrome nightmare in *A Portrait of the Artist as a Young Man* (1914-15). In the latter, lustfully goatish creatures, 'faces grey as indiarubber', like the satyr's horns, close in on him in a weed-choked field,[3] the same location as much of Stow's film.

The second trickfilm, *An Easy Way to Pay Bills* (Italy, 1909), features serial comic André Deed. Deed, who began work in the early French industry, made his name in Italy from 1908 playing 'Cretinetti', known as 'Foolshead' in English. *An Easy Way*'s madcap vanishings and re-appearances, not only confirm Joyce relished, and thought the Dublin public would too, the tradition of visual conjuring initiated by George Méliès and Alice Guy-Blaché in France as early as 1896, but that he was also familiar with the use of 'object animation',[4] essentially achieved by the same 'stop motion' process. Double-exposure renders Foolshead spookily transparent so he can walk through walls, etc., but he mostly evades his massing creditors by leaping in and out of a magic carpetbag, which moves around with a life of its own, quite literally a displacement of a human presence into an object – a sort of 'living' metonymy. Animism – what Vachel Lindsay in his *The Art of the Moving Picture* (1915) (perhaps the earliest 'serious' critical study of film) called 'a yearning for personality in furniture' – was rife in early cinema, most obviously in trickfilms and cartoons.[5] This helps to corroborate the theory (advanced by Austin Briggs and Thomas L. Burkdall) that Joyce drew on stop-motion in the fantastic drama of 'Circe',[6] though I intend to show that he may also have been influenced by its logical extension, graphic, or 'cartoon', animation. Indeed no early cinema-goer could fail to notice the medium's childlike fascination with 'autokinesis', the basic principle of moving images, whether of people, objects or drawings. As Alan Spiegel has argued, it is possible to trace Joyce's innovative treatment of objects along a kind of spectrum, from the subtly symbolic in his earlier writings to the fantastically literal in *Ulysses*.[7] In *Dubliners* (1914) and *A Portrait of the Artist as a Young Man*, Joyce uses metonymies to signify emotional states and situations. Well-known examples are the 'close-up' of the limp boot in 'The Dead' which figures Gabriel and Gretta's sexual anti-climax, or the 'tracking shot' of the napkin ring rolling across the floor, which prolongs the tension of the Christmas dinner row in the Dedalus household after Dante storms from the table.[8] But in *Ulysses* objects increasingly have a life of their own, from the automatic printing press Bloom watches in 'Aeolus',[9] to fully 'animated' objects in 'Circe'. Lindsay also noted that the complementary tendency of cinematic animism was objectification of people: in 'all photoplays ... human beings tend to become dolls and mechanisms, and dolls and mechanisms tend to become human' (*Art of the Moving Picture*, p. 53). However, the transformational devices of *Ulysses'* mockalyptic climax move beyond the staginess of stop-motion trickery and into parallels with early graphic animators. As Donald Crafton argues, Leo Bloom's contemporary, Felix the Cat, displayed a 'polymorphous plasticism', through which his body or anything in his environment could be instantly reshaped.[10] Joyce's effects, especially in the case of Bloom's corporeal deformations, even, arguably, anticipate today's computer generated digital imaging, which can render actuality footage into virtual 'polymorphousness'.

In Homer's *Odyssey*, Chapter X, the witch, Circe, turns men into swine, i.e. visible embodiments of their animal appetites. The Latin root gives us the familiar word for living creatures (i.e. 'animals'), but also soul or life ('anima'). It is arguable that relations between soul and body, subject and object are never under greater strain in *Ulysses* than in Chapter XV. Significantly, the 'technic' designated for 'Circe' by Joyce in the Linati schema was *'Visione animata fino allo scoppio'*, which Ellmann translated as 'Vision animated to bursting point'.[11] Moreover, 'Circe's' form – which switches into a kind of fantastic 'play' – is one in which people, things, objects are constantly being transformed, transfigured and interfused. Everything in effect becomes 'animated' or given grotesque and phantasmagoric life, like tropes – metaphoric or metonymic – made visually literal. For example, the lemon soap Bloom carries rises from his pocket into the sky like a cartoon sun, singing, in a kind of prosopopoeia anticipating the soundtrack:

THE SOAP
We're a capital couple are Bloom and I;
He brightens the earth, I polish the sky.

The shopkeeper Bloom bought it from then pops up as a visual 'insert': '(*The freckled face of Sweny, the druggist, appears in the disc of the soapsun.*) (*Ulysses*, p.419) Similarly, a flock of come-hither kisses flutter around Bloom, murmuring provocatively:

THE KISSES
(*Warbling*) Leo! (*Twittering*) Icky licky micky sticky for Leo! (*Cooing*) Coo coocoo! Yummyumm Womwom! (*Warbling*) Big comebig! Pirouette! Leopold! (*Twittering*) Leolee! (*Warbling*) O Leo!

(They rustle, flutter upon his garments, alight, bright giddy flecks, silvery sequins.)

(Ulysses, p. 449)

Appropriate to his fetish for ladies' garments and accessories, when Bloom encounters the dominatrix madame, her fan talks portentous arousal:

(*Bella approaches, gently tapping with the fan*)

BLOOM
(*Wincing*) Powerful being. In my eyes read that slumber that women love.

THE FAN
(*Tapping*) We have met. You are mine. It is fate.

(Ulysses, p. 495)

Bloom kneels to unlace her boot, now metamorphosed into a hoof making erotic threats to titillate his masochistic streak:

THE HOOF
Smell my hot goathide. Feel my royal weight.

BLOOM
(*Crosslacing*) Too tight?

THE HOOF
If you bungle, Handy Andy, I'll kick your football for you.

(Ulysses, p. 497)

It is such increasingly bizarre effects which make 'Circe' possibly *Ulysses'* most experimental, even 'postmodern', chapter. The effect is the most extreme version of the discontinuity in the novel between an apparently empirical world, existing in real space and time (created by infinitesimally painstaking mimesis) and a self-contained 'elsewhere' with its own physical rules, just like the screen.[12] I suggest the inspiration for Joyce's technique is best understood in relation to logically inter-connected developments in early film.[13] Before the first rudimentary cinemas, films, especially comedies, were often first shown as elements in variety stage shows. It is arguable 'Circe' retraces this exhibition history, by moving from vaudeville, to trickfilm to animation (also derived from Latin *animatus*, 'filled with life, and *anima*, air, breath, soul, mind'.[14] It has often been noted that 'Circe' is literally unstageable (despite brave efforts such as Zero Mostel's *Ulysses in Nighttown* (1973)), because of the 'special effects' its bizarre stage-directions demand.[15] Of course, as is nearly always the case in Joyce, there are multiple influences behind the drama of 'Circe'. It is almost certainly a parody of the *Walpurgisnacht* scene in Goethe's *Faust*, Part I (1808), as well as developing the folktale style of Ibsen's *Peer Gynt* (1867). Significantly, Joyce's more contemporary models, German Expressionist theatre and art, themselves aspired towards a filmic dynamism in presentation of space, time and subjectivity.[16] Moreover, in the preface to his *A Dream Play* (1901) (another well-known influence), August Strindberg famously described his scenario in terms which already strain against the limitations of the stage towards a kind of cinematic visualisation of the unconscious.[17]

Filmic 'spacetime' was perhaps more able than any other narrative medium hitherto to visualise magical and instantaneous shifts and metamorphoses. In 'Circe' dimensions of figures alternate between dramatic compression and enlargement, as well as abrupt chronological cuts backwards and forwards, but always with the paradoxically cinematic effect of 'one continuous present tense', as Briggs notes (*'Circe' and the Cinema*, p. 153).[18] This makes 'Circe' (*pace* Eisenstein)[19] perhaps most fundamentally like early film of all chapters in *Ulysses*, because its naturalistic and phantasmagoric aspects are 'granted equal authenticity' (Briggs, *'Circe' and the Cinema*, pp. 48-49). These discursive dimensions co-exist in Joyce's chapter, as in the dual Lumière/Méliès tradition, as if there were no ontological contradiction between them. In what Lindsay dubbed 'the picture of Fairy Splendor', the camera wielded 'a kind of Hallowe'en witch power' (*Art of the Moving Picture*, p. 59). Especially when we consider 'Circe's' art (according to the Gilbert schema) was magic, the medium seems most closely analogous to all its instantaneous costume changes, 'sound effects', rapidly changing 'sets' and dis/appearing, metamorphosing cast. As was recognised by early commentators, such as Leo Tolstoy and Hugo Münsterberg, as well as Lindsay, lumbering stage machinery could not begin to duplicate cinema's capacity to conjure in ways which render its technological legerdemain invisible in the trick itself.[20] Consequently, 'Circe's' art 'jumps and jerks and flickers through its astonishing transformations and wonders', as magically as film seemed to its first audiences (Briggs, *'Circe' and the Cinema*, pp. 150-52).

Joyce even seems to allude to the actual process of stop-motion trickery (by which anything can be made to dis/appear or be substituted with something else). Bloom ambiguously vanishes in a flash, only to re-materialise a split-second later: *'At Antonio Rabaiotti's door Bloom halts, sweated under the bright arclamps. He disappears. In a moment he reappears and hurries on.'* (*Ulysses*, p. 413) As Ian Christie notes, central to Méliès' imaginary worlds 'was the idea of *transformation* – something or someone turning magically into something else',[21] just as shape-shifting is central to 'Circe', where traditional plot (minimal in *Ulysses* anyway) almost vanishes completely, replaced by protean metamorphosis as the principle narrative motor. Indeed Méliès' *The Temptation of St Anthony* (1898) is one of the possible sources for its *Walpurgisnacht* style (Méliès also filmed episodes from the *Odyssey* as *L'Île de Calypso: Ou, Ulysse et le Géant Polypheme* (1905)). Méliès' work often featured a sensational generic blend of 'sex, horror and sentimentality', as Briggs puts it (*'Circe' and the Cinema*, p. 150), all elements of popular culture also incorporated in Joyce's writing, as typified by 'Circe'. This is particularly marked in the collapsing of moral and sexual oppositions, when Méliès' hallucinating hermit watches Jesus materialise from a contemplated skull, only to metamorphose into a naked woman, then back into a skeleton. Indeed, Virag's head-unscrewing 'finale' (*Ulysses*, p. 491) would have been a 'commonplace miracle' (Briggs, *'Circe' and the Cinema*, p. 151)[22] in Méliès' movies (for example, in his *The Man with the India-rubber Head* (1902 and 1903) which swells up elastically until it bursts and/or grows back in six different forms) and those of his French contemporaries.

However, 'stop-motion' dis/appearance and metamorphosis are not the only cinematic techniques Joyce emulates. Another early moment, when Bloom catches sight of himself in a shop window, heralds the extreme expressive deformation to come. Joyce ingeniously suggests visual distortions with his own phonetic deformations, expanding and contracting syllables duplicating their shapes like miniature 'concrete poems':

On the farther side under the railway bridge Bloom appears flushed, panting, cramming bread and chocolate into a side pocket. From Gillen's hairdresser's window a composite portrait shows him gallant Nelson's image. A concave mirror at the side presents to him lovelorn longlost lugubru Blooloohoom. Grave Gladstone sees him level, Bloom for Bloom. He passes, struck by the stare of truculent Wellington but in the convex mirror grin unstruck the bonham eyes and fatchuck cheekchops of Jollypoldy the rixdix doldy. (*Ulysses*, pp. 412-13)

As Bloom sees three views of himself in the shop pane mirrors (amongst the movers and shakers of Irish history), his human form, as Spiegel puts it, 'is treated with the elasticity of a rubber band',[23] flexing between lugubrious elongation, sober proportionality and corpulent compression. (It is also arguable Bloom momentarily doubles into the classic Chaplin-Arbuckle, Laurel-and-Hardy, pairing of comic opposites.) Comparable effects were achieved in the 1920s by German expressionist film-makers using anamorphic lenses,[24] but they also parallel the stretching and compression of figures in early animated cartoons, such as Winsor McCay's *Little Nemo in Slumberland* (1911). The 'plausible impossibilities' of graphic animation, in their turn, granted the polymorphous words and images of Lewis Carroll and John Tenniel new, kinetic life.[25] (Cartoons were also perfect for their kind of visual punning: in *Little Nemo*, a dragon's jaws open to become a coach, just as in 'Circe' Bloom sees a fogbound sandstrewer, '*its huge red headlight winking, its trolley hissing on the wire*', as a saurian monster (*Ulysses*, p. 414).)

Indeed much of 'Circe's' later expressive deformation finds its closest contemporary counterpart in graphic animation. By the time of *Ulysses*' publication, this had already reached a high degree of sophistication, thanks to pioneers such as Anglo-American James Stuart Blackton and Frenchman Émile Cohl (who became 'the Méliès of the cartoon'),[26] among others. Moreover, the concept of animation – in the broadest sense of the principle of the moving image itself, of endowing stills with appearance of life – was crucial to early film as a whole.

The nineteenth century closed with a virtual 'explosion of graphic imagery' (Christie, *Last Machine*, p. 83), made possible by the development of cheap new printing technology and bringing illustrated publications to a mass market. It is well-known Joyce reflected this in multiple public and privy moments in *Ulysses*, not just in Bloom's job as advertising canvasser, but the popular papers, magazines and handbills so many characters are seen reading, the numerous posters and, especially, the nymph, cut out of *Photo Bits*, who witnesses the secrets of the Blooms' marriage bed at 7 Eccles Street in 'Calypso'. Blackton was a news illustrator by training, but film animation and the strip cartoon were particularly closely interactive, as the migration between them by other artists such as McCay shows. (Edwin S. Porter's *Dream of a Rarebit Fiend* trickfilm (1906), was based on McCay's popular New York *Telegram* strip. MacCay's animated cartoon *Little Nemo* (1911) was probably the first strip (this time from the New York *Herald*) adapted more or less directly by its originator.)[27] Indeed, the strip cartoon 'created a purely visual form of narrative' which continues to influence cinema (Christie, *Last Machine*, p. 83). Manually animated drawings even arguably predate moving photographic ones, as at Émile Reynaud's Parisian Optical Theatre, from 1892. The revolutionary 'cel' process (the basis of animated drawings until computer graphics), allowing backgrounds to be drawn directly onto celluloid so only figures needed retouching for each movement, was patented by Earl Hurd as early as 1914, though pioneered by others well before that (see Crafton, *Before Mickey*, pp. 150-3). Moreover, originally little practical distinction was made between animation and live action: film itself was simply known as 'animated pictures' (the first recorded use of 'animated cartoon' dating only from 1915).[28] British pioneer R.W. Paul's version of the cinema-apparatus (developed in 1896) was patented as the 'Animatographe' and his compatriot Cecil Hepworth, who published the first manual on moving pictures, significantly titled it *Animated Photography* (1897). It was inevitable that early filmmakers would quickly discover the illusion of movement, produced by the 'persistence of vision' effect, could be logically extended from people, to objects, to drawings.

Perhaps the first graphic animation proper consisted of Méliès' 1896 footage of a music-hall 'lightning sketch', using stop-motion for each sheet. Though Méliès did not follow this up, the same kind of act was filmed by Blackton at least as early as 1898. His elaborated 1900 version, *The Enchanted Drawing*, features the animator himself, manipulating his picture's facial expressions, thus demonstrating the intermingling of live action and graphic 'magic' dates from the very beginning of film cartooning. *The Enchanted Drawing*, also typically, draws attention to the animation process itself. The cartoonist appears to take objects – wine-bottle, glass, etc. – in and out of the picture, alternating between two- and three-dimensional effects. Blackton's formula was quickly imitated (e.g. in Edwin S. Porter's *Animated Painting* (1904)), although his own 1906 *Humorous Phases of Funny Faces*, which appear to draw and metamorphose themselves, is usually seen as marking the 'conjuring of a fictional world entirely by graphic means' (Christie, *Last Machine*, p. 84).

Animation technique became common on both sides of the Atlantic in the early twentieth century, allowing both graphic elements and objects to come to life, with comic and/or supernatural effect. Blackton's internationally successful (and again widely imitated) *The Haunted Hotel* (1907) used a single frame exposure technique to move things around by 'unseen' agency, thus inspiring Cohl's object animations. Cohl's *The Tenants Next Door* (1909) used magical transformations equivocally, to both gratify and punish voyeurism, anticipating Circe's metamorphoses and scenarios. *Le Garde-Meuble automatique* ('The Automatic Moving Company') (Pathé-Comica 1912) was a 'Cohlesque' masterpiece of the genre.[29] The broom which sweeps up (accompanied by Dukas' *Sorcerer's Apprentice*), after the furniture has decamped unaided, self-consciously alludes to the film's own visual wizardry. Cohl quickly applied the same principle to animating graphics. His *Fantasmagoria* featured magical metamorphoses of line-drawn figures and objects as early as 1908. *The Neo-Impressionist Painter* (1910) has a live action setting in an artist's studio, but the bizarre drawings shown to a potential buyer become literally animated pictures: e.g. a devil playing billiards, or a fish presenting a bouquet to a washerwoman.

Cohl eventually emigrated to train the first generation of American cartoonists and start the earliest continuity character series, though retaining his uncanny edge. In his first US work, *Professor Bonehead Is Shipwrecked* (1912) (possibly a comic take on Wells's evolutionary throwback story, 'Aepyornis Island' (1894)), the professor hatches a giant avian *Doppelgänger* which pursues him. Cohl's explicit parodies of modern art could also have inspired Cubists and Futurists in their 'playful reflexivity' and 'questioning of illusionism', exploiting the full resources of contemporary picture-making (Christie, *Last Machine*, p. 85). Animated cartoons developed with an inherent sense of the 'metafictional', of breaking through the frame of one discourse into another in a kind of vernacular anticipation of postmodernism.[30] McCay's *Little Nemo* shows the process of animating its 4,000 drawings against its live action. His *Gertie the Dinosaur* (1914) went further. Betting he can restore a fossil to life, McCay orders the resulting cartoon about, finally 'climbing' into the picture for a ride. The most explicitly metafictional moment in *Ulysses* is Molly Bloom's appeal to her author in 'Penelope' to rescue her from the midden of prurient detail in which she is sinking: 'O Jamesy let me up out of this pooh' (*Ulysses*, p. 719). Molly's wish might well have been granted, in a cartoon of the period, such as Earl Hurd's *Bobby Bumps Puts a Beanery on the Bum* (1918), which climaxes with perhaps the earliest use of the 'ladder' gag, where the animator's hand draws in the means to escape a tight situation.

Certainly, early animation's fascination with 'autokinesis' and its own processes often seems 'like a popular version of the same concerns that pushed "serious" artists into Modernism.' (Christie, *Last Machine*, p. 85) René Clair, in his Surrealist phase, was amongst 'the leading filmmakers excited about animation' (*Before Mickey*, pp. 257-8). Clair incorporated a whimsical cartoon sequence in his time-freezing *Paris qui dort* (*The Crazy Ray*) (1923) and some choreographed matches in *Entr'acte* (1924), inspired by Cohl's *The Bewitched Matches* (1908) (so popular Cohl remade it at least twice). *Entr'acte*'s accelerated-motion, driverless hearse chase might also have been inspired by Cohl's bizarre, autokinetic comedies, such as *The Pumpkin Race* (1908), in which Hallowe'en vegetables rampage over town, before 'reversing' back into their cart.[31] Another prominent example is Fernand Léger's 1924 *Ballet Mécanique*.

This incorporated both object animation sequences and a dancing cutout of Chaplin, recalling the 'Charlot' cartoons of wartime, which naturally extended one comic mode into another, just as Joyce does in 'Circe'.[32] Even Jean Cocteau's initial (1929) conception for his *Le Sang d'un Poète* was a feature-length cartoon. Indeed, Crafton suggest multiple affinities between early animated films' vernacular or proleptic surrealism and Surrealism proper:

> Almost all ... begin by establishing an 'alien universe' into which the spectator may project himself. Although the creators of the first animated films were not surrealists or even cognizant of that movement, they inadvertently made films that demonstrated a disregard for everyday existence, normal logic, and causality, and a propensity for dreamlike action which André Breton and his followers admired. (*Before Mickey*, pp. 258 and 348-49)

Correspondences between cartoons and the emerging antirealist aesthetic were voiced as early as 1925 by Gus Bofa, in an article called 'Du Dessin animé'. Similarly, abstract art historian and *Académie Française* member, Marcel Brion, in 'Felix le chat, ou la poésie créatrice' (1928), argued 'creative power of the dream and this surrealist formation of the object give to these fantastic images the means by which the mind enjoys free play.'[33] Such developments measured how serious criticism and the avant-garde were catching up with what had been possible in animation from the beginning.

Iris Barry, a London Film Society founder and *Daily Mail* movie critic (1925-30), praised Felix in *Let's Go to the Pictures* (1926), one of the first serious British studies of film, by a writer closely associated with Modernists such as Wyndham Lewis. Barry recognised the animated feline was a hybrid of the fantastic acrobatic comedy of Chaplin and Keaton with the venerable tradition of anthropomorphism handed down through Æsop, Swift and Carroll. However, she did not want disclosure of technical processes to 'take the bloom off his furry coat', because 'Felix must be respected: he is an institution, a totem.' Like Lindsay, she argued cinema programmes possessed greater generic range and dramatic fluidity than the stage, precisely because they encompassed 'Clyde Cook comedy, a travel picture, Felix the Cat, Mr. Cecil B. de Mille, Mr. Lubitsch and staggeringly serious pictures from Sweden or Germany or Russia.' Barry acknowledged this variety, like 'Circe's', derived from a mix of popular traditions and visual media: 'all the realm of the legitimate theatre, the music-hall, the circus, the penny peep-show, the toy kaleidoscope and the rural pageant'.[34] Her compatriot, Virginia Woolf, (hardly renowned for receptiveness to 'mass' cultural forms) in her 1926 essay 'The Cinema' argued the mimetic glibness with which film appeared to simply *re*present reality was a handicap to its aesthetic development. Even the celebrated graphic expressionism of *Caligari* (1919) failed to pinpoint the medium's inherent potentials for Modernist discourse. However, an accidental shadow (probably caused by projector fault) during Woolf's viewing made her feel 'thought could be conveyed by shape more effectively than by words', because momentarily, 'The monstrous quivering tadpole seemed to be fear itself'. Consequently, Woolf groped speculatively towards what sounds like a form of *abstract* animation, through which other emotions, such as anger, might be figured by 'a black line wriggling upon a white sheet.' Thus, she wondered, might some unconscious 'secret language which we feel and see, but never speak ... be made visible to the eye?' Cinema only needed to discover a new vocabulary of non-naturalistic symbols to 'animate the perfect form with thought'. By mixing its modes, a medium, squandered primitively on spectacle, could visualise its true potentials: 'Then as smoke pours from Vesuvius, we should be able to see thought in its wildness, in its beauty, in its oddity, pouring from men with their elbows on a table; from women with their little handbags slipping to the floor.'[35]

In Weimar Germany, the connection between experimental animation and advertisement films was particularly strong: Walter Ruttmann, Lotte Reiniger and Oscar Fischinger all cut their teeth in the industry. Ruttmann's commercials subsidised his early career as a leading abstract filmmaker. His 1920 tyre promotion, *Der Sieger*, already displays 'the fascination with wave forms and moving geometric shapes' which mark his 'Opus' series (see Crafton *Before Mickey*, pp. 231-2). There is a clear genealogical link with Ruttmann's later career, through the famous 'Falcon's dream' cartoon insert he animated for Fritz Lang's epic *Die Nibelungen* (1922-4) and also the undulant visual prologue of his own *Berlin: Sinfonie einer Großstadt* (1927) (often compared to Joyce's *Ulysses*, as an avant-garde depiction of a day-in-the-life of a contemporary city), as well as in the play between visually saturated realism and abstract, rhythmic patterning throughout the documentary itself.[36] Even the godfather of Soviet *cinéma verité*, Dziga Vertov, recognised animation's importance, by commissioning cartoon sequences in *Kino-Pravda* newsreels from 1922 onwards. Vertov's own Debrie camera was shown performing object-animation stunts on its stand in his meta-cinematic masterpiece, *The Man with a Movie Camera* (1929). Indeed, Vertov recognised animation as *the* fundamental cinematic principle, as well as linking it with the Einsteinian spacetime paradigm, in the first manifesto of his *kino-eye* group:

> Cinema is...the *art of inventing movements* of things in space in response to the demands of science; it embodies the inventor's dream – be he the scholar, artist, engineer, or carpenter; it is the realization by *kinochestvo* of that which cannot be realized in life.
>
> Drawings in motion. Blueprints in motion. Plans for the future. The theory of relativity on the screen.[37]

In 1923, Einstein himself collaborated with Max and Dave Fleischer on a cartoon account of his theory, as the natural popular medium for explaining spacetime to the lay public. His approval of the results recognised the 'visual relativity' of cartoons themselves, lending weight to animation's analogy with and/or influence on 'Circe', *Ulysses'* most dimensionally flexile chapter.[38] However, this didn't mean the current of influence between animation and modern art and science flowed all one way. One probable reason why early serial characters 'Mutt and Jeff' (by Raoul Barre and Charles Bower) stuck in Joyce's memory, to re-emerge in *Finnegans Wake* (1939)[39] was because such cartoons sometimes reproduced developments in painting and optics as sight gags. In *Mutt and Jeff in the Flood* (c.1918), for example, Mutt arcs across the water, creating a bridge out of his multiplied image for Jeff to cross. The effect recalls the kinetic 'retinal afterimages' of numerous Futurist paintings, or Marcel Duchamp's Cubist *Nude Descending a Staircase, No.2* (1912); alternatively, the rhythmic curves into which Charles Étienne Marey transformed the subjects of his Chronophotographic studies of motion in the 1880s.[40]

Polymorphous distortions and mutations of the body in early animation were indeed a vernacular surrealism. The humour of trickfilms often seems 'sardonic and physically violent' (Christie, *Last Machine*, p. 86). Immediate conversion of living animals into sausages in *Mechanical Butchery* (Lumière 1895) provides a good example of the closeness of realist and fantastic tendencies made possible by stop-motion, but such macabre corporeality was also passed on into forms of animation. The highly un-Disneyesque climax of Walt Disney's *Alice's Mysterious Mystery* (1925), for example, features sausages, made from dognappers' victims, revenging themselves. Though rooted in the robust routines of music-hall and pantomime, such jokes played on atavistic fears of the body under a kind of 'Circean' possession. Early films exhibited a positive delight in amputation and dismemberment, often nonchalantly taking the body apart and reassembling it (as when a caveman is chopped in half, runs around and is then rejoined, in Willis O'Brien's 'Mannikin Comedy' *10,000 BC* (1916)). Animated cartoons could gratify this ever more inventively and with weaker undertow of sensory and moral revulsion, because of their distance from mimesis. Christie suggests this was both a modern form of perversely pleasureable objectification and a kind of collective imagining of the carnage of the trenches, in which the body would be literally deformed and dissected by technological means (Christie, *Last Machine*, p. 86).[41]

Protean deformation of time, space, body and identity in both early graphic animation and in 'Circe', is matched only by jointly conspicuous zoomorphism, not just in the literal menagerie swarming through Joyce's text and its saturation with animalistic metaphors for human traits and behaviour. Typically, Paddy Dignam transforms from beagle hound, with 'grey scorbutic face', 'to human size and shape' (he also manages an impression of the famous HMV dog trademark, in the process (*Ulysses*, pp. 447-8)). Grandpapachi Virag, like Professor Bonehead's *Doppelgänger*, acquires scraggy bird-features, with '*yellow parrotbeak*', talons, storklike legs and moulting plumage, finally exiting with a 'Quack!' (*Ulysses*, pp. 484-91). 'Circe's' pantomime black mass climaxes in reversal of divine into canine, of 'the Lord God Omnipotent reigneth' into 'Htengier Tnetopino Dog Drol eth' (*Ulysses*, pp. 556-57). Similarly, Tony Sarg's shadow-puppetry in *Adam Raises Cain* (1920) brought to life a whole bestiary of fantastic and extinct species, but some of the bizarrest 'humanisations' took place in Russia in the 1910s. A vogue for micro-photographic documentaries led to the proto-surreal 'entomological animation' of Wladislaw Starewicz, in a logical extension of the Victorian tradition of 'humorous taxidermy'. In his satirical masterpieces reanimated insect specimens act out dramatic roles. Besides possibly influencing Kafka's *Metamorphosis* (1915) and the Capeks' *Insect Play* (1921), Starewicz even made a version of the Æsop/Krylov fable, *The Ant and the Grasshopper* (1911) (one of the first Russian films seen widely by foreign audiences), which Joyce also rewrote as the 'Ondt and Gracehoper' in *Finnegans Wake*.[42] Starewicz's *The Cameraman's Revenge* (1912) was a self-reflexively cinematic tale of infidelity. In one of 'Circe's' fantasy sequences, Bloom masochistically offers to snapshot Boylan's liaison with Molly through the keyhole as public proof of his own cuckolding (*Ulysses*, p. 527). In Starewicz's animation, a voyeuristic grasshopper similarly films adulterous Mr Beetle *in flagrante*, then exposes him on the local screen. By the mid-Twenties, some of Hollywood's biggest cartoon stars were animals with human traits, often spun off established comic acts. Felix (conceived by Pat Sullivan and Otto Messmer in 1920) was arguably the first animated character to have a distinctive, easily-identifiable personality, like a live action star.[43] (Significantly, in *Felix in Hollywood* (1925), Chaplin accuses the cat of stealing his act, when he detaches his tail and twirls it like Charlie's trademark walking stick). Though sometimes the mutation was the other way: the Fleischers' 'Betty Boop' made her debut as a puppy with the same gooey eyes.[44] Disney's *Puss in Boots*, dating from the year of *Ulysses'* publication, is a typically self-conscious extension of the anthropomorphic tradition. This modernised fairytale (one of a series of six *Laugh-O-Grams*), includes a sequence where puss inspires his master to romantic heroism by taking him to a 'Rudolph Vaselino' movie. Similarly, in *Felix in Fairyland* (1925), the cat enters a universe entirely populated from folklore and *double entendre*.

Alternatively, Victor Bergdahl's *delirium tremens* cartoon, *Captain Grogg Among Other Strange Creatures* (Sweden 1920), fuses classical mythology with the contemporary: a centaur beats his mate for flirting with the drunken skipper. Thus animation turned out to be the natural home for a 'vernacularly postmodern' anachronism which also seems to parallel Joyce's parodic revisitings of the past, especially in sending up its primal machismo. O'Brien's *10,000 BC* was stop-motion model animation based on this principle: for example, the mailman delivers by brontosaurus, well before the *Flintstones*. Similarly, in his *The Dinosaur and the Missing Link* (1917) – not unlike the mischievous captions in Joyce's 'Aeolus' or the clashing narrative registers in 'Cyclops' – intertitles point up satirical parallels and disjunctions between 'civilised' present and cave-dwelling prehistory: for example, 'Mr Rockface and his Daughter Araminta in the drawing room of their country home.' In *The Lost World* (1925), O'Brien optically inverted relative sizes of live actors and model dinosaurs to adapt Conan Doyle to the screen. Is the dimensional switch of this proto-*King Kong* altogether dissimilar to the gargantuan perspectival changes achieved in 'Cyclops', *Ulysses*' most technically and thematically 'monstrous' chapter?

Despite the ostensible frivolity of early animators' work, they also lined up on either side of the most serious and controversial topics of the age, just as the contemporary Boer War fuels the trivial confrontation between Stephen and the English squaddies in 1904 Dublin. Early cartoons, like other film genres, were rapidly mobilised for propaganda, especially in the debate over ending American neutrality in the Great War. John Randolph Bray's *Colonel Heeza Liar at Bat* (USA 1917) satirised hotheaded motives for intervention which might have appealed to pacifist Joyce in Switzerland. The Munchausenish colonel rushes off to the Western Front after reading inflammatory newspaper reports. He kicks enormous shells as if they were footballs and bats away enemy fire, like a kind of proto-Superman. However, the joke is that he gets so disorientated by shellshock he ends up playing from the German trenches. On the other side, as the first real animated feature, McCay's *The Sinking of the Lusitania* (1918) was an apocalyptic early disaster movie. The *Titanic* of its day, it mixed live action and animation sequences to fan anti-German sentiment. Crafton argues what is surprising about the output of the early animated film industry is not its scarcity, but sheer volume and diversity, even though much has probably been lost (*Before Mickey*, p. xviii). The thousands of cartoons produced in different genres and countries make it extremely unlikely a regular film-goer and polyvisual writer like Joyce would not have been familiar with their basic techniques and themes by the time of writing *Ulysses* ('Circe' itself was completed only in 1920).[45]

Another early investigation of cinema, Hugo Münsterberg's *The Photoplay: A Psychological Study* (1916), argued film's narrative discourse was closer to the 'language of the mind' than any previous cultural form. This was because cinema had an unprecedented ability to rapidly rearrange appearance, dimension and motion at will, to achieve simultaneity and to visualise the impossible as if actual: 'The photoplay tells us a human story by overcoming the forms of the outer world, namely space, time, and causality, and by adjusting the events to the forms of the inner world, namely attention, memory, imagination and emotion'. Cinema images, albeit imprinted from objective realities, were recomposed to 'reach complete isolation from the practical world'.[46] Lindsay too believed special effects could go beyond mere entertainment into psychology: 'the possible charm in a so-called trick picture is in eliminating the tricks, giving them dignity till they are no longer such, but thoughts in motion made visible' (*Art of the Moving Picture*, p. 142). And if the unconscious play of the inner mind could be approximated in actuality footage subjected to editorial sorcery, how much more freely could it be achieved by animation?

Similarly, Joyce's technique strives to 'make visible' on the page the agitated, teeming life of the unconscious with its repressions, complexes and wish-fulfilments.[47] As in 'Cyclops', there is an extreme split in 'Circe's' narrative method. There remain intermittent sequences of naturalistic realism, like 'live action' film, but their diegetic continuity and logic is interrupted by sudden dilations into a fantastic parallel dimension (usually triggered by some kind of symbolic link), which resembles various forms of animation effects. Here Joyce's implicit third-person narrator (locatable now only in the 'stage directions') becomes not just a film editor, but a kind of mock-psychoanalytic animator, making his characters assume the secret identities of their phobias and lusts. 'Circe's' restless shape-shifting corresponds to the continuous displacement and condensing of symbolic meanings by the unconscious, from one word or object on to another. Cartoonlike 'polymorphous plasticism' in both its characters and scenes mimics, as it were, desire's 'polymorphous perversity'. 'Circe's' sheer anarchic animatedness, in that sense, matches Freud's description of the Id as 'a cauldron of seething excitations', knowing neither time, nor space.[48] Joyce learned that humour could be used subversively against repression and censorship, to help confront and purge anxieties and complexes. This intensified his interest in the vernacular surrealism and therapeutic potentials of comic film and animation.

Indeed, the representation of dream, fantasy, wish-fulfilment and anxiety achievable in trickfilms, became ever freer in cartoon animation, as in McCay's highly influential *Dream of a Rarebit Fiend* series, which migrated between the two forms. Porter's (1906) trickfilm version, opens with 'nighttown' live action drunkenness and gluttony, not unlike Joyce's naturalistic setting, but, similarly, rapidly gives way to hallucinatory superimpositions over a swaying lamppost. Tiny female devils hack at the rarebit fiend's sleeping head, before his wildly bucking bed flies out of the window, with the same ambivalent blend of Freudian eroticism and nightmare punishment Joyce combined. The rarebit fiend ends up hooked on a steeple weathercock by his nightshirt, before falling through the ceiling and waking up. In a 1921 cartoon number from the series animated by McCay himself, the fiend's wife dreams he converts their house into a flying-machine to avoid ground-rent. This whisks them off on an interplanetary voyage, reworking early trickfilms which move seamlessly between reality and dream as in Méliès' *Journey Across the Impossible* (1904), but with greater *panache* and fluidity.

Another significant point that 'Circe' and early animation share is their mixing of modes. In postmodern culture, beings/figures from different universes and/or genres and modes interact intertextually and transgressively, as if no logical, epistemological, or ontological boundaries were recognised or operative. This is precisely what happens in Joyce's breakthrough experimentalism (which, of course, set an important precedent for the metafictions of full-blown literary Postmodernism)[49] and, more vernacularly, in cartoons of the time. Besides their own memories and ghosts, Bloom and Stephen encounter characters from all sorts of discourses and contexts, and with varying existential bases – Joyce's actual contemporaries, historical figures, characters from other fictions, from popular culture, allegory, legend, myth, etc. Similarly, *Felix in Hollywood* runs through every conceivable movie genre established by the mid-Twenties. Besides meeting his counterpart comics, such as Chaplin and Ben Turpin (who confesses, Bloomishly, to going cross-eyed peeping through dressing-room keyholes), the cat impersonates stars of western, romance and adventure pictures during his 'screentest'. Similarly, early mixing of live action and cartoon animation (a common practice, as we saw above) led to the development of distinctive styles by the immediate post-Great War period. These were based on the reversible principle of superimposing graphic characters against 'real' backgrounds, or vice versa, again paralleling 'Circe', which either inserts 'unreal' figures into the naturalistic setting, or transports Bloom into hallucinatory 'elsewheres' in past or future. In the Fleischers' *Out of the Inkwell: Perpetual Motion* (1920), the animator breathes on an ink blob to create Koko the Clown, who promptly escapes from page into live action. After numerous pranks, he then dissolves himself back into the word: 'Stung!' Another cartoon from the same series, *Modeling* (1923), incorporates a 'claymation' bust. Koko ('AWOL' from his graphic frame again) climbs inside it, causing its nose to elongate, wiggle, detach and run all over the studio. Earlier, in Willie Hopkins's 'Animated Sculpture' *Swat the Fly* (USA, 1916), a chameleon head changes faces, moves and reshapes its ears, etc. Both films anticipate or parallel the expressive distortions of Bloom's features in 'Circe' (see below), as well as recalling recent literary precedents for such effects in H.G. Wells.[50]

Raoul Barre's *The Hicks in Nightmareland* (1915) similarly begins with live action – people at the beach reading a handbill for the cartoon itself – but then alternates modes, reflecting their flirtations and jealousies grotesquely in the content and style of animated sequences. Conversely, in 1923, Disney and Ub Iwerks created a 'Through the Looking Glass' world in which anything was possible, in their 'Alice in Cartoonland' series, but by reversing the Fleischer format, using a live girl (Margie Gay) against animated backgrounds instead.

When cartoons entered the talkie era (fully synchronised sound was first used successfully in 1927, making Disney's *Steamboat Willie*, 'the *Jazz Singer* of animation' (see Crafton *Before Mickey*, p. 5)), anything could suddenly speak, as well as come to life. Although this post-dates the prosopopoeia of objects in 'Circe', Joyce was certainly aware of the possibilities of the soundtrack at least as early as the 'opera films' he intended screening at the Volta, which maintained crude synchronicity by accompanying phonograph.[51] The mechanical 'voices' of both gramophone and pianola feature prominently in 'Circe', especially in some of its 'aural' distortions. As we saw in the examples discussed above, the most insignificant object in 'Circe' is 'animated' and gets a speaking role. Bloom's trouserbutton even assumes a crucial bit part. The strain of following the *Photo Bits* nymph (now a literally moving and talking picture herself, decamped from her frame),[52] into the dimension of mystical purity in order to escape his sexual problems, proves too much for Bloom's earthbound bodiliness. In effect he is saved by a classic slapstick gag – his pants suddenly fall down:

(Bloom half rises. His back trousers' button snaps.)

THE BUTTON

Bip!

(Ulysses, p. 516)

Despite the ingenuity of trickfilm makers, it is arguable that until recent developments in digital-manipulation and computer generated imagery (which have made the 'morphing' of actors and objects commonplace in films since Charles Russell's *The Mask* (1994)), some of the protean transformations and 'expressive distortions' in 'Circe' would only have been visualisable on screen in 1922 using the graphic devices of the animated cartoon to make figures and dimensions infinitely malleable. For example, Bloom also undergoes a paranoid martyrdom. Like other fantastic sequences, this is a dilation between two bits of dialogue occurring in naturalistic space and time. Zoe's sarcastic rejoinder, 'Go on. Make a stump speech of it.' cues Bloom's transformation into a soap-box campaigner, who rises in a series of edited jumps to global eminence and seems destined to lead humankind into the comic Utopia of the 'New Bloomusalem' (projected in the shape of the pork kidney he burnt at breakfast), as King Leo or the new Elijah. 'If I ruled the world' fantasies were common in early film, as were ambivalent visions of the future. Paul Peroff's *Willis Zukunfts-Traum* (Germany 1920) was a cutout Wellsian Utopia, which turns into a Dystopian nightmare about modernity. A naughty boy dreams up a futuristic consumer paradise, complete with *Metropolis*-like cityscapes and aerial traffic. Bunking off school (taught by tele-screen), the globe-trotting truant is apprehended and spanked by a robot. Bloom's zany rise to power, results in a symmetrically improbable fall from grace. From being saviour against all ills, Bloom becomes their scapegoat and is finally burnt at the stake. However, though the sequence ends with Bloom's body 'mute, shrunken, carbonised', he then springs miraculously back to life, just like an indestructible character in a cartoon, where, as Joseph C. Voelker puts it, 'violence is by convention inconsequential'.[53]

This political fantasy is one of the most successfully adapted sequences in Joseph Strick's 1967 film. Indeed 'Circe' is one of the few chapters from which some of the novel's cinematic potentials are effectively realised on screen, precisely because Strick used the resources of 'stop-motion' and montage editing, in a style which deliberately recalls the conjuring and exoticism of early trickfilms. However, the segment leaves out other special effects which could still arguably only have been replicated even in 1967 by mixing live action with animation footage.[54] In the course of the text, Bloom's actions and metamorphoses increasingly resemble the wackiest kind of visual tropes and bodily distortions comparable only to the plausible impossibilities and polymorphous plasticism of contemporary cartoons. For example, after having already changed sex and given birth to eight male heirs, Bloom is called upon to prove he is Ireland's saviour:

A VOICE

Bloom, are you the Messiah ben Joseph or ben David?

BLOOM

(*Darkly*) You have said it.

BROTHER BUZZ:

Then perform a miracle.

BANTAM LYONS

Prophesy who will win the Saint Leger.

(*Bloom walks on a net, covers his left eye with his left ear, passes through several walls, climbs Nelson's Pillar, hangs from the top ledge by his eyelids, eats twelve dozen oysters (shells included), heals several sufferers from king's evil, contracts his face so as to resemble many historical personages, Lord Beaconsfield, Lord Byron, Wat Tyler, Moses of Egypt, Moses Maimonides, Moses Mendelssohn, Henry Irving, Rip van Winkle, Kossuth, Jean Jacques Rousseau, Baron Leopold Rothschild, Robinson Crusoe, Sherlock Holmes, Pasteur, turns each foot simultaneously in different directions, bids the tide turn back, eclipses the sun by extending his little finger*) (*Ulysses*, pp. 466-7.)

It is possible some of Bloom's shape-shiftings, for example impersonations of famous people, could have been achieved by 'mixes' (as with the protean disguises of the eponymous villain shown at the beginning of Fritz Lang's *Dr Mabuse, der Spieler,* also released in 1922). But others, such as the physically distortive ear and eyelid tricks manifestly couldn't, without resorting to animation. It is very significant that in the 1967 film all that's left of Bloom's 'miracles' is the racing tip.

And if more proof were needed that in 'Circe' *Ulysses* seems nowhere more at home than in 'toontown',[55] Strick's film omitted other highlights of Joyce's 'all-singing, all-dancing' mockalypse. Consider, for example, how the vision of Doomsday (literalising a snatch of mystical dialogue Bloom overhears in 'Lestrygonians' (see *Ulysses,* Ch.VIII, pp. 157-58.) could have been embodied in any other way, either in 1922 or 1967?

(A rocket rushes up the sky and bursts. A white star falls from it proclaiming the consummation of all things and second coming of Elijah. Along an infinite invisible tightrope taut from zenith to nadir the End of the World, a twoheaded octopus in gillie's kilts, busby and tartan filibegs whirls through the murk, head over heels, in the form of the Three Legs of Man.)

THE END OF THE WORLD
(*With a Scotch accent.*) Wha'll dance the keel row, the keel row, the keel row?

(*Ulysses,* p. 477)

Notes

1   For details and images of the Volta venture, see, among others: Richard Ellmann *James Joyce,* New and Revised Edition (Oxford: Oxford University Press, 1982), pp. 300-04 and 310-12; Gösta Werner 'James Joyce, Manager of the First Cinema in Ireland', in *Nordic Rejoycings – 1982* (Norberg, Sweden: James Joyce Society of Sweden and Finland, 1982), pp. 125-36, and Liam O'Leary *Cinema Ireland 1896-1950.* (Dublin: National Library of Ireland, 1990).

2   (Letter of 4 December 1898, in Jean G. Aubry (ed.) *Joseph Conrad: Life and Letters.* Vol.I. (London: Heinemann, 1927), pp. 259-60

3   James Joyce, *A Portrait of the Artist as a Young Man.* (1914-15; repr. Oxford: Oxford University Press, 2000) Ch.III, p. 116.

4   Significantly, Deed had worked with Méliès from roughly 1901-6 (See the entry on Deed (which also discusses *An Easy Way*) in Glenn Mitchell, *A-Z of Silent Film Comedy: An Illustrated Companion* (London: Batsford, 1998), pp. 79-80). Méliès

claimed that his training of Deed ensured the latter's future success in *Mes Mémoires* (1938) (repr. in Maurice Bessy and G.M. Lo Duca (eds.), *Georges Méliès, Mage* (Paris: Éditions Jean Jacques Pauvert, 1961), pp. 168-217, especially 194). The Volta showed at least three Cretinetti reels, as well as other trickfilms and 'object animations', such as Pathé's *Le Château hanté* (1908), during its 'Joycean' period of less than four months (I am indebted for that invaluable information to Luke McKernan's research into the Volta's programmes for the BFI, from the Liam O'Leary archive). During his 1904 sojourn in Paris, Joyce may also have seen some of the trickfilms Méliès was showing near his hotel (See Robert Ryf, *A New Approach to Joyce: A Portrait of the Artist As a Guidebook* (Berkeley: University of California Press, 1962), p. 174. A professional magician, Méliès is usually credited with discovering film's inherent 'narrative potential' (See David A. Cook, *A History of Narrative Film* (New York and London: Norton, 1981), pp. 13-14). According to Méliès, his screen conjuring with space and time, principally by means of editing, emerged quite accidentally when filming a Parisian street in the Autumn of 1896. His camera jammed just as an omnibus exited a tunnel. The resulting interruption in the continuity of the footage seemed to magically transform the bus into a hearse and men into women (Méliès account is translated in John Wakeman (ed.), *World Film Directors*, Vol.I (New York: H.W. Wilson, 1987), p. 750). Apocryphal or not, this story encapsulates how Méliès and other pioneers such as Britons G.A. Smith and James Williamson discovered how film could function as a kind of parallel reality yet with separate structural laws (see Paul Hammond *Marvellous Méliès* (London: Gordon Fraser, 1974), p. 34). Austin Briggs points out this is exactly the kind of 'Viconian transformation Joyce would have relished.' (Austin Briggs, "'Roll Away the Reel World, the Reel World'': ''Circe'' and the Cinema', in Morris Beja and Shari Benstock (eds.), *Coping With Joyce: Essays From the Copenhagen Symposium* (Columbus: Ohio State UP, 1989), pp. 145-56, especially , 150.) Alice Guy Blaché, the world's first female filmmaker, was also directing trickfilms as early as 1896 for Gaumont. For example, *La Fée aux choux* (from the French fable about a fairy who makes children in a cabbage patch) was full of magical effects, but also, arguably, a feminist satire of the mystification of sexuality and childbirth (see Ally Acker, *Reel Women: Pioneers of the Cinema 1896 to the Present* (London: Batsford, 1991), pp. xxiv and 3-12).

5   Vachel Lindsay, *The Art of the Moving Picture* (1915. Revised 1922; repr. New York: Liveright, 1970), pp. 61-3. (Henceforth all page references to *Art of the Moving Picture* will be given in brackets in the text.) Lindsay included a whole chapter on 'Furniture, Trappings, and Inventions in Motion', but his most detailed example was Pathé's 'Moving Day', i.e. very probably Émile Cohl's object animation, *Le Mobilier fidèle*, discussed in note 28. Cf. also literary anticipations such as *The Invisible Man*, in which 'He's put the sperits into the furniture!' (See H.G. Wells, *The Invisible Man* (1897; repr. London: Pan, 1987), p. 29.)

6   See Austin Briggs, '"Circe" and the Cinema', in Beja and Benstock (eds.) *Coping With Joyce*, pp. 145-56. (Henceforth, all page references to Briggs's essay will be given in brackets in the text.) Also Thomas L. Burkdall, 'Cinema Fakes: Film and Joycean Fantasy', in Morris Beja and David Norris (eds.), *Joyce in the Hibernian Metropolis: Essays*. (Columbus: Ohio State UP, 1996), pp. 260-69. (This essay is revised as Ch.V of his *Joycean Frames: Film and the Fiction of James Joyce* (New York and London: Routledge, 2001), pp. 65-80.)

7   Alan Spiegel, *Fiction and the Camera Eye*. (Charlottesville: UP of Virginia, 1976), pp. 134-40.

8   See James Joyce *Dubliners* (1914; repr. Oxford: Oxford University Press, 2000), pp. 175, and *A Portrait*, Ch.I pp. 32-33.

9   'Sllt. The nethermost deck of the first machine jogged forward its flyboard with sllt the first batch of quirefolded papers. Sllt. Almost human the way it sllt to call attention. Doing its level best to speak. That door too still creaking, asking to be shut. Everything speaks in its own way. Sllt.' (James Joyce, *Ulysses* (1922; repr. Oxford: Oxford University Press, 1998), p. 117. (Henceforth, all page references to *Ulysses* will be given in brackets in the text.) The famous final scene of Fritz Lang's film *Dr Mabuse, der Spieler*, released the same year, features a literally animated printing press, with monstrously anthropomorphic features hallucinated by the master criminal after his breakdown.

10   Donald Crafton, *Before Mickey: The Animated Film 1898-1928*, Revised edition (Chicago and London: University of Chicago Press, 1993), p. 329. (Henceforth all page references to *Before Mickey* will be given in brackets in the text.)

11   See Richard Ellmann *Ulysses on the Liffey* (Oxford: Oxford UP, 1972), Appendix pullout between pp. 188-89.

12   In his *Finnegans Wake* workbook entry for 'Circe', Joyce made the connection between the chapter and cinematic trickery retrospectively explicit: 'cinema fakes, drown, state of sea, tank: steeplejack, steeple on floor, camera above: jumps 10 feet, 1 foot camera 6 foot pit' (See James Joyce . *Scribbledehobble: The Ur-Workbook for Finnegans Wake*, ed. Thomas E. Connolly (Evanston, Illinois: Northwestern UP, 1961), p. 119.

13   Craig Wallace Barrow, reading the novel in terms of Eisenstein's theories, comments that in 'Circe', the simultaneous montage of the interior monologues, finally breaks out into primary montage, which it has 'threatened to become throughout *Ulysses*', by mixing fantasy and realism. However, Barrow's comparison with a Fellini scenario seems rather after-the-event considering the wealth of filmic analogies contemporary to Joyce's text (see his *Montage in James Joyce's* Ulysses (Madrid: Studia Humanitatis, 1980), pp. 138 and 146.

14   Kevin Jackson, *The Language of Cinema* (Manchester: Carcanet, 1998), p. 14.

15   Cf. 'Circe's' influence on Dylan Thomas's own 'play for voices', *Under Milk Wood* (1954), which also begins in a kind of 'Nighttown' scenario and dramatises the

unconscious, 'dream-lives' of its inhabitants in the alternative, 'blind' medium of radio. An interesting sidelight is also cast on 'Circe' by cartoonist Winsor McCay's first attempt to adapt his *Little Nemo in Slumberland* strip, as an three-act operetta in 1908 (see Charles Solomon, *Enchanted Drawings: The History of Animation* (New York: Wing Books, 1994), p. 16).

16   Lotte H. Eisner established this in her classic study *The Haunted Screen: Expressionism in the German Cinema and the Influence of Max Reinhardt*, trans. Richard Greaves. (London: Thames and Hudson, 1969). For a recent discussion of 'Circe's' use of Expressionism, see Sherill Grace, 'Midsummer Madness and the Day of the Dead: Joyce, Lowry and Expressionism', in Patrick A. McCarthy and Paul Tiessen (eds.), *Joyce/Lowry: Critical Perspective* (Lexington: University Press of Kentucky, 1997, pp. 9-20.

17   ...the author has attempted to imitate the disconnected but yet seemingly logical shape of a dream. Anything can happen, everything is possible and probable. Time and space do not exist. Upon an insignificant background of real life, the imagination spins and weaves new patterns; a blend of memories, experiences, pure inventions, absurdities, and improvisations.... The characters split, double, redouble, evaporate, condense, fragment, cohere. But one consciousness is superior to them all: that of the dreamer. For him there are no secrets, no inconsistencies, no scruples, no laws,. He neither condemns not acquits, only relates. And since dreams are more often painful than happy, a tone of melancholy and of compassion for all living things, runs through the swaying narrative.' ('Author's Note' in August Strindberg *Five Plays*, trans. Harry G. Carlson (Berkeley and Los Angeles: University of California Press, 1983), pp .205-06.) Alternatively, Michael Meyer translates 'swaying' as 'flickering', compounding the play's cinematic aspirations (see August Strindberg *Plays: Two*, ed. and trans. Michael Meyer (London: Methuen. 1982), p. 175).

18   Cf. the tense of Shem's writing as described in *Finnegans Wake* (1939; repr. London: Faber, 1975), pp. 185.36-186.1.

19   In his detailed discussions of the filmic aspects of *Ulysses*, Sergei M. Eisenstein concentrated on Bloom's interior monologues, largely ignoring other possibilities. (See, for example, 'A Course In Treatment' (1932), in his *Film Form: Essays in Film Theory*, ed. and trans. Jay Leyda (London: Dennis Dobson, 1963., pp. 84-107, especially p. 104.) For the fullest account of the Eisenstein/Joyce encounter so far, see Gösta Werner 'James Joyce and Sergej Eisenstein', trans. from Swedish by Erik Gunnemark, in *James Joyce Quarterly* XXVII, No.3 (Spring 1990), pp. 491-507.

20   Like the transformation between naturalism and the 'sinful' fantasies of 'Circe', 'how much more quickly than on the stage the borderline of All Saints' Day and Hallowe'en can be crossed', argued Lindsay (see *Art of the Moving Picture*, pp. 65-66). In 1908 Leo Tolstoy predicted the revolutionary effect 'this little clicking contraption with the revolving handle will make ... in the life of writers', instancing his own difficulties with stage transitions: 'When I was writing 'The Living Corpse,' I tore my hair and

chewed my fingers because I could not give enough scenes, enough pictures, because I could not pass rapidly enough from one event to another. The accursed stage was like a halter choking the throat of the dramatist; and I had to cut the life and swing of the work according to the dimensions and requirements of the stage... But the films! They are wonderful! Drr! and a scene is ready! Drr! and we have another! We have the sea, the coast, the city, the palace... ('A Conversation with Leo Tolstoy' in Jay Leyda *Kino: A History of the Russian and Soviet Film* (London: Allen and Unwin, 1960), pp. 410-11) As Spiegel points out, Tolstoy was not simply describing motion in the phenomenal world so much as narrative movement within the medium itself, between one shot and another, i.e. montage, *avant la lettre*, which creates the unique rhythm of film spacetime (see Spiegel, *Fiction and the Camera Eye*, p. 163). Münsterberg also noted film's technical advantages over traditional drama: 'No theater could ever try to match such wonders ... Rich artistic effects have been secured, and while on the stage every fairy play is clumsy and hardly able to create an illusion, in the film we really see the man transformed into a beast and the flowers into a girl. The divers jump, feet first, out of the water to the springboard. It looks magical, and yet the camera man has simply to reverse his film and to run it from the end to the beginning of the action. Every dream becomes real, uncanny ghosts appear from nothing and disappear into nothing, mermaids swim through the waves and little elves climb out of the Easter lilies.' (Hugo Münsterberg,. *The Photoplay: A Psychological Study* (1916; repr. as *The Film: A Psychological Study* (New York: Dover Publications, 1970), pp. 14-15)

21   Ian Christie *The Last Machine: Early Cinema and the Birth of the Modern World* (London: BBC/BFI, 1994), pp. 118-19. (Henceforth, all page references to *Last Machine* will be given in brackets in the text.)

22   Briggs's examples are largely taken from John Frazer, *Artificially Arranged Scenes: The Films of George Méliès* (Boston: G.K. Hall, 1979).

23   Spiegel, *Fiction and the Camera Eye*, pp. 148-49.

24   Anamorphic distortion of objects and people occurs most impressively in Karl Heinz Martin's *Von Morgen bis Mitternacht* (1920), F.W. Murnau's *Der letzte Mann* (1924), Ernö Metzner's *Überfall* (1928) and Alfred Abel's *Narkose* (1929).

25   *The Plausible Impossible* was the title of Walt Disney's TV broadcast (31 October, 1954). In this he explained how animation techniques often function on a logical basis, albeit of a purely visual kind: e.g. when a character goes down or up in a lift gravity seems to make it elongate, and vice versa. (For details of the programme, see, among others, Dave Smith, *Disney A-Z: The Official Encyclopaedia* (New York: Hyperion, 1996), p. 390.) For McCay's precedents in Carroll and Tenniel, see Crafton *Before Mickey*, especially pp. 124-26, and Solomon *Enchanted Drawings*, p. 14, which shows the hand-tinted images.

26   See G.M Lo Duca *Le Dessin animé: Histoire, Esthetique, Technique*. (Paris: Prisma, 1948), p. 128.

27 So smooth and 'realistic' was the animation in McCay's cartoon (which was hand-tinted to match the colours of the newspaper strip) to audiences hitherto only exposed only to moving line-drawings, that they often assumed its artistry was achieved with live actors and trick photography, much to McCay's chagrin (see Solomon *Enchanted Drawings*, p. 16).

28 Jackson cites the OED record for *Harper's Weekly* (11 December, 1915): 'Even cartoons began to come in – "animated" cartoons as they are called.' (See Jackson *Language of Cinema*, p. 14)

29 According to Crafton, *Le Garde-Meuble* was by Cohl's disciple Roméo Bosetti, although it is often confused with Cohl's own *Le Mobilier fidèle* (1910), whose scenario it reworks (see Donald Crafton, *Émile Cohl, Caricature and Film*. (Princeton: Princeton UP, 1990), pp. 154-55, also note 5 on Lindsay above).

30 Even one of Walt Disney's early *Laugh-O-Grams* (1918) featured the animator himself, 'caught redhanded' limning a burglar.

31 Again there is some dispute as to whether the 'Cohlesque' *Pumpkin Race* was actually by the master or some of his juniors at Pathé (see Crafton, *Émile Cohl*, p. 116).

32 For example, Pat Sullivan contracted with Chaplin himself for a 1916 cartoon series based on his screen character and working from films and photographs. Similarly, Howard S. Moss's 1917 'Motoy Films' series, featured animated puppets which often burlesqued film stars such as Chaplin, Mary Pickford and Ben Turpin. As Crafton points out, the development of continuity series based around individual cartoon characters was an inevitable corollary to Hollywood's emerging star system (see *Before Mickey*, pp. 304, 265 and 271-2, respectively.)

33 These articles (quoted by Crafton (*Before Mickey*, pp.348-49)) featured in 'serious' journals, *Les Cahiers du Mois* 16-17 (1925), 53, and *Le Rouge et le Noir* (July 1928).

34 Iris Barry *Let's Go to the Pictures* (1926; repr. as *Let's Go to the Movies* (New York: Payson and Clarke, 1972), pp. 11-12, 17-18 and 185.

35 Virginia Woolf, *Collected Essays*, ed. Leonard Woolf, vol. II. (London: Hogarth, 1964), pp .268-72, especially 270-72.

36 For Joyce and Ruttmann, see my forthcoming essay 'Symphonies of the Big City: Modernism, Cinema and Urban Modernity', in Paul Edwards (ed.), *The Great Vortex: Modernist London 1910-30* (Bath: Sulis Press, 2003).

37 Dziga Vertov, 'We' (1922), in *Kino-Eye: The Writings of Dziga Vertov*, ed. Annette Michelson. (Berkeley and London: University of California Press, 1984), pp. 5-9, especially 9. Vertov's neologism, *kinochestvo*, is translated by Michelson as the special 'quality' of the cinema-eye, its 'way of seeing', in effect (see her note on pp. 5-6).

38 The result was the hour-long 'mixed mode' animation *The Einstein Theory of Relativity* (1923), presented by Edwin Miles Fadman. For details, see Leslie Cabanga *The Fleischer Story* (revised edition) (New York: Da Capo, 1988), pp. 29-30. Also Solomon *Enchanted Drawings*, p. 32, and Shamus Culhane *Talking Animals and Other*

People: the Autobiography of a Legendary Animator (New York: Da Capo, 1998), p. 56.

39   Mutt and Jeff feature in an early dialogue and later in all kinds of syllabically mutated guises (see Joyce, *Finnegans Wake*, pp. 16-18, also (for example) 273).

40   For Joyce's precocious interest in series photography and interrelated attempts to render motion in painting, see my 'Joyce and Early Cinema', in *The James Joyce Broadsheet* (February, 2001), p.1., and Archie K. Loss, *Joyce's Visible Art: The Work of Joyce and the Visual Arts, 1904-1922* (Ann Arbor, Michigan: UMI Research Press, 1984), especially pp. 62-64.

41   As confirmed in Sassoon's use of the screen flicker to represent the 'unreal' violence of the first fully-mechanised modern war (see his poem 'Picture Show', in Philip French and Ken Wlaschin (eds.) *The Faber Book of Movie Verse* (London: Faber, 1994), p. 38).

42   See *Finnegans Wake*, pp. 414-18.

43   For Felix's genesis, see Leslie Cabanga, *Felix: the Twisted Tale of the World's Most Famous Cat* (New York: Da Capo, 1996). Crafton argues the continuity series characters of the Twenties were based around particular stars, as in the case of both Messmer and Disney: 'If Felix's balletic movements and victimization by his environment are seen as derived from Chaplin's screen character, then Oswald may be viewed as closer to Keaton and his ability to transform the absurd mechanical environment of the modern world into something useful and humane.' (See *Before Mickey*, pp. 295 and 308)

44   See Crafton, *Before Mickey*, pp. 292-97, and Culhane (who worked on the actual transformation) *Talking Animals*, pp. 52 and illustration 55.

45   See Ellmann, *James Joyce*, pp. 486 and 490.

46   Münsterberg, *Photoplay: a Psychological Study*, pp. 72, 84 and 14-15, respectively.

47   For the evidence supporting 'Circe' as a comically sceptical rendering of Freud's theories, see Ellmann, *Ulysses on the Liffey*, pp. 138-41, and *The Consciousness of Joyce* (London: Faber, 1977), pp. 54-56 and *James Joyce* (1982), pp. 495 and 509. For a round-up of more recent views on 'Circe', as a possible joint parody of Expressionism *and* psychoanalysis, see Weldon Thornton, *Voices and Values in Joyce's Ulysses* (Gainesville: University Press of Florida, 2000), pp. 154-70.

48   See 'Infantile Sexuality' (1905) and 'The Dissection of the Psychic Personality' (1933) in Sigmund Freud, *The Essentials of Psychoanalysis*, ed. Anna Freud (Harmondsworth: Penguin, 1986), pp. 330-31 and 498-99.

49   For example, in Flann O'Brien's 1939 *At Swim Two Birds* (a 'template' Postmodern metafiction, which teems with figures from Irish literature and myth, and itself a parody of Joyce's *Portrait*), a gang of cowboy desperadoes escape the 'frame' of the pulp western to highjack a corporation tram in a shoot-out with the Dublin police (see *At Swim Two Birds* (1939; repr. Harmondsworth: Penguin, 1975), pp .55-59). Similarly, in Patrick Hamilton's *Impromptu in Moribundia* (published the same year

and set on a planet in which media words and images reify and interfuse with organic reality) commodities literally move and speak to consumers, as if in anthropomorphising animated cartoons (see *Impromptu in Moribundia* (1939; repr. Nottingham: Trent Editions, 1999), pp. 88-89).

50   See, for example, 'The Temptation of Haringay' (1895) and 'The Magic Shop' (1903) in *The Complete Short Stories of H.G. Wells*, ed. John Hammond (London: Dent, 1998), pp. 37-41 and 429-37.

51   See Werner 'James Joyce', in *Nordic Rejoycings*, p.128.

52   In an advertising film made by Méliès for Dewar's, ancestral portraits are similarly lured out of their frames by the whisky's irresistibility (see Erik Barnouw, *The Magician and the Cinema* (Oxford: Oxford University Press, 1981), p. 101. He also brought photographs to life in *The Spiritualistic Photographer* (1903) (see Hammond *Marvellous Méliès*, p. 90).

53   Joseph C. Voelker 'Clown Meets Cops: Comedy and Paranoia in *Under the Volcano* and *Ulysses*', in McCarthy and Tiessen (eds.) *Joyce/Lowry*, pp. 21-40, especially 39.

54   It will be interesting to see what techniques are employed to visualise 'Circe' in the new film of *Ulysses* (directed and adapted by Sean Walsh and starring Stephen Rea as Bloom), which commenced production on Bloomsday 2001.

55   The Hollywood suburb where animated characters reside in Robert Zemeckis' mixed mode parody of *film noir*, *Who Framed Roger Rabbit?* (1988).

Bridges

7

Len Lye and Laura Riding in the 1930s: the Impossibility of Film and Literature

Tim Armstrong

This essay concerns itself with one episode in the intersection of film and writing in modernism, the brief collaboration of the experimental film-maker Len Lye and poet Laura Riding in the early 1930s. It was a collaboration which saw Riding and Graves publish some of Lye's writings, use his illustrations for book covers for their Seizen Press, and Riding and Lye produce a film script and a joint film manifesto, as well as other related writings. In part I simply want restore Lye to the picture, since his trajectory is a fascinating one, emblematic of a second-wave British modernism characterised by its dialogue with Surrealism, its satirical stance, its collaborative work, and by such fluid movements between genres and media as we see in Lye (and in other figures such as his friend Oswell Blakeston, film-maker, artist, novelist, poet, editor, travel-writer). In terms of the concerns of this collection, I want to look at a form of cinema which sees itself as inscription, and a form of writing which seems to partially conceive itself in terms of cinematic technology. Ultimately, what will be described is, paradoxically, both collaboration between poet and film-maker and a mutual rejection of the intersection of literature and film.

I

Some biography is probably necessary for most readers.[1] Born in Christchurch, New Zealand in 1901, Lye was from a fairly poor family; for a while they lived in a remote lighthouse. A rather isolated modernist in the antipodes – he later described his excitement at finding Pound's *Gaudier-Brzeska* in Wellington around 1920 – he worked in Australia and spent time in Samoa studying tribal art before his arrival in London in 1926. He stayed almost two decades, painting as a member of the 'Seven and Five Society,' the group around Ben Nicholson, writing as a member of the Graves-Riding circle, and making some famous films for Grierson's GPO film unit, before departing for the USA in 1944.[2] There he acted briefly as a political advocate for his own idiosyncratic theories of human fulfilment, and made more films; but for much of his later career he worked as a kinetic sculptor, a well-known figure in the New York avant-garde. His work featured prominently in the 2001 Kinetic Art exhibition at the Hayward Gallery in London. He died in New York in 1980, having – paradoxically, after decades of exile – see some of his more technologically-demanding sculptural projects realized by supporters in his homeland, New Zealand.

Like Riding in her 'Histories', Lye produced much of his work in the thirties in dialogue with Surrealism – he admired Miró, and wrote prose pieces in an 'automatic' style indebted to Breton and Stein. A collection of these was published by Graves and Riding as one of the first Seizen press books, *No Trouble*, in 1930.[3] He exhibited work at the London International Surrealist Exhibition in 1936 and in later Surrealist shows, and practiced automatic doodling, a technique, Wystan Curnow and Roger Horrocks report, which was 'increasingly important for him as a source of images and "energy signs", and as a methods of transferring power from the "new" brain to the old' (*FM*, p. xiii). Lye preferred the term 'old brain' to the 'unconscious', partly because of his interest in 'primitive' (Aboriginal, Samoan and Maori) art, and partly because his evolving theories of motion – which after the war took on a more biological and evolutionary slant – involved notions of empathetic registration in which the artist takes the motion he or she sees in the world and translates it into a form dependant on their individual body and its accidentals. He later commented that 'I got my feeling for motion down to the most subtle of empathies, such as the way both ends of a pen waggled in relation to one another as I write, or how my eyeballs moved in their sockets as I scanned lines of print' (*FM*, p. 82). The art of movement is, then, founded on vitalistic notions of encounter and translation, rather than mechanical registration.

Lye had begun with scratching on film when he was working as a scenario writer in Australia in the early 1920s, noticing the random scratches in film leaders and making his own experiments. He revived the idea in London in 1934, using film stock friends gave him, producing 'direct' films set to music: *Colour Box* (1935), *Kaleidoscope* (1935); *Rainbow Dance* (1936) and others, films which combine animation techniques and colour patterns – lines, grids, dancing blobs – directly applied as a lacquer, sometimes to already used documentary footage, with Post Office advertising slogans added at the end. The films were popular for their startling colour; and for the playful yoking of rhythmic image and jazz music achieved by the sound editing of Lye's Australian collaborator Jack Ellit. They have inspired many later animators; even Disney purchased and studied them for *Fantasia*.[4] In his post-war films, without the funding he needed, Lye returned to the solitary technique of scratching onto films, producing dancing, twisting lines set to African drums. All Lye's 'direct' films have a remarkable vibration intensity; the vibration produced by the fact that directly-painted lines and colours can never achieve the precise registration of a photographed object or of cartoons laid in a frame. For Lye, this jumpiness was a desirable effect; an intimation of life. We might compare it to the 'jerkiness' and 'vibration' or 'syncopation' which (as Michael North explains) Cocteau and others admired in Chaplin: a mechanical rhythm which disrupts the surface of cinematic realism and foregrounds, rather than effacing, the comic dissonance of the human body and the machine.[5]

What does it mean to scratch or paint directly onto film? For Lye the 'direct film' means a return to the origins of film in the play of light of the magic lantern, and to a version of the pre-Griffith 'cinema of attractions'; the cinema which astounds technically. But direct film is more radical that. Bypassing the origins of film in photography and the observation of actual movement – in Marey and Muybridge – direct film can to work without a camera, using the projector as its medium, and producing an art of *pure* movement, abstract and animated. If one were to succumb to a Foucaultian moment, it might be said that this marks a radical epistemic shift: movement, *perhaps for the first time in the history of representation*, free of the direct trace of the human hand at the level of production (which remains present, of course, in abstract painting) or of realism at the level of representation. To be sure, a few other artists also experimented with 'direct' film in this period; though surely Lye is the most accomplished. But Lye's 'direct film' is, to return to the point, often free from the figure moving in the spectator's vision, as in the theatre or naturalistic film, or from what remains at least a displaced representation of bodies in motion in most animated film – Lye commented that Mickey Mouse was just the Griffith continuity rules applied to animation. The individual frame may be produced by hand-painting, but what the spectator sees is not; it is produced instead by of successive frames moving through a projector's gate, that is a series of quanta integrated in the physiology of perception. This foregrounds the technology of presentation rather than registration, as Lye himself acknowledges when he stencils film-sprocket motifs onto his film; or when he breaks down three-colour processes and applies its components abstractly to a ground of black and white film. But Lye does more than that: he uses the projector as a colour mixer, noting that 'a few frames of blue followed by a few frames of yellow appears as a vivid green' (*FM*, p. 44). Indeed, in its constant re-codification of colour values and its break between the production of visual information and its reception Lye's work looks forward to digitalisation, as at least one recent manifesto of digital film acknowledges; that is partly why *we* look at it with such easy recognition.[6]

In a recent article on Lye, Paul Watson argues that Lye's work deconstructs the distinction between so called 'live' film and animation, and in fact exposes the way cinema constructs motion: 'it is only through the dual logic of animation – to endow with life and impart motion to – that cinema can define itself as cinema.'

There is, he argues, 'nothing less live about animation than live action; both create an illusion of life through what is first and foremost an animation apparatus'.[7] This is undoubtedly true; but what if we take Watson's argument a stage further, and accept Lye's own claims that what his animation offers us is less an 'illusion' than a form of life, mediated by the 'empathy' that allows the artist to translate external motion or sub-cellular events into film. One might want to say that it is, in some Deleuzian sense, a new mode of *being* – it isn't surprising that Lye later described his early work *Tusalava* in terms of viral or mitochondrial (energy-carrying) life. Compare Lewis Mumford, writing in the 1930s: 'Without any conscious notion of its destination, the motion picture presents us with a world of interpenetrating, counter-influencing organisms: and it enables us to think about that world with a greater degree of concreteness.'[8] Film as an organism, animated and moving in time to music: for Lye, the beat of life is a techno beat.

Finally, 'Animation' in the abstract sense is an interesting subject in early cinema, and is worth lingering over for a moment. Early film criticism repeatedly describes film as revealing the 'life of *things*', that is as fetishistically endowing inanimate objects with life by isolating and enlarging their presence. Such terms recall the nineteenth-century anthropological debates on two broadly opposed ways of explaining similar phenomena in 'primitive' societies: animism and fetishism.[9] Broadly speaking, animism (associated with the British anthropologist E. B. Tylor) represents the worship of totemic objects as an intimation of the soul, the kernel of all later vitalisms and idealisms. For Auguste Comte and Karl Marx, on the other hand, the fetish represents a way of thinking about materiality and its relation to the human – for Marx commodity fetishism represents the alienation of value from its sources, as well as the source of social desire itself; implicitly, the troubling intersection of an idealist category (ideology) and the real. If Marx's definition of fetishism as 'the religion of sensuous desire' seems to offer a general reflection on Hollywood cinema as an institution – what does cinema do if not present an abstract, alienated investment in the glittering world of the *mise en scene*? – then Lye's animation refuses such pleasures as they might be invested in the object, focusing on the process itself; the vibrating images of the hand-painted film bypass the object in favour of that which animates. 'Animism' in Lye's filmic anthropology might thus represent a vitalism conceived as intrinsic to the medium, a kind of film which cannot be the vehicle of illusion, and so cannot be demystified (in this he differs from the Surrealists, for whom filmic fetishism is, broadly speaking, to be put to subversive uses in more direct opposition to realism). Animism vs. fetishism, animation vs. representation; these are the oppositions which define Lye's direct films, which demand the sensuousness of the 'real', and ultimately life itself, at the level of presentation rather than representation.

II

How does all this relate to Riding and her collaboration with Lye? First, a brief sketch of that collaboration: Lye, singly and then with his first wife Jane, was one of the inner members of the Riding-Graves circle in the 1930s. Lye produced book jackets and designs for their Seizin Press, which in turn published his *No Trouble*. His collaboration with Riding produced a film scenario, 'Description of Life', related in turn to the John Aldridge-Riding collaboration *The Life of the Dead*; and Riding suggested the project for Lye's 'Quicksilver', a fantastic musical comedy based on space travel.[10] The piece which Lye and Riding wrote together, the manifesto (if we can call it that) 'Film-making', appeared in 1935 in the first volume of *Epilogue*, the occasional journal which Riding and Graves published. She then published a 46-page pamphlet *Len Lye and the Problem of Popular Films* (1938) – a pamphlet now so rare that there are only a few locatable copies in the world.[11]

One answer to the question above is that Lye's stress on directness of communication matches Riding's. He was willing to apply his ideas to literature, attempting to translate poetry into 'direct film' in a 7 minute film called *Full Fathom Five* (1937), with Gielgud reading passages from Shakespeare. In a 1936 article he suggested voice-and-colour films or television, with 'colours rising up off the pages of a book to fill the screen as a person reads from it . . . This fresh acceptance would isolate the words from their recording in abstract type and present them as "immediate" mental stimuli' (*FM*, p. 44). This proposal seems to find an echo in Riding's stress on the immediacy of poetry, and, in 'Come, Words, Away', her desire to remove language from the accidentals of its presentation:

> Come, words, away to where
> The meaning is not thickened
> With the voice's fretting substance,
> Nor look of words is curious
> As letters in books staring out [...]

> (*P*, p. 134)[12]

The 'Film-making' manifesto begins with an attack on all thinking which stresses form as an achieved reality rather than the context-bound movement which creates form. This error informs the tendency to read 'truth-signs where there are only life-signs'; whereas movement is the 'language of life', and 'the earliest language'. Movement is Being, 'physical things'; the world of the senses rather than meaning. They continue:

But the arbitrary realities of life do not explain themselves. We cannot expect them to tell what they are as against other things which are. We can only expect a physical accuracy of them, physical explicitness – movement. And this is why a strict historical analysis of life is necessarily cinematographic. It is not what is called 'history': because it is the object of professional history to find truth in life, and this is neither physically appropriate nor possible. History imposes on life a kind of accuracy of which it is innocent, an accuracy of self-explanation; whereas life has only physical accuracy. (*FM*, p. 39)

With their stress on the movement and origins of life as opposed to analytic frameworks, these formulae recall Bergson; the difference, is of course, that for Bergson the 'cinematographic' is the enemy, the analysis which cuts the flow of being into segments – since Bergson thinks of film in terms of the work of his famous colleague at the Collège de France, E. J. Marey.[13] This alerts us to the *recuperative* position of film here. Echoing the Surrealist stress on film as defamiliarisation, as a re-seeing of the world, the manifesto aims to return movement to the eye, to prise it away from language: 'To extricate movement from the static finalities or shapes which the mind imposes on living experience is *to translate the memory of time back into time again* – to relive experience instead of merely remembering it' (*FM*, p. 41, emphasis added). In some ways this is akin to Riding's translation procedure in *The Life of the Dead* (1933), the poetic sequence which she wrote first in French, she explained, because that language is more literal and anti-poetic (*P*, p. 360).

That evocative formula, 'to translate the memory of time back into time again,' touches on a debate which threads its way through turn of the century psychology, psychophysics and philosophy – on the issue of the *lost present*; the moment which for James and Bergson is spread across an echoing continuum; which for Helmholtz is lost in reaction-time and processing; which for Husserl is a kind of retrospective fiction. The present is ineffable; cannot be captured; but film offers at least the possibility of re-presenting it.[14] For the Surrealists, the recaptured moment is most often a sublime flash or shock which ruptures the continuity of habitual perception; for Lye, the moment is realised by its translation into what he later called 'figures of motion' or 'Aesthetic Kinesthesia' (*FM*, p. 78-9), that is by the empathetic and non-mimetic reproduction of the energies of the world in the art-work (and it is interesting in this respect that he was willing to re-edit actual motion, like the man's swinging arm in *Trade Tattoo*, to fit the music). Lye bypasses the problem of strict 'accuracy' (*FM*, p. 39): life cannot be relived *as representation*, but it can be imitated.

Time, and the reclamation of time, is a preoccupation for the later Riding: poetry, as her 1938 preface explained, arguing for a state in which 'we are so continuously habituated that there is no temporal interruption between one poetic incident (poem) and another' (*P*, p. 413). Time and history almost always linked to 'the curse of thought's construction'; it is the self-conscious 'historical effort' that blights poetry.[15] The former phrase is from her poem 'March, 1937', which describes the way 'vision [is] now a thing of thinking', in a world of mediated or fictionalised time. Riding's poem turns us away from this time of 'story', contained within the 'envelopes' of years, months, days:

> The poem takes the story away.
> We have left nor a month nor its least cruel day.
> Nor the envelope without the envelope
> Without the envelope within.
> This is the poem.
> Are we so naked then of life,
> Stripped to the death?
> Is this the promised core of us?
> Come closer, let us not shudder so, shiver,
> We are not ill, nor dead – nor uncovered
> In the lost shame of ordeal.
> There is something so good in this
> That, despite worry, hope, and no letter,
> I scarcely dare let myself wish for better.

(P, p. 312)

What is arrived at is the *moment* – which in this formula is the moment of an encounter; an empathetic moment, in Lye's terms – and of a new representation, the poem. As she later wrote, 'I put religious trust in the predictiveness of poetry as an immediacy, not a future in the making' (*P*, p. 3). For Riding, this moment is typically that of love, containing a 'promise of the words all yearned to hear from one another' (*P*, p. 3). In 'Friendship on Visit' she writes 'Yet must the picture be a talk-lit darkness, / Of flickering instances, for so it was', evoking cinema's flashing instances in the birth of passion.

We can also turn to Riding's 'Poet: A Lying Word', with its many resonances, including *A Midsummer Night's Dream* and Plato's allegory of the cave. The distinction here is between the false wall, the poet who is like a ladder or a monument to be scaled, and the true wall which is the poet only visible as her poem. Thus, 'And the tale is no more of the going: no more a poet's tale of a going false-like to a seeing. The tale is of a seeing true-like to a knowing: there's but to stare the wall through now, well through' (*P*, p. 216).

Can we think of this wall which we must stare through as akin to the film itself for Lye? – the film which is not a going to a seeing (by the camera and director), but rather something more unmediated, seeing and knowing in closer relation, seeking nothing beyond the liveliness of the representation. What is produced is something precisely located in time, 'a written edge of time' – the end-of-time which Riding equates with the production of meaning; not the metaphorical weather of the poetic career but the presence of the body as it moves through time:

> It is not a wall, it is not a poet. It is not a lying wall, it is not a lying word. It is a written edge of time. Step not across, for then into my mouth, my eyes, you fall. Come close, stare me well through, speak as you see. But, oh, infatuated drove of lives, step not across now. Into my mouth, my eyes, shall you thus fall, and be yourselves no more.
>
> Into my mouth, my eyes, I say, I say. I am no poet like transitory wall to lead you into such slow terrain of time as measured out your single span of broken turns of season once and one again. I lead you not. You have now come with me, I have now come with you, to your last turn and season: thus could I come with you, thus only.
>
> [. . . . .]
>
> This body-self, this wall, this poet-like address, is that last barrier long shied of in your elliptic changes: out of your leaping, shying, season-quibbling, have I made it, is it made. And if now poet-like it rings with one-more-time as if, this is the mounted stupor of your everlong outbiding worn prompt and lyric, poet-like – the forbidden one-more-time worn time-like.
>
> (*P*, p. 216-17)

The poem as a site of encounter with *time worn time-like* – recalling that earlier phrase, 'to translate the memory of time back into time again'. *Time worn time-like* is time returned to the poem itself, the time of 'have I made it, is it made'.

One further example might be adduced: Riding's 'How Now We Talk', with its stress on directness and precision pointing towards her later position on language. Here it is in the moment of encounter, a moment of 'physical accuracy' (as film is described above), perhaps even a form of poetry written in what we could call the cinematographic mode, where 'accuracy' must replace the uncertainties of past or future:

> For what we now talk of is all true
> Or all false, since all is words, no doing to do
> Or prospect to wage or more going to go
> Or grief to be old or delight to be new.
> We must keep faith with what we say
> And every coxcomb ghost of fancy lay,

> Forbearing from the tales which cloy
> The ears of time and drive the future away.

(P, p. 283)

In this state 'only the present is left to promise / And for air the breath of our words must suffice' – language taking on a physical immediacy, a naked presence.

A final question: what might all this have to do with Riding's famous abandonment of poetry at the end of the 1930s? Film, or rather Lye's version of film, may have supported her evolving suspicion that poetic language is embodied, immanent; it may have helped her escape from what Jerome McGann calls the 'Kantian ghetto' of poetry, into a poetry in which the presence of language is attested.[16] Riding's view of film can be allied to a poetry of being; a poetry poised on the moment's edge represented by the encounter of self and other. This is in turn related to her later belief that poetry is the product of an instantaneous apperception, and the related belief that only the 'instant' understanding of a poem is acceptable – that the poem must be released from mere meaning into being.[17]

But film, for that reason, helps Riding to separate meaning from poetry, and to see the potential redundancy of the poem. One corollary of the stance of 'Film as Motion' is that the cinema produces only a caricature of language if it tries to be literary or historical in the discursive sense:

> The language of cinema is movement. When it attempts to make of movement a literary language the result is a physical-intellectual caricature-language which furnishes stories of life as something half-true, half-ridiculous (the result of such films as *Henry VIII, Catherine the Great, Christina of Sweden*). The language of the film, that is, becomes the language of hysteria; people have been trained to go to the cinema to enjoy respectable hysteria, not to know, physically and soberly, 'life'. And so they enjoy films more than proper stage drama because the excitement of feeling unreasonably and irresponsibly in contact with 'meanings' is on a larger scale than with stage drama [. . .]

(FM, p. 40)

The 'language of hysteria' is the mixing of the somatic and linguistic: 'sentimentalities'. This shares its structure with Riding's post-war position on poetry – seeing it as a hopelessly mixed discourse, confusing truth with the merely pleasurable image, sound-effect or play of connotation – as, in effect, a product of *techne*. If film is the language of being, and rational prose the language of truth or meaning, then in so far as poetry mixes those elements it becomes 'hysterical'.

This has been, in part, a story of modernist refusal of what André Bazin called a 'mixed cinema', a cinema in which the values of literature and film mix productively rather than becoming opposed.[18] For Lye, the 'literary' in the sense of discursive meaning and narration is not a part of his cinema, eschewed for a technology of sensation and being. For Riding, poetry may aim to be part of being and even, for a moment, find a kind of ally in film – an ally against the abstractions of 'history'. But ultimately she comes to equate poetry with a disabling mechanics of pleasure, with the fall into the body which she and Lye had equated with the cinema of 'hysteria'.

As a coda, a final irony. Riding's career after her return to America and marriage to Schuyler Jackson was dedicated in large part to a project for a philosophy and dictionary of rationalised concepts – an idea still in process at her death, and subsequently edited by William Harmon as *Rational Meaning: A New Foundation for the Definition of Words* (1997).[19] As if in parallel, when Lye arrived in the USA in 1945 he came to make a series of six 10-minute black and white films entitled *Basic English*, sponsored by 'The March of Time' and supervised, of course, by I. A. Richards.[20] It seems that if the modernist dream of unmediated communication of being or meaning, mind to mind, cannot be achieved in poetry or film, one might settle for mere accuracy. And that, tragically some would say, is what Riding spent so many decades doing in that lonely house in Florida, up to her death in 1991. And one wonders if she ever went to the movies.

Notes

1   Roger Horrocks's recent *Len Lye: A Biography* (Auckland: Auckland University Press, 2001) brings Lye's long career and many contexts for the first time into detailed focus. See also the essays collected in *Len Lye*, ed. Jean-Michel Bouhours and Roger Horrocks (Paris: Centre Pompidou, 2000). For Lye's own work, the best source is Len Lye, *Figures of Motion: Selected Writings*, ed. and intro. Wystan Curnow and Roger Horrocks (Auckland: Auckland University Press, 1984), cited below as *FM*. This text includes a comprehensive bibliography and filmography. Lye's films are currently available in various collections, including animation videos in the GPO Classic Collection (issued by the BFI) and *Free Radicals*, a compilation issued by the Len Lye Foundation in New Zealand.

2   See Horrocks, *Len Lye*, chs. 12-31. Another recent text describing Lye's London context is Michel Remy, *Surrealism in Britain* (Aldershot: Ashgate, 1999). His films are described briefly in the standard accounts of British film of the 1930s by Rachael Low and others, and in most histories of film animation. The collaboration is, however, barely mentioned in Deborah Baker's *In Extremis: The Life of Laura Riding* (London: Hamish Hamilton, 1993) and in other accounts of Riding.

3   Len Lye, *No Trouble* (Deya: Seizin Press, 1930); reprinted in *FM*, pp. 99-113.

4   Horrocks, *Len Lye*, pp. 163-4.

5   See Michael North, *Reading 1922: A Return to the Scene of the Modern* (New York: Oxford University Press, 1999), pp. 170-71.

6   See e.g. Lev Manovich, 'What is Digital Cinema?' (1995), *Teleopolis* Film archive, http://www.heise.de/tp/english/special/film/6110/1.html.

7   Paul Watson, 'True Lyes: (Re)Animating Film Studies', *Art & Design* 53 (1997), pp. 46-49.

8   Lewis Mumford, *Technics and Civilization* (London: Routledge, 1934), p. 343.

9   For historical and theoretical accounts of these ideas, see, respectively, George W. Stocking, *Victorian Anthropology* (New York: Free Press, 1987), 192ff; William Pietz, 'Fetishism and Materialism: The Limits of Theory in Marx', in *Fetishism as Cultural Discourse*, ed. Emily Apter and William Pietz (Ithaca: Cornell University Press, 1993), pp. 119-51.

10   See Horrocks, *Len Lye*, pp. 129-30. As well as the collaborative texts listed, a statement by Lye on politics was included in Riding's compilation *The World and Ourselves [Epilogue* 4] (London: Chatto & Windus, 1938).

11   Joyce Piell Wexler mentions the text under this title in *Laura Riding: A Bibliography* (New York: Garland, 1981), p. xxi; her reference was based on a list of publications drawn up by Riding in collaboration with Alan Clarke. Curnow and Horrocks list it (incorrectly) as *Len Lye and The Problem of Popular Film, FM,* p. 148. Copies exist in New York (MOMA) and Michigan; I have located no copy in UK libraries.

12   Laura (Riding) Jackson, *The Poems of Laura Riding* (1938; Manchester: Carcanet, 1980). Here and subsequently cited in text as *P*.

13   Riding, in fact, attacks Bergson (in her rather peculiar understanding of his work as representing a philosophy of the 'Zeitgeist') in *Contemporaries and Snobs* (London: Jonathan Cape, 1928), pp. 145, 184.

14   Recent discussions of this issue include Mary Anne Doane, 'Temporality, Storage, Legibility: Freud, Marey and the Cinema', *Critical Inquiry* 22 (1996), pp. 313-43; Leon Charney, *Empty Moments: Cinema, Modernity and Drift* (Durham, NC: Duke University Press, 1998), pp. 15-25. Doane's position is ultimately more pessimistic than Chaney's: cinema also operates under the sign of loss, since its intervals can never recapture time's flow.

15   Laura Riding and Robert Graves, *A Survey of Modernist Poetry* (London: Heinemann, 1927), p. 259.

16   See Jerome McGann, 'Laura (Riding) Jackson and the Literal Truth', *Critical Inquiry* 18 (1992), pp. 454-73.

17   See Peter S. Termes, 'Codes of Silence: Laura (Riding) Jackson and the Refusal to Speak', *PMLA* 109 (1994), pp. 87-99.

18   Andre Bazin, 'In Defense of Mixed Cinema', *What is Cinema?*, selected and edited by H. Gray (Berkeley: University of California Press, 1967), pp. 53-75.

19   Laura (Riding) Jackson and Schuyler B. Jackson, *Rational Meaning: A New Foundation for the Definition of Words*, ed. William Harmon, intro. Charles Bernstein (Charlottesville: University Press of Virginia, 1997).

20   The series is described (without any mention of Lye) in John Russo's *I. A. Richards: His Life and Work* (London: Routledge, 1989), pp. 435-37; Russo also details Richards's negative response to the Riding-Jackson linguistic project.

8

Writing the Alphabet of Cinema: Blaise Cendrars

Eric Robertson

The biography of Blaise Cendrars is the stuff of legend: in the summer of 1912, the twenty-five year old Swiss Freddie Sauser boarded a ship in New York bound for Paris, with a new poem in his suitcase and a new identity. Blaise Cendrars the poet was born. It was not long before this name was associated throughout France with one of the most distinctive poetic voices on an avant-garde scene fascinated with fast travel, telegraphy and scientific progress. What makes Cendrars unusual, though, is the extent to which his art is an extension of his life. His pre-First World War poetry, like that of his friend and contemporary Guillaume Apollinaire, expresses wonderment at the advent of the flying machine; unlike Apollinaire, though, Cendrars actually worked with Blériot on his first aeroplanes. His entry to the film world was no less wholehearted. At the age of twenty-two, while staying in London in 1909, he shared a miserable room with an aspiring entertainer by the name of Charlie Chaplin. A decade later he collaborated with Abel Gance on *J'Accuse* and *La Roue,* and wrote the screenplay of another project, *Les Atlantes.* The early 1920s saw him making a film entitled *Black Venus* at the Rinascimiento studios in Rome, and he refers in a number of quasi-autobiographical essays to having made documentaries in the mid-1920s in Sudan and Brazil;[1] none of these, however, has survived, and it is tempting to speculate as to whether such accounts as these owe more to Cendrars's self-mythologising than to fact.

What lies beyond doubt, on the other hand, is that his nine volumes of collected works testify to a long-standing fascination with the creative possibilities opened up by film.[2] These fall into quite distinct generic categories: on the one hand there are the critical essays, written chiefly in the inter-war period, which alternately extol the virtues of Gance and Griffith, Survage and Léger, even Disney and Chaplin, and decry the soulless factory productions of Hollywood.[3] And then we find writings, dating from the years 1917–1924, which adopted the discourse, technical detail and structure of screenplays in an effort to bring these to the attention of a literary readership. As we shall argue, Cendrars's first forays into

137

the film world owed much to his experience of the First World War. Even in his pre-war poetry, however, there is compelling evidence to suggest his keen preoccupation with a peculiarly cinematic form of visuality and motion.

Pre-War Poems

In the period 1912–14, Cendrars was at pains to evolve a radically new poetic idiom whose main characteristics were immediacy of notation, speed of discourse and a violent dynamism. Just as Apollinaire defined his Calligrams as a means of renewing poetry at a time when its existence was threatened by the phonograph, so can Cendrars's early poems be seen as an attempt to approximate the new syntax of cinema and appropriate it within a poetic context. Two long poems written before the First World War bear out René Clair's dictum that 'if there is an aesthetics of cinema [...] it can be summarized in one word: "movement".'[4] The first of these is *Prose of the Transsiberian and of Little Jeanne of France*, published in 1913 and billed as 'the first simultaneous book' by virtue of the largely abstract 'simultaneous colours' by Sonia Delaunay that accompany and encroach on the text.[5] Underpinning its experimental format, and its title, is a radical challenge to traditional reading methods and the elitism all too often associated with poetry. As Cendrars explained in 1913: 'Poem seemed too pretentious to me, too closed. Prose is more open, popular.'[6]

   This provocative and highly ambitious agenda is reflected in the physical format of the work, which consciously eschews literary conventions. Gone is the virginal vertical fold of the page so revered by Mallarmé; in its place, a new aesthetics of the broadsheet and the billboard. Like the *papiers collés* of Picasso and Braque, whose appropriation of newspaper, wallpaper and the techniques of painter-decorators had challenged the centuries-old assumptions of academy painting, Cendrars and Delaunay sought to rejuvenate the very nature of the reading process. In its original edition, the work consists of a single sheet, some two metres in length, which could be folded and unfolded like a map; the text, which descends the entire length of the sheet, occupies its right-hand side; alongside it runs a largely abstract design by Delaunay. No mere background illustration, this pictorial element occupies a very central role in the work, not least in the use of bold, spectral colours that run to the very borders of the text and occasionally spill over it. The colours, in fact, fill every gap surrounding the text, which itself emphasises its pictorial character by incorporating left, right and centre-justified margins, various letter sets and sizes, and several colours of print. The sheer length of the work forces the reader to scroll down it, taking in the lines of text and the areas of colour simultaneously. Reading and viewing thus combine in one dynamic movement. Cendrars boasted that the one hundred and fifty copies published would, if placed end to end, reach the height of the Eiffel Tower, anticipating by a decade Jean Epstein's prediction that filmmakers would make cinematographic poems one hundred and fifty metres long.[7]

As if to assert the quasi-documentary authenticity of this hybrid artefact, the map of the route of the Transsiberian express appears directly above the title. Far from creating a harmonious whole, these various pictorial and verbal elements were intended to generate a dynamic tension stemming from the fundamentally different receiving activities they demand of the reader/ viewer. In the author's words, 'The simultaneous contrasts of the colours and the text create depths and movements which are the new inspiration.'[8] These terms are clearly indebted to Bergson's theories on memory and duration; but Cendrars's efforts to overcome the static nature of poetry do also owe much to the chronophotography of Muybridge and Marey, and to other late-nineteenth century optical inventions such as Wheatstone's stereo viewer of 1870, which called upon its user to view simultaneously two parallel strips of images.[9] Cendrars's text employs a montage technique, cutting abruptly between its many different spatial and temporal levels. While the conjunction of speed and violence suggests a strong parallel with the Italian Futurists, the repeated allusions to the train's revolving wheels also prompt structural analogies with early cinema (the verb 'tourner', which is especially prominent in the text, can mean both to turn and to film). The vertiginous movement of Cendrars's train could not fail to recall the many early films featuring speeding trains, from Louis Lumière's pioneering *Arrival of a Train at La Ciotat* of 1895 to Hale's Tours, which became a popular success in the U.S.A. after their introduction in 1904. To experience these, 'passengers' would pay to enter a narrow viewing room shaped like a railway carriage for the projection of a train journey.[10] And of course, from the chronophotographic experiments of Muybridge and Marey to the travelling shots of early films, cameras running on rails had played a crucial functional role in creating the impression of movement. In the *Prose of the Transsiberian*, the circular movement generated by the train's wheels is associated with a particularly violent dynamism. The conflation of rapid trains and violence, too, was a feature of early films, especially the western, which became a staple of popular cinema after Edwin S. Porter's *The Great Train Robbery* of 1903.

A second long pre-war poem, *Panama or the adventures of my seven uncles*, has much in common with the *Prose of the Transsiberian* besides its epic length and the theme of rail travel. Devoid of punctuation, conjunctions and all expressions of causality, the poem calls upon the reader to negotiate its many blank spaces, which frequently mark abrupt temporal and spatial shifts. A full decade before Aragon used the technique in his Surrealist narrative *Paris Peasant*, here we find Cendrars splicing an extraordinarily incongruous textual ready-made into the body of the text. The insertion in question is a prospectus advertising

Denver. Curiously enough, this splicing occurs within a reference to another cutting action, that of the guillotine:

> The guillotine is the masterpiece of plastic art
> Its click
> Perpetual movement[11]

Both in the process of montage and in the image of the guillotine's blade, the cutting room seems to be raising its shadow in this metonymy. The slicing motion and clicking sound of the blade evokes the act of splicing and the cinematic cut that generates movement. As if to accentuate the loss of aura that Walter Benjamin would famously associate with film, Cendrars re-used these lines in another poem written the same year, 'La Tête' ('Head'), inspired by Archipenko's eponymous sculpture.[12] Once more, the cut is a catalyst for movement, but on this occasion, the motion has a concentric circular direction:

> The guillotine is the masterpiece of plastic art
> Its click
> Creates perpetual motion
> Everyone knows about Christopher Columbus's egg
> Which was a flat egg, a stationary egg, the egg of an inventor
> Archipenko's sculpture is the first ovoidal egg
> Held in intense equilibrium
> Like an immobile top
> On its animated point
> Speed
> It throws off
> Multicoloured waves
> Coloured zones
> And turns in depth
> Nude.
> New.
> Total.[13]

Some months after Cendrars's poem was published in *De Stijl*, the same journal printed an essay by Theo Van Doesburg on the abstract films of Viking Eggeling and Hans Richter. Van Doesburg cites exactly this combination of stasis and mobility as the very basis of a new film aesthetic of mechanical objectivity.[14] He goes on to evoke a future abstract film art whereby movement would be produced, not by human intervention, but by an electric current.[15]

In many respects, the poems cited above alternate between a highly subjective first-person voice and an impersonal, one might say mechanical, narrating presence. Cendrars's frequent use of monolexical lines and his elliptical syntax, which jettisons verbs and any stable narrating identity, combine to create the impression of autonomous, self-generating imagery whose subjectivity is not that of the seeing eye, but rather that of Vertov's Kino-Eye, anticipating what Paul Virilio terms the 'machine of vision':[16] this can be seen in 'Contrasts', written in 1913 and published in Cendrars's collection of *19 Elastic poems*:

> It's raining light bulbs
> Montrouge Gare de l'Est Métro Nord-Sud Seine omnibus world
> One big halo
> Depth[17]

This segment typifies the cosmic imagery, syntactic economy and concentric circular patterning of many of the *Elastic Poems*. At around the time these poems were written, Cendrars was on close terms with the artist Robert Delaunay, husband of Sonia, and conveyed to him the colour theories of Goethe and Schopenhauer, which fed into Delaunay's own reading of Chevreul's theories of colour contrasts based on chromatic discs. And so the halos and concentric circles to which Cendrars alludes became the basis of an entire series of quasi-abstract circular paintings that Delaunay produced in 1913. Just as clearly as these hark back to Newton's glass discs, they may be seen to point ahead both to Duchamp's *Rotoreliefs* of the mid-1920s and to Oskar Fischinger's abstract films of the 1930s such as *Circles* or *Allegretto*, which in their different ways explore the disruption of naturalistic illusionism through the physical movement of geometric forms. In this way, both Duchamp and Fischinger continue an aesthetics that Thierry de Duve, referring to Delaunay, has defined in terms of 'the ideological constitution of painting in language.'[18]

The cinema of war

Paul Virilio has argued suggestively that the birth of cinema is inextricably connected to the birth of modern warfare.[19] Indeed, as early as 1882, Marey had produced 'a photographic gun', inspired by the Colt pistol, which, its inventor boasted, 'kills nothing and which takes the picture of a flying bird or running animal in less than 1/500 of a second.'[20] Before his death in 1905, Marey's expertise in chronophotography would be used for military research into movement. And when war was declared in the summer of 1914, a year after the *Prose of the Transsiberian* was published, less innocuous kinds of guns than the photographic kind would begin to figure prominently in Cendrars's life. As a

Swiss national, he had no obligation to fight in the Great War, but in August 1914, the poet volunteered for what was to become the French Foreign Legion, and with fellow poet Ricciotto Canudo published an 'Appel à tous les étrangers', an emotive text calling upon their fellow foreigners in France to 'offrir leurs bras' ('give up their arms') for the French nation.[21] A year later, the wording of this text would seem uncannily prescient: by a macabre stroke of fate, on 26 September 1915, Cendrars lost his right arm in an attack of machine-gun fire on the battlefields of Champagne.

In his 'Small History of Photography', Walter Benjamin summed up the appropriateness of the camera to the new age of modern warfare that took form during the First World War. Unlike the artist, he argues, the cameraman has a quasi-surgical power to 'operate' on the subject by penetrating more deeply into the tissue of its reality (*ins Gewebe der Gegebenheit*).[22] Besides this ability to reveal the hidden recesses of the self, which he terms 'the optical unconscious', the camera also has the power to extend *beyond* the body's normal field of perception: quoting Benjamin again, 'mass movements, including war, constitute a form of human behaviour which particularly favours mechanical equipment... [for] mass movements are usually discerned more clearly by a camera than by the naked eye.'[23] This function of the camera as a kind of prosthetic limb might help to explain the appeal of film for Cendrars, a point to which we will return later.

Benjamin, as we have seen, considered the camera to be a highly apt medium in the context of modern warfare, and indeed the Great War bore this out with horrific clarity: the war of entrenchment which superseded the short-lived war of movement brought about a new remoteness in which the machine gradually supplanted human vision, and hand-to-hand combat gave way to more remote, dehumanised forms of death. By the time he was wounded and discharged, Cendrars had witnessed both phases of the war, and both forms of combat; but by comparison with Apollinaire, or indeed with other writers involved in the hostilities such as Barbusse and Duhamel, he is surprisingly reticent about his experience of war, a fact which some critics have ascribed to the profound trauma caused by the loss of his right (and writing) arm. This thesis is supported by the fact that Cendrars's best known work on the subject, the autobiographical text *La Main coupée*, was begun in draft form as early as 1918, but was only published in reworked form nearly thirty years later, in 1946. Moreover, the narrative ends, tantalisingly, before the events of September 1915 that would lead to his injury.

The absence of an explicit literary account of his wound has another possible explanation: namely, that on his return to civilian life, Cendrars's focus was increasingly shifting away from literature and towards cinema. Indeed, it was at this time that he became closely acquainted with the filmmaker Abel Gance, working as his assistant and general dogsbody during the filming of *J'Accuse*, which was completed in 1919. Fittingly enough, the plot of Gance's film has as its central character a poet who is driven by personal tragedy to make the ultimate sacrifice in the Great War. Gravely wounded in battle, he returns home to admonish his fellow villagers for failing to appreciate fully the debt they owe to the soldiers. His last words before dying in the arms of his beloved are a warning that the war dead will return to haunt the people until their sacrifice is shown to have been worthwhile. The ensuing scene, in which thousands of war dead rise up on a huge plain, played a crucial part in earning Gance widespread critical acclaim for the film.[24] And clearly visible in this scene is one Blaise Cendrars, complete with authentic war wound.

This haunting scene arguably exceeds the signifying power of any written text, and might be seen as Cendrars's most telling gesture relating to the Great War. By contrast with the ostentation of this performance, Cendrars's reluctance in his writings to broach the subject of his wound is all the more surprising. But this should not prevent us from examining his literary output from this period, especially as his interactions with visual artists in the pre-war years had been highly fruitful for his poetic activity. As Deleuze has asserted, Cendrars had a marked influence on Gance's ideas, conveying to him the spiritual connotations of circular movement that Cendrars had assimilated from the paintings of the Delaunays.[25] Equally clear is that the medium of film had a profound effect on Cendrars's writing of this time. And this is perhaps most evident in *J'ai tué*, his only text devoted to the war which was both written and published during the hostilities. Dated Nice, 3rd February 1918, the essay was first published three days before the Armistice, and reprinted the following year. Jean Mitry reports that Cendrars was involved in the filming of *J'Accuse* in early 1918, and so it seems probable that the text was written concurrently with this.

Certainly, in terms of its style, *J'ai tué* has a distinctly cinematic quality. Written exclusively in the present tense, using factual, prosaic vocabulary, it employs predominantly short, abrupt sentences entirely devoid of conjunctions or expressions of cause and consequence. The reader is carried along by its breathless momentum, which leaves little time for overt explanation, reflection or literary niceties. Claude Debon has commented on the fact that, rather than a historically accurate and coherent depiction of a single episode of the war, Cendrars has interwoven chronologically discrete episodes into a single narrative. I would argue that the principle of montage most accurately describes the structure of this text, as it is characterised less by narrative continuity than by its succession of juxtaposing points of view. These contrasts offer the reader a series of radically diverse perspectives on the action, rather like the mobile eye of the camera. Richard Abel has noted the effective use Gance makes in *J'Accuse* of just such a 'rhythmic montage' based on the constant interplay of similarities and differences and on the film's extensive use of rhetorical images.[26] Cendrars's text, likewise, juxtaposes three principal perspectives:

(i)   firstly, the huge-scale movement of troops, portrayed in terms that evoke a textual equivalent of the wide, sweeping panoramic shot. (Here, the predominance of the personal pronoun 'on' establishes complicity with the reader, while retaining a degree of generality). This perspective is momentarily interrupted, without warning, by a second level of narration:

(ii)   this takes the form of fragmentary, fleeting images of a more personal kind, seen from the perspective of an individual ['je']. The shift from the plural to the singular, from external observation to inner reflection, might be compared to the superimposition or montage of literal and figurative images in cinematic terms.

(iii)   The text culminates by cutting with increasing frequency between the two perspectives described above, the global (or long shot) and the first person singular (or close-up), before closing in on the latter for a dramatic conclusion.

The text is largely devoid of similes and metaphors, and of the few that do appear, a high proportion allude to water imagery. As Deleuze has remarked, this was a characteristic motif used by early filmmakers such as L'Herbier, Epstein, Renoir, Vigo and Grémillon as a means of shifting from the literal to the abstract plane while 'endow(ing) movements with an irreversible duration independently of their figurative character'.[27] Other metaphors in the text have a recurrent circular pattern, reminding us of the *Prose of the Transsiberian* and its conflation of dynamism, circular movement and violence: 'Straightaway the German submachine guns ticktock. The coffee mills turn. The bullets crackle.' Both in its imagery and in its telegrammatic syntax, this extract has a distinctly filmic quality: conjunctions or expressions of cause and consequence are replaced here by a kind of cinematographic, visual logic based on the association of images. These sentences function like a montage sequence of film shots, employing metonymy to suggest a connection between the rotating coffee mill and the ammunition chamber of the submachine guns.

The cinematic structure of this text is most clearly apparent in its series of fragmentary images that gather momentum towards the horrific, and highly problematic, conclusion. This final sequence, with its juxtaposition of global and individual perspectives, could be seen as a corollary to what Canudo, referring not to this text but to Gance's *J'Accuse*, described as 'the collective body acting as a single individual':[28] in a breathless paragraph, delivered largely in the present tense, Cendrars's first-person narrator reels off a long list of all the industry, all the raw materials brought from every corner of the globe, that have gone into the uniform he is wearing and the knife he is carrying – a huge wealth of human effort of which he is the sum total.

A thousand million individuals have devoted their entire day's work to me, their strength, their talent, their knowledge, their intelligence, their habits, their feelings, their heart. So here am I today with the knife in my hand. [...] I have braved the torpedo, the cannon, the mines, the gunfire, the gas, the submachine guns, all the anonymous, demonic, systematic, blind machinery. Now I am going to brave man. My fellow creature. An ape. An eye for an eye, a tooth for a tooth. It's just the two of us now. With fists and knives. Without mercy. I jump on my opponent. I strike him hard. His head is nearly off. I've killed the Hun. I was sharper and faster than he was. More direct. I hit first. I, the poet, have a sense of reality. I've acted. I've killed. Like one who wants to live.[29]

How are we to respond to this apparent celebration of violence? Claude Debon has pointed out that the manuscript draft of this text begins with some lines of text, deleted from the final, published version, which, had they been retained, would have cast a far more negative and ironic light on its political and ethical implications.[30] Admittedly, even without these lines, the text can be read in an ironic light: the concluding passage seems to imply that this act of barbarism is the sum of all the world's progress: technology has merely returned civilisation to its origins; modern man has reverted to an ape. But the irony is, to say the least, mitigated by the final lines, with their seeming affirmation of the act of killing as a defining moment of reality.

I believe that Cendrars's decision not to include the opening lines in the published version, nor to allude to the loss of his arm, may be attributed to his appropriation of the cinematic paradigm. The tripartite structure of the action, its pivotal conflict between the protagonist and his nemesis in which a life-or-death decision leads to a resolution, and the overall emphasis on action rather than inner motivation: all of these have become stock traits of classic Hollywood-style films.[31] In distilling his experience thus into a mini-scenario, and fictionalising it in the process, Cendrars has, arguably, displaced its most painful associations. In the concluding lines, the first-person narrative voice, which straddles the dividing line between autobiography and fiction throughout Cendrars's entire œuvre, nudges the text towards the latter category, conferring on it the status of fictional discourse mediated by a first-person narrator rather than the straightforward narration of first-hand experience. Given Cendrars's proximity to the film aesthetic and to filmmakers such as Gance at the time of writing *J'ai tué*, it seems all the more compelling to situate the final scene in an indeterminate space between autobiographical narrative and a more symbolic mode of narration. As Deleuze asserts with reference to Gance's *La Roue*, one distinguishing feature of the French school of cinema, especially perceptible in the relationship between the individual and the machine, was its tendency to conceive cinematic unity in terms of a shift from the individual to the global.[32]

Claude Leroy has recently proposed an alternative version of the circumstances surrounding Cendrars's mutilation, a version corroborated by two of the poet's close friends: they maintain that Cendrars himself used his knife to remove what little remained of his right arm after the machine gun had done its work. If this interpretation of events is accurate, then the cinematic analogy arguably gains validity: the writer/ editor's cut would stand for another, unspeakable one. Through the writer's metaphorical 'camera', mourning is deferred, and suffering is sublimated, deferred, and projected from self onto other.[33]

In Praise of living dangerously

A decade after he sustained his wound, Cendrars published an essay entitled 'Eloge de la vie dangereuse'. Set, not on the battlefield, but in the rainforests of Brazil, where Cendars was living at the time, this essay too suggests that violence – here in the form of street fighting – can, by virtue of its sheer intensity, be a life-affirming act. And, like *J'ai tué*, this essay unites the language of cinema and the theme of killing around the idea of the cut. As before, we are left with the a sense that writing and viewing can help to sublimate violence:

> Hey you all, city crowds who go to the cinema every evening, watch this, pay attention. This tree that invades the screen is 75 metres high. Its crown blocks out the sky and its branches are a mass of little monkeys and screaming parakeets. [...] Look at the tiny white mark at the foot of the tree, on the right. That's me, as fat as a flea dressed in white. By closing in, you will see me get bigger before your eyes and fall on top of you. Hold. That's me in close-up. Here is the assassin's knife. I rip open a box of crackers.[34] I cut a slice of venison. Ever since, I have cut my bread with it. I cut my books open. I cut my book open. This book.[35]

The owner of the knife then offers it to the narrator as a memento, 'because I had lost my arm in the war.' Once more, then, the act of violence is replaced with the acts of filming and of writing. Here again, Cendrars raises the spectre of his war wound, but once more stops short of confronting it directly in his writing. Instead, the quasi-cinematic text, with its camera instructions and its present-tense narration, becomes the site of displacement, of transfer, of projection. And all the while one senses that the complementary acts of writing and filming are shown to be therapeutic, necessary aids in exorcising the ghosts of memory.

Theorising film: the inter-war essays

In the years following the war, Cendrars devoted his creative energies to film. The early 1920s saw him working as assistant director of Gance's next film, *La Roue* (1921-22), writing a string of scenarios and even helping to develop a new literary genre, the *ciné-roman*, which allied a consciously flat language to the notational system of *découpage*.[36] Such was Cendrars's reputation as an advocate of cinema that Fernand Léger, writing to René Clair in 1923, referred to him as a film-maker rather than a writer. In this letter Léger anticipates the emergence of 'a cinematographic concept that will find its own means... As long as film has literary or theatrical origins, it will be as nothing... New men such as Messrs Abel Gance, Blaise Cendrars, Jean Epstein will be, I hope, the new directors in this domain that I can only begin to anticipate.'[37]

In an essay of 1919 devoted to *Coloured Rhythms*, Léopold Survage's abstract film experiments, Cendrars for his part explores what he calls 'photogenic' writing, which amounts to a breathless, elliptical discourse peppered with asyndeton and parataxis. 'I shall try to render, in words as *photogenic* as possible, the bold manner in which Monsieur Léopold Survage manages to recreate and decompose the circular movement of colour.'[38] The 'photogenic' writing in question shares the very same truncated, elliptical syntax and montage techniques as we find in the *19 Elastic poems*: 'Orange and violet devour each other, tear each other [...]. Evanescence into white. The white steadies and hardens. It freezes. And all around, the void hollows out. The disc, the black disc reappears and obstructs the visual field.'[39]

'Profound today', written in 1917, shows this cinematic writing already in action: although this essay is not explicitly about cinema, its flickering shadow can be felt both in its paratactic structure and in its very thematics:

> A blue eye opens. Red closes. Soon all is colour. Co-penetration. Disc. Rhythm. Dance. Orange and purple consume one another.
> [...]
> Prodigious today. Wave. Antenna. Door-face-whirlwind. You live. Off-centre. In complete isolation. In anonymous communion. [40]

In the Paris-based *Editions de la Sirène* which he directed, Cendrars published Jean Epstein's *Bonjour cinéma* and an essay of his own, 'L'ABC du cinéma' ('The ABC of cinema'), in which he hails Gance and Griffith as the inventors of a new language, the *only* language equipped to reflect a world whose points of reference had been upturned by scientific discoveries and new technologies. As Cendrars states, both Griffith and Gance speak in terms of their having had to learn a new, visual alphabet. Cendrars links this to the role of Cadmus in ancient

Greece who had revolutionised communication by replacing the then existing pictograph with the Phoenician alphabet, thereby opening up a whole new range of expressive possibilities. This he describes as the first world revolution. The second, he argues, was the discovery of oil painting and Gutenberg's invention of the printing press in the fifteenth century. The third revolution is the explosion of communication in the early twentieth century: 'The entire world is caught in a network of railways, cables, terrestrial, maritime, aerial lines. All peoples are in contact. The telegraph sings.'[41]

Cendrars concludes by relating this profusion of new technologies to the emergence of a new cinematic alphabet. Its first three letters relate to the different scales on which the cinematic experience operates: the mobile camera, the moving eye of the spectator, and the crowds of people across the globe simultaneously flooding the streets as they emerge from cinema halls. The final letter of the new alphabet, its point of arrival and its raison d'être, is a revolution of the soul that affects the individual 'au fond du cœur'. For Cendrars, this new medium has fundamentally affected the spiritual make-up of modern society.

> A hundred worlds, a thousand movements, a million dramas simultaneously enter the visual field of this eye that the cinema has given mankind. [...] The brain is overwhelmed. [...]
>
> Reality no longer makes any sense. Has any meaning. All is rhythm, word, life. There is no more demonstration. We commune. [...][42]

Fifty years after Daguerre's invention of photography, the cinema emerges. Cendrars sees this as nothing less than the manifestation of a new stage in the evolution of mankind:

> All indications suggest that we are heading towards a new synthesis of the human mind, a new humanity, and that a breed of new men will appear. Their language will be cinema.[43]

Cine-novels

Given such a sustained fascination with the cinema, it is not surprising that Cendrars would explicitly appropriate the structural and discursive characteristics of film scenarios as a new hybrid literary genre. The first of these *ciné-romans* is *La Fin du monde filmée par l'Ange Notre-Dame*, published in 1919. Although this text bears the generic subtitle 'fantasy novel', its very conception embraces the structures and forms of film in a highly overt way. It is divided into fifty-one numbered short scenes, written in a telegraphic style almost entirely in the present tense. The text explores a number of cinematic effects such as different speeds and a montage technique, and employs some proto-surreal *mises en abyme* to comic effect: God is cast as a Hollywood-style director complete with fat cigar and green sun shield; the Angel of Notre Dame is his cameraman. In the final sequence, the projector catches fire, causing the entire film to rewind. In spite of these filmic borrowings, however, this text remains rooted in a fundamentally literary discourse: the short scenes are divided into seven chapters, and the narrative only occasionally provides explicit technical details such as camera angles, or shifts in distance. At times, the instructions provided are so vague as to be of questionable use to a director, e.g. scene 41: 'A dark eye closes on all that has been.'[44] Moreover, the narrative frequently falls back on literary techniques such as metaphor and simile to generate effects; added to this, the vast, cosmic scale of the action depicted would doubtless have posed serious problems of cinematic realisation to any prospective director, suggesting that Cendrars considered this work above all as a text to be read, rather than as the basis of a film.

A far more wholehearted adoption of cinematic techniques is to be found in *La Perle fiévreuse* (*The Feverish Pearl*), published in serial form in 1921 and 1922.[45] The title page describes the book rather misleadingly as a novel (*roman fantaisiste*), whereas in fact it is a *découpage*: the text is divided into some eight hundred and fifty shots, with technical instructions as to the different sizes of lens to be used, the various camera angles and effects (travelling shots, close-up, *plongée, contre-plongée*, etc); moreover, it employs intertitles, flashbacks, fade and superimposition. The plot is a satirical send-up of the crime serials which had become popular at the time: the list of secondary characters includes fictional heroes of serials including the Surrealists' favourite, Fantômas, alongside creators of the genre such as Arthur Conan Doyle and Gustave le Rouge. But as much as Cendrars's text is intended to mimic this popular literary form, it is also a mise en abyme of cinematic production, written consciously for the benefit of a reading public unfamiliar with the discourse of film, as is clear from the title of the first section: 'That's cinema. How to produce a scenario découpage'.[46] In spite of this confident assertion, this text too has its fair share of logistical complexities for a prospective director: the list of extras alone includes two great danes and a small bear.

Lack of commercial success and the onset of the talkie killed off Cendrars's cinematic aspirations by the end of the 1920s. He did, however, come tantalisingly close to a major breakthrough: a meeting with none other than Sergei Eisenstein in Paris led to the latter pursuing the adaptation of his novel *L'Or*. Such was Eisenstein's enthusiasm for the project that he even wrote a scenario himself and submitted it to Paramount, complete with a detailed production schedule.[47] The project was rejected on grounds of its excessive cost; an unauthorized adaptation, meanwhile, was produced by Luis Trenker in Nazi Germany in 1936, under the title *The Emperor of California*, and to add insult to injury, it won the Mussolini Cup at Venice. The outbreak of war prevented the court case from reaching completion.[48]

Ironically, the same year marks the date of Cendrars's visit to Hollywood, the fruit of which was not a film but an essay, 'Hollywood, Mecca of Cinema'. It expresses both fascination with its stars and leading lights such as Walt Disney, and disgust with its blatantly commercial interests and factory-style production. One huge sentence enumerates the panoply of technicians, engineers, assistants, secretaries, costume and make-up artists, drivers and hangers-on who populate the set for the painstaking and time-consuming takes and retakes of a simple close-up shot of a screen kiss. All this happens under the critical eye of the cigar-puffing producer, his wife and her friends. Cendrars observes drily:

> So there are well over fifty people, and the whole lot are chatting, quibbling, gossiping, comparing, giving their opinion, commenting, guffawing, laughing, envying, censoring, applauding this kiss – this false kiss – and when it's over, the entire beskirted and prattling bunch goes off into town to drink a cocktail, a 'kiss-me-quick' [...].[49]

For all his irritation with the paraphernalia of the industry, he recognises the power that a single shot can wield, when viewed by millions across the globe. In a semi-autobiographical short story entitled 'Pompon', written in 1925, Cendrars expresses fascination with the quasi-surgical invasiveness of filming. The story relates the tragedy of its eponymous heroine, a young French woman with whom he became acquainted while he was filming in Rome, and who would ultimately commit suicide. Cendrars's first-person narrative reflects on how an early intervention with the camera could have saved her life. A long paragraph lists in detail the types and sizes of cameras he would have used, describing their respective properties. These, he claims, would have had the capacity to pin down and bind the subject, dope her and put her to sleep like chloroform. The passage culminates thus:

> [...] intervening at top speed with my Akeley Camera, like a surgeon armed with his scalpel or a Chinese executioner with his large sword [...], taking wide, incisive panoramic swipes, I would have externalised and brought Pompon's despair to light. It would have done her good, as if she had had a cyst removed.[50]

Here, Cendrars anticipates by some years Walter Benjamin's discussion of the camera's capacity to expand the sensory perception of the body. In his 'Small History of Photography', Benjamin famously likens the incisive action of the camera to that of the surgeon's scalpel, with its ability to penetrate deep under the skin and reveal hitherto invisible layers. 'The nature that speaks to the camera is different from the one that speaks to the eye; above all different in the sense that a space interwoven with human consciousness gives way to one that is unconsciously interwoven.'[51]

Cendrars went on to write a series of radio plays in the 1950s, and when they were published in 1959 he gave them the collective title *Films sans images (Films without images)*, as if to assert his new affiliation with the auditory in place of the visual. In the foreword to this volume, Cendrars underlines the populism inherent in all of his work:

> [...] the poetry of our time (and others) feeds on legends and voices: you can discover it by turning the button on a radio.
>
> Let's just say it's all about popular poetry, and everyone will be happy, including the authors.[52]

This remark brings us full circle, echoing as it does the intentions behind *Prose of the Transsiberian*, and stressing the common ground underpinning Cendrars's work at all stages of his career. It also reasserts his fascination with film and, latterly, radio, as 'prosthetic' media with the power to extend the body's sensory capacity. Cendrars's wonderment at the simplicity of the radio carries echoes of early Kodak advertisements promising the would-be photographer, 'Hold it steady. Pull a string. Press a button. This is all we ask of *you*, the rest *we* will do'.[53] With this in mind, and in the light of Cendrars's uncharacteristic reluctance to discuss the loss of his arm in his prose, I should like to return briefly to the still photograph from *J'Accuse* in which the character played by Cendrars leads the march of the dead. Commenting on this film in his masterly study of early French cinema, Richard Abel mistakenly states that it was Cendrars's *left* arm that was lost in the war.[54] It is tempting to speculate as to whether this uncharacteristic error stems from a misreading of this still, in which the trick of perspective appears to restore to Cendrars his right arm (what appears to be his raised right arm in fact belongs to the figure standing behind him).

In a very literal, graphic way, this example could be seen to bear out Walter Benjamin's definition of the camera lens as a prosthetic limb capable of covering over the body's deficiencies and creating a semblance of totality. Of course, this is an artificial device which is no more able to restore the mutilated body than the cinema screen is able to turn its flickering shadows into flesh-and-blood human beings. Limited though it may have been, the film medium in its various guises nevertheless offered Cendrars the opportunity to project suffering from self onto other, and to restore the *appearance* of normality, while allowing him time for the real processes of healing and mourning to take place.

Notes

1. On the Brazilian film project, see 'Etc, Etc. (un film 100% brésilien)'. Cendrars recounts the filming of *La Vénus noire* in the essays 'Un Homme heureux' and 'Pompon'. His text 'Chasse à l'Éléphant', closely based on poems from his 1924 collection *Documentaires*, makes reference to a film about the life of elephants made in Egypt and the Upper Sudan. All four essays are reprinted in the collection *Trop c'est trop* (1957). Unless otherwise stated, reference to works by Cendrars are from Blaise Cendrars, *Œuvres Complètes,* Tomes I–VIII (Paris: Denoël, 1961–65), henceforth *O.C.*. Here, *O.C.* IV, pp. 135-310. Unless otherwise indicated, translations of works by Cendrars are my own.

2. See, e.g., Philippe Pilard, 'Cendrars: cinéma de rêve, rêve de cinéma', in *SUD: Blaise Cendrars. Colloques poésie Cerisy 18e année* (1988), pp. 123-132.

3. See, e.g. 'Si j'étais...', 'Charlot', in *O.C.* VIII, pp. 275–289; 'Hollywood, la Mecque du cinéma', *O.C.* IV, pp. 385–467.

4. Cited in Siegfried Kracauer, *Theory of Film: The Redemption of Physical Reality* (London and New York: Oxford University Press, 1960; Princeton: Princeton University Press, 1997), p. 34.

5. The text is reprinted, without the visual element, as 'Prose du Transsibérien et de la petite Jeanne de France', in Blaise Cendrars, *Du Monde entier: Poésies complètes 1912-1924* (Paris: Gallimard, 'Poésie', 1947, 1967), pp. 27–45 (28). The original edition, with the slightly different title 'La Prose du Transsibérien et de la petite Jehanne de France', is displayed in the opening pages of Miriam Cendrars's *Blaise Cendrars: l'or d'un poète* (Paris: Gallimard, 'Découvertes', 1996).

6. Letter in *Der Sturm*, vol.184/5, November 1913, 127. Cited in Blaise Cendrars, *Aujourd'hui 1917-1929* suivi de *Essais et réflexions 1910-1916* (Paris: Denoël, 1987), pp. 193-4.

7. Jean Epstein, 'Le Cinéma et les lettres modernes', in *La Poésie d'aujourd'hui: un nouvel état d'intelligence* (Paris: Editions de la Sirène, 1921), pp. 169-180. Cited in Richard Abel, *French Cinema: The First Wave, 1915-1929* (Princeton University Press, 1984), p. 300.

8. 'Le simultanisme de ce livre est dans sa présentation simultanée et non illustrative. Les contrastes simultanés des couleurs et le texte forment des profondeurs et des mouvements qui sont l'inspiration nouvelle.' Blaise Cendrars et Sonia Delaunay, letter to André Salmon, in *Gil Blas*, Paris, 12 October 1913.

9. See Brian Coe, *Muybridge and the Chronophotographers* (Exhibition catalogue, London: British Film Institute / Museum of the Moving Image, 1992), pp. 10-11.

10. *L'Arrivée d'un* train à *La Ciotat* was famously screened to astonished audiences in 1895. Edwin S. Porter's *The Great Train Robbery* (1903), the first western film to be made, was one of many early films to exploit the dramatic potential of a fast train. For

stills of both films, see Emmanuelle Toulet, *Cinématographe, invention du siècle* (Paris: Gallimard, 'Découvertes', 1988).

11 In Blaise Cendrars, *Complete Poems*, translated by Ron Padgett, introduction by Jay Bochner (Berkley and Oxford: University of California Press, 1992), p. 43.

12 This short poem was written in 1914, a month after completing *Le Panama*, and was published without his authorization in the review *De Stijl* in August 1918, a year before Cendrars included it in *19 Elastic poems. O.C.* I.

13 Cendrars, *Complete Poems*, trans. Ron Padgett, p. 79, slightly modified.

14 *De Stijl*, IV, 71. Cited in H.L.C. Jaffé, *De Stijl 1917–1931: the Dutch Contribution to Modern Art* (Cambridge, Mass. and London: Harvard University Press, 1986), p. 189.

15 *De Stijl*, IV, 75. in Jaffé, *Op. cit.*, p. 189.

16 Paul Virilio, *La Machine de vision* (Paris: Editions Galilée, 1998).

17 Cendrars, *Complete Poems*, p. 59, slightly modified.

18 Thierry de Duve, *Nominalisme pictural* (Paris: Editions de Minuit, 1984), pp. 211-227.

19 Paul Virilio, *War and Cinema: the Logistics of Perception* (London: Verso, 1989).

20 Cited in Brian Coe, *Muybridge and the Chronophotographers* , p. 26.

21 Text cited by Jean-Jacques Becker, 'La Vision de la guerre chez Cendrars', in Claude Leroy (ed.), *Blaise Cendrars et la guerre* (Paris, Armand Colin, 1995), p. 14.

22 Walter Benjamin, 'Kleine Geschichte der Photographie' (1931), in Walter Benjamin, *Das Kunstwerk im Zeitalter seiner technischen Reproduzierbarkeit: Drei Studien zur Kunstsoziologie* (Frankfurt a. M.: Suhrkamp, 1963), p. 32.

23 Benjamin, 'Kleine Geschichte der Photographie', pp. 45-64.

24 Jean Mitry, who is otherwise highly critical of the film's 'débordements sentimentaux' and 'symbolisme outrancier', praises the visionary power of this scene, which he finds worthy of Victor Hugo. In Jean Mitry, *Histoire du cinéma, 2: Art et Industrie 1915-1925* (Paris: Editions universitaires, 1969), p. 259.

25 Gilles Deleuze, *Cinéma 1: L'Image-mouvement* (Paris: Minuit, 1983, Collection 'Critique'), pp. 65 and 72.

26 Richard Abel, *French Cinema: The First Wave, 1915-1929*, p. 300.

27 Deleuze, *Cinéma 1*, p. 65.

28 Ricciotto Canudo, 'Préface: Paris, décembre 1922', in *La Roue, après le film d'Abel Gance*, 4. Cited in Richard Abel, *French Cinema: The First Wave, 1915-1929*, p. 300.

29 Cendrars, *Aujourd'hui*, p. 22.

30 See Claude Debon, 'La Littérature à l'eustache: *J'ai tué*', in Claude Leroy (ed.), *Blaise Cendrars et la guerre*, pp. 64-70 (70).

31 See, e.g. Roy Armes, *Action and Image: Dramatic Structure in Cinema* (Manchester and New York: Manchester University Press, 1994), especially Chapter 9, 'The Individual as Protagonist: *The Big Sleep*', pp. 125–139.

32 Deleuze, *Cinéma 1*, p. 64.

33 Musing on Cendrars's bilingual, bicultural Swiss origins, Leroy advances the theory that the poet's automutilation symbolises a separation from his own Germanic roots.

See Claude Leroy, *La Main de Cendrars* (Villeneuve d'Ascq: Septentrion, 1996), pp. 21-43.

34   The original French text uses the verb 'éventrer', meaning literally to disembowel.

35   Cendrars, 'Eloge de la vie dangereuse', in *Aujourd'hui*, pp. 25-31 (31).

36   Cendrars worked for the Rinascimento studios in Rome on the mise en scène of *La Vénus noire/ La Venere Nera*. In 1929 Eisenstein considered making a film based on Cendrars's novel *L'Or*. See Philippe Pilard, 'Cendrars: cinema de rêve, rêve de cinéma', pp. 123-132 (125).

37   Fernand Léger, letter to René Clair, 1923, cited in Pilard, op. cit., p. 124. My translation.

38   Cendrars, *Aujourd'hui*, p. 73.

39   *Ibid.*, pp. 73-4.

40   *Ibid.*, pp. 13–14.

41   *Ibid.*, p. 38.

42   *Ibid.*, pp. 36-38.

43   *Ibid.*

44   Cendrars, *La Fin du monde*, in *O.C.* II, p. 44.

45   The text appeared in four successive numbers of the journal *Signaux de France et de Belgique*.

46   Cendrars, *O.C.* IV, p. 17.

47   An extract of the screenplay, entitled *Sutter's Gold*, is reproduced in Sergei Eisenstein, *The Film Sense* (London and Boston: Faber and Faber, 1943, 1986), pp. 191–6.

48   The rights were eventually bought by Universal Pictures, allowing James Cruze to make 'a mediocre film with huge resources.' Miriam Cendrars, *Blaise Cendrars: L'or d'un poète*, p. 72.

49   Cendrars, *O.C.* IV, pp. 433–4.

50   Cendrars, *O.C.* VIII, p. 272.

51   Walter Benjamin, 'Kleine Geschichte der Photographie', in *Das Kunstwerk im Zeitalter seiner technischen Reproduzierbarkeit: Drei Studien zur Kunstsoziologie* (Frankfurt am Main: Suhrkamp, 1963), pp. 45-64 (50). My translation.

52   Cendrars, *O.C.* VIII, p. 312.

53   Advertisement for the Eastman Dry Plate and Film Co., cited in Clive Scott, *Reading the Rhythm: the Poetics of French Free Verse 1910–1930* (Oxford: Clarendon Press, 1999), p. 157.

54   Richard Abel, *French Cinema: The First Wave*, p. 302. Abel also mistakenly identifies Cendrars in a still from the 'walking dead' scene of *J'Accuse* reprinted on p. 301 of his book.

9

The Grammar of Time: Photography, Modernism and History

Elena Gualtieri

To Siegfried Kracauer writing in 1927, photography appeared as 'the *go-for-broke game* [*Vabanque-Spiel*] of history',[1] the ultimate, desperate gamble of a historical process faced with its own bankruptcy. Indissolubly linked through their origins in the nineteenth century, photography and historiography stood for Kracauer in a dialectical relation that turned photography both into the ultimate realisation of a certain conception of history and into its downfall. Born from the process of industrialisation and acting as a reflection of the alienation of nature brought about by it, photography is joined to nineteenth-century historicism by a certain geometrical model that figures time and space as interchangeable dimensions.[2] Just as historicism believes that it 'can grasp historical reality by reconstructing the course of events in their temporal succession without any gaps',[3] so photography constructs space as an uninterrupted surface where 'the spatial appearance of an object is its meaning'.[4] One figuring time as a linear vector, the other assimilating space to the two-dimensional plane of the photographic print, photography and historicism mark the reduction of what were previously categories of experience to abstract dimensions. There is a deadly danger in this reduction, as consciousness becomes further and further alienated from 'a mute nature which has no meaning', but there is also a potential for liberation in it, as a consciousness emancipated from 'natural bonds'[5] might prove to be equipped for harnessing nature itself to its own development.

Like all other forms of technology, photography is Janus-faced, with the potential both for destruction and for liberation. This is a well-known dialectical view of the character of technological inventions and interventions,[6] but what is especially useful in Kracauer's argument is the identification of photography as the technological realisation of a certain conception of history. This conception rests on a linear model of temporality which marks the past off as a separate dimension, as the object of historical knowledge rather than as an integrated part of lived experience. It is this particular kind of past that becomes materialised

155

with the advent of photography and its tendency to abstract objects from their contextual meaning. As Kracauer points out in the opening pages of his 1927 essay, the photograph of the diva which circulates in illustrated magazines contributes to depleting the photograph of the grandmother of the personal and familial meaning with which memory would have invested it. As we shall see, this opposition between photography and memory runs through the modernist reception of the medium and even extends well beyond it. In what follows I shall be tracing a sort of archeology of the conditions from which this opposition emerged through a comparative reading of Marcel Proust's *In Search of Lost Time* and Robert Musil's *The Man Without Qualities*.[7] Each of them central to the canon of their respective linguistic communities, Proust's and Musil's texts take shape through a sustained engagement with the cultural meaning of photography which makes of photography one of the privileged locations for modernism's negotiation with the historical process.

1. Photographic Essayism

While chronology would require that we discuss Proust first, it is in Musil's later text that we find outlined the conception of photography on which Proust's work builds its poetics of memory. This reversal of the chronological order reflects the condition of belatedness or anachronism which is often ascribed to *The Man Without Qualities*.[8] Published in the 1930s but set in the year before the beginning of the Great War, Musil's text hovers in between the two sets of dates, offering us a glimpse of a society caught between the tantalising possibility of what could have been and the ineluctable reality of what we know will happen. Just like the state of Kakania in which the action is set, this text enacts the troubled relation to temporality which for Musil defines the paradoxical experience of modernity. It is both a product of its time and severely lagging behind it, a reluctant passenger on 'the train of time' who is driven forward by 'a longing to be stopped, to cease evolving, to stay put, to return to the point before the thrown switch put us on the wrong track' (*MWQ*, 8, p. 28).

This troubled relation to temporality is articulated in the text through a series of encounters which see its protagonist, Ulrich, repeatedly confronted with photographic images both of a familial, personal character and of a more contemporary, public one. In one of these encounters, Ulrich finds himself tracing back 'the disorder called modern times' to a crucial moment of transition in the history of the European bourgeoisie. Leafing backwards through a family album, he observes that,

> the closer he came to the beginnings of that new art of picture-taking, the more proudly, it seemed to him, the subjects faced the camera. There they were, with

one foot placed on a pile of cardboard boulders wreathed in paper ivy . . . the emancipated men stood their ground in creaseless trousers that rose up like curling smoke, in coats with a bold romantic sweep to them, as though a gale had blown away the dignified stiffness of the bourgeois frock coat. The time must have been between 1860 and 1870, when photography had emerged from its earliest stages, when the revolutionary forties were remembered as a wild, chaotic time long gone and life had become subtly different, though no one could say exactly what the new elements were; even the tears, embraces, and confessions in which the new middle class had tried to find its soul in its early days were no more, but as a wave runs out over the sands, this noble impulse had now come to express itself in the way people dressed and in a certain personal buoyancy [*Schwunghaftigkeit*] for which there may be a better word, but for the moment all we have is the photographs.

(*MWQ*, 99, pp. 497-98)

Far from supporting the sense of historical destiny which the photographs' subject display, Ulrich's family album in fact traces the movement of decline that flattened the political and moral aspirations of the European bourgeoisie into the two-dimensional space of the photographic portrait. As the 'new art' which offered for the first time the opportunity for immortalisation to common citizens, photography effectively arrests the movement of history into a series of frozen moments that have lost the ability to transform themselves. The distance that separates the revolutionary forties from the conservative sixties becomes translated into a succession of poses where 'the dignified stiffness of the bourgeois frock coat' gives way to 'trousers rising like curling smoke and coats with a romantic sweep to them'. As history cedes its place to fashion, the new becomes simply a different image to be added to the existing sequence in an infinite extension of the same basic structure. This structure cannot itself be adequately explained or articulated in language, which is forced into the awkward formulation of the simile to convey the sense of resilience and yet also of passivity that marks the post-revolutionary bourgeoisie. Etymologically related to 'swing', *Schwunghaftigkeit* suggests the continued momentum of a social and intellectual class that has been swung like a buoy by changes in the political currents of contemporary Europe. What remains of the grand aspirations of the revolutionary bourgeoisie of the 1840s is only the technological invention of photography, which finds itself recording the process of decline that it had initiated.

Ulrich's trawl through his family album leads him to identify in photography a technological process whose invention had changed the very conception of history. The shift from a revolutionary class to a conservative one is presented here not just as a shift in political allegiances and interests, but rather as a fundamental epistemological change in the very substance of the historical process and in the means of recording it. Just as the bourgeoisie becomes politically more conservative, its appearance takes on that romantic flair which was missing from the austerity of its earlier, revolutionary incarnation. This signals a shift of meaning from substance to appearance for which photography is explicitly held to be responsible. But this shift in meaning becomes also a change in structure, as historical narrative detaches itself from the referential ground and is turned into a sequence of images which are depleted of historical meaning and reduced to the function of marking the passage of time.

Although it is in his family album that Ulrich identifies the origins of this reduction of historical experience to a series of self-contained moments, its consequences become visible for him in the public and contemporary photographs reproduced in illustrated magazines.[9] These photographs confront him with an image of modernity which is assembled by jumbling together different temporal planes. In this assemblage the absolute novelty of female sportswomen exposing their bodies to the camera lens is also traversed by a series of more archaic elements which introduce within these images of modernity the incongruous traces of different contexts. The tennis player portrayed with 'one leg exposed above the garter, the other flung up toward her head' also carries 'on her face the expression of an English governess'. The swimmer who is shown 'being massaged after a contest' presents herself clinically exposed to 'two women dressed in street clothes', the male masseur and, of course, the public looking on from the other side of the camera (*MWQ*, 16, p. 57). Yet the pose of her 'knee drawn up in a posture of sexual abandon' (*MWQ*, 16, p. 58) belongs to an earlier type of iconography, suggesting a more intimate kind of setting which is at odds with the clinical atmosphere of the modern changing room. As images of modernity these photographs show a series of ruptures in what was once the complacent pose of the post-1848 bourgeois subject. This rupture is itself produced by the incongruous juxtaposition of time frames and planes which turns these modern images into the photographic equivalent of a cubist painting, where temporal axis and semantic circles do not quite square up.

Within *The Man Without Qualities*, photography maps, then, a process of transformation of the related categories of temporality and historical experience. It participates in the reduction of the historical experience of the bourgeoisie to a sequence of images which have gradually emancipated themselves from the historical reality to which they initially referred. This emancipation of the image from its referential ground in its turn produces modernity as the contiguous coexistence of different temporal frames on the same spatial plane.[10] As this 'infinitely interwoven surface' of disparate images, modernity is clearly identified by Ulrich as marking the end of the 'elementary, narrative mode of thought' which had provided a 'refuge from chaos' to the nineteenth-century bourgeois subject (*MWQ*, 122, p. 709).

Ulrich's own experience of the death of narrative occurs during a nocturnal stroll through the city. This brings back to him 'for no special reason' a recent memory of what it felt like to be looking at his own childhood photographs:

> from what a distance he had regarded the little boy, with the beautiful woman [his mother] in an old-fashioned dress happily smiling at him. There was that overpowering impression of the good, affectionate, bright little boy they all felt him to be; there were hopes for him that were in no way his own; there were the vague expectations of a distinguished, promising future, like the outspread wings of a golden net opening to enfold him. And though all this had been invisible at the time, there it was for all to see decades afterward in those old photographs, and from the midst of this visible invisibility that could so easily have become reality, there was his tender, blank baby face looking back at him with the slightly forced expression of having to hold still. He had felt not a trace of warmth for that little boy, and … he had on the whole the impression of having narrowly escaped a great horror.
>
> (MWQ, 122, p. 707)

Photography works here as a trap that catches Ulrich as a boy in the meshes of a story that is not his own. Its rigidity is that of 'a character, a profession, a fixed mode of being' (*MWQ*, 62, p. 269) from which Ulrich, the man endowed with qualities that refuse to stick to him, is determined to escape. The present Ulrich inhabits is emphatically not the future that his childhood photographs projected in front of him as if it were a reel of film. Although motionless and fixed to a very distant point in his past, these photographs contain within themselves the seeds of a story into which Ulrich refused to grow. This refusal did not simply erase the other story that had been drawn around the child's face as if in invisible ink. Rather it is precisely Ulrich's distance and detachment from that story which makes it become visible. It is as if Ulrich were standing at a street corner watching the man he could – and perhaps should – have become go by, existing in a parallel universe of possibilities of which his childhood photographs are the only remaining traces.

But the future which was in store for Ulrich and the present in which he finds himself living are not simply equally valid alternatives, different versions of the same basic narrative structure. In fact, the present from which Ulrich looks back at his childhood self exists only as a defect in his ability to follow what he calls 'the law of narrative order'. Ulrich's decision to hesitate before committing himself to a definite future has halted the progress of his life-story in a way that cannot be remedied by simply reinstating the chronological order of events, since his hesitation has opened up gaps in that order which reveal its illusory character. If narrative consists in the simple ability to say "'First this happened and then that happened'" (*MWQ*, 122, p. 708), it is for Ulrich an illusory construct which does not resolve incongruence or inconsistencies but 'makes them disappear, the way the gaps between trees disappear when we look down a long avenue of them'. Narrative order fulfils the same function as the law of perspective in the field of vision, where 'the relationships of things always shift to make a coherent picture for the eye, one in which the immediate and near at hand looks big, while even the big things at a distance look small and the gaps close up and the scene as a whole ends by rounding itself out' (*MWQ*, 122, p. 707). Just as space can be re-organised to give the impression of depth, so time may be arranged on a continuum that makes past, present and future appear as successive stops on the same line.

But if linear temporality emerges precisely from this coincidence of narrative order and visual perspective, it is the dissolution of this coincidence that comes to define the modern condition. Ulrich's inability to relate to the photographic image of his own childhood self measures the distance that separates him from the order that had given at least the appearance of coherence to the European bourgeoisie of the nineteenth century. This order was predicated on the idea that temporality could be mapped onto a spatial category such as perspective thus producing the illusion that sequence, 'first this happened, then that happened', is sufficient to generate meaning. Musil's text exposes this illusion by portraying his central character as he takes 'a year's leave of absence from his life' (*MWQ*, 13, p. 44) so that 'the given order of things' may be treated as 'a hypothesis that has not yet been surmounted' (*MWQ*, 62, p. 269), just one possibility (*Möglichkeit*) among the many that could have been realised. As Ulrich chooses to model his life on the form of the essay,[11] his absence from the narrative that should have constituted his life pries apart the apparent coincidence of sequence and consequence, chronology and causality on which narrative rests. It is in the space opened up by the dissolution of this coincidence that Musil inserts his essayistic prose to delay the ineluctable historical fact of the First World War and the end of the Hapsburg Empire and perform the endless amplification of the one-year interval that separates 1913 from 1914.

While Musil's essayistic practice works to undo the narrative drive towards closure, the fictional photographs that punctuate the movement of his prose constantly reintroduce the model of temporality that the essay is trying to undo.[12] Within *The Man Without Qualities* photography comes to stand in for the old nineteenth-century order and for the convergence of narrative sequence, linear temporality and Albertinian perspective which structured that order. It acts as a temporal catalyst, hurrying time and ushering in modernity, but a modernity that is also running out of steam and rushing head on towards its conflagration in World War I. As we saw through Ulrich's reaction to the picture of himself as a child, photography represents an intrusion within the text of the relentless historical process from which Musil's protagonist is helplessly trying to untangle himself. Musil's struggle to produce a convincing release for his hero (the text was left unfinished at his death in 1942)[13] demonstrates, though, how difficult it may be to discard the historical order generated by photography.

2. From the Literary Preterite to the Photographic Aorist

Musil's analysis of the structural affinity that links photography, narrative order and linear temporality invites us to reconsider some of the issues that have been fundamental to the understanding of linguistic structures and modernist texts elaborated in the last few decades. In this context the question posed by Barthes in 1966, 'Is there an atemporal logic lying behind the temporality of narrative?',[14] becomes the product of a post-photographic situation where narrative time appears to presuppose another, non-temporal structure or matrix that would produce narrative temporality according to its own combinatory logic. From this point of view, narrative has already lost that link to experience and shared knowledge that characterised the ancient art of story-telling[15] and is rather conceived as a semiotic structure that produces meaning through the organisation of events into a sequence. The question raised by Barthes is, then, whether narrative temporality constitutes a by-product of this semiotic structure or whether it is in fact the most fundamental part of the structure, the meaning which narrative itself sets out to produce:

> To put it another way, one could say that temporality is only a structural category of narrative (of discourse), just as in language [*langue*] temporality only exists in the form of a system; from the point of view of narrative, what we call time does not exist, or at least only exists functionally, as an element of a semiotic system. Time belongs not to discourse strictly speaking but to the referent; both narrative and language know only a semiotic time, 'true' time being a 'realist', referential illusion...[16]

The answer to Barthes's question about the existence of an 'atemporal logic' is therefore a qualified 'yes'. It is a 'yes' because insofar as temporality is a product of narrative, that product is the effect of an 'illusion', of a trick being played on us by our willingness to believe in the referential power of language and by narrative's constitutional propensity to reinforce that belief. But it is a *qualified* 'yes' because the question is itself not the 'right' question to ask. The issue at stake here is not so much whether the temporality of narrative is produced by an underlying, structural system that is itself not temporal. Rather, the two systems – temporality per se, the 'atemporal' logic of narrative on the other hand – are for

Barthes incommensurable categories, the former belonging to the referent, the latter to the realm of signification. The question that seemed to address itself to an atemporal logic turns out to be an insidious question, postulating of necessity the existence of a bond or relationship between the world of reference and the world of semiosis. It is precisely this bond that Barthes's structuralist approach to narrative aims to undo or expose as the product of a long-cherished 'illusion'.

While in Musil this 'illusion' had been produced by the convergence of space and time marked by the invention of photography, for Barthes its origins are not technological but linguistic. *Writing Degree Zero* (1953) explicitly traces back the slippage between historical reality and semiosis that is characteristic of narrative structure to the use of the preterite which in French is exclusive to historical and fictional narratives.[17] Obsolete in spoken language, the preterite no longer works for Barthes as a grammatical category but rather as an ideological tool whose function is 'to reduce reality to a point of time, and to abstract, from the depth of a multiplicity of experiences, a pure verbal act, freed from the existential roots of knowledge, and directed towards a logical link with other acts'. Abstract and isolated from the other verb tenses, the preterite functions as the motor of narrative itself, 'call[ing] for a sequence of events' that would place the actions inscribed by it into some 'intelligible' context.[18] In this sense, the preterite comes very close to functioning as that atemporal structure or matrix from which the 'illusion of temporality' is itself produced. Through the preterite, the distinction between abstract temporality, unhinged and separated from the experiential ground, and atemporal structure, a linguistic model that only exists in the abstract, is whittled down. If the preterite produces, as Barthes puts it in relation to Balzac, 'a view of History which is harsh, but coherent and certain of its principles',[19] it also fathers the structuralist conception of a *langue* [language] that can be abstracted from the everyday, historical occurrence of *parole* [utterance].[20]

As this marker of abstract temporality, the preterite returns also in Barthes's discussion of photography in *Camera Lucida* (1980). Taking up its Greek name of 'aorist', the un-defined, this verb tense that is restricted to historical and fictional narratives becomes in *Camera Lucida* a sort of knot or juncture that mediates photography's relation to historicity. From the beginning, *Camera Lucida* sets up an equivalence between photography and verbal forms which appears to contradict flatly Barthes's discussion of narrative temporality in the 'Introduction to the Structural Analysis of Narratives' and *Writing Degree Zero*. Just as in *The Man Without Qualities* Ulrich uncovered the emergence of the temporality of modernity by moving backwards through the albums of family photographs, so *Camera Lucida* sees Barthes identifying the true referent of photography at the end of a trawl through time that leads him to the discovery of the Winter Garden photograph in a family album. This movement back through time reveals that the photograph's ultimate referent is in fact not the object depicted, but an irreducible experience of temporality that is not susceptible to transformation or sublimation. Since the referent of the photograph is 'not the *optionally* real thing to which an image or sign refers, but the *necessarily* real thing which has been placed before the lens',[21] the photograph attests to the existence of that particular object at the particular time it was taken. This 'certificate of presence'[22] produces 'a superimposition . . . of reality and of the past'[23] which precisely mirrors the effect of the preterite in the classical novel. But while *Writing Degree Zero* claimed that this collapse of the real into the past was an ideological effect, a sort of linguistic false consciousness produced by the preservation of an obsolete verbal form in written French, *Camera Lucida* insists that this collapse is brought about by the chemical reaction of photography. Rather than producing 'a "copy" of reality', photography offers 'an emanation of *past reality*'[24] whose 'testimony bears not on the object but on time'.[25]

Photography as analysed in *Camera Lucida* therefore marks a convergence between the temporality of narrative as inscribed by the French use of the preterite and the temporality of the real which 'Structural Analysis' had dismissed as lying outside the bounds of semiosis. This convergence places the past that is inscribed by both narrative and photography beyond the grasp of human consciousness. The astonishment to which Barthes confesses when faced with the existential vertigo produced by historical photographs testifies to the essentially in-human character of the past that is materialised in photography. As he warns, 'not only is the Photograph never, in essence, a memory (whose grammatical expression would be the perfect tense, whereas the tense of the Photograph is the aorist), but it actually blocks memory, quickly becomes a counter-memory'.[26] Rather than making that past available to consciousness and recovery, the photograph marks it as a dimension that exists independently of any human agency and indifferent to it. The 'harsh view of History' that *Writing Degree Zero* had identified with Balzac's novels turns out to be in fact the only real one, or rather, the real as captured in the photograph is revealed to coincide with the fictional construction of an abstract, mechanical temporality.

3. Photography and Writing: Technologies of Repetition

Barthes's sharp distinction between photography and memory as ways of conceiving and relating to the past is very clearly indebted to Proust. His warning that there is 'nothing Proustian in a photograph'[27] underscores the radical opposition between the temporality of continuity and memory inscribed by the perfect and that of discontinuity and history inscribed by the aorist. This opposition clearly rewrites the Proustian differentiation of memory into voluntary and involuntary forms. At a simple level, photography works within *In Search of Lost Time* as the technological equivalent of *mémoire volontaire*, a lifeless, detached representation which does not engage the full sensory apparatus in the way in which the madeleine, the uneven cobblestones, the crisp napkin do. Rather than bringing back the past, the photographic snapshot or *'instantané'* puts it beyond the reach of the present, forever frozen into the abstract, detached temporality of the preterite. Irreducible and not susceptible to transcendence, photography stands in stark opposition to the work of revivification carried out by (involuntary) memory – it is, as Barthes points out, a 'counter-memory'.

At this thematic level, the technological intervention of photography is presented within Proust's text as marking a clear distinction between two different conceptions of temporality. On the one hand there is the temporality of repetition, recovery and return within which both past events and the subject who experienced them continue to exist, in a realm that is both 'outside Time' and always potentially capable of irrupting into the present. As the narrator reflects on the 'happy impressions' brought to him by the madeleine and the napkin, 'they had in them something that was common to a day long past and to the present, . . . in some way they were extra-temporal' just as the subject who experienced them 'made its appearance only when, through one of these identifications of the present with the past, it was likely to find itself in the one and only medium in which it could exist and enjoy the essence of things, that is to say, outside time' (*S*, 6, pp. 222-3).

But access to this kind of extra-temporal dimension is normally barred by the everyday experience of time as an arrow relentlessly pointing towards the future, whose inevitable end is death. This is the type of temporality that is summed up by Proust's narrator in his last appearance at the Guermantes', where he observes a spectacle of ageing that 'was something much more valuable than an image of the past: it offered me as it were all the successive images – which I had never seen – which separated the past from the present, better still it showed me the relationship that existed between the present and the past; it was like an old-fashioned peepshow, but a peepshow of the years, the vision not of a moment but of a person situated in the distorting perspective of Time' (*S*, 6, p. 292).

The confrontation between these two models of time, one cyclical and eternal, the other mechanical and linear,[28] takes place in Proust through the well-known episode of the photograph of the grandmother taken by Saint-Loup during the first visit to Balbec. Following the logic of the *Search*, this episode is in fact modulated into three movements that map successive stages in the protagonist's development and understanding. In the first one, Marcel witnesses his grandmother's sudden conversion to photography at Balbec, as she prepares to pose for Saint-Loup with what he thinks is a childish concern for her own appearance (*S*, 2, pp. 423-4). In the second episode, it is Marcel who finds himself transformed into the mechanical, unfeeling objective of the photographic camera as he returns to Paris from Doncières unannounced. Unexpected and unseen, he is confronted by the sight of his grandmother as an 'overburdened old woman', 'red-faced, heavy and vulgar, sick and day-dreaming, letting her slightly crazed eyes wander over a book' (*S*, 3, p. 157). In the third and final modulation of this episode, the hidden meaning of the first photograph is revealed to Marcel by Françoise on their return to Balbec after his grandmother's death and just as he finally experiences the full extent of his loss (*S*, 4, pp. 180-207).

Through the repetition and revisiting of the motif of the grandmother's photograph, we witness Marcel struggling to come to terms with the experience of loss and mourning that is associated with linear temporality. In the first episode in Balbec, Marcel fails to comprehend the significance of his grandmother's desire to be photographed, mistaking it for the revelation of a form of vanity of which he had never thought her capable. His failure to understand has, however, the paradoxical effect of bringing to light the hidden text behind his grandmother's desire to be photographed. With 'a few sarcastic and wounding words calculated to neutralise the pleasure which she seemed to find in being photographed' Marcel strips away the veil of her 'joyful expression' (*S*, 2, p. 424) to expose that 'sentence of death' (*S*, 4, p. 207) which he will only become capable of seeing on his return to Balbec, in the third modulation of this theme.

This first instalment announces the motif of the camera as, in a sense, death-giving, which the second episode develops by confronting Marcel himself with the spectacle of his grandmother as she appears to 'the witness, the observer in travelling coat and hat, the stranger who does not belong to the house, the photographer who has called to take a photograph of places which one will never see again' (*S*, 3, pp. 155-56). Transformed into the unfeeling, detached eye of the camera, Marcel is faced with the picture of a woman whom he does not recognise as the grandmother who existed for him 'always in the same place in the past, through the transparency of contiguous and overlapping memories'. If that grandmother was seen through the sight of 'my own soul' (*S*, 3, p. 157), the picture taken by eyes 'work[ing] mechanically, like film' (*S*, 3, p. 156) suddenly reveals 'for the first time and for a moment only' the existence 'of a new world, that of Time, that which is inhabited by the strangers of whom we say "He's begun to age a good deal"' (*S*, 3, p. 157).[29]

The mental picture of his grandmother which Marcel takes on his return from Doncières in fact already reveals to him the secret behind the first, actual picture at Balbec – even though, and this is crucial, the two episodes will only become connected for him in the third stage of his coming to terms with the significance of this photograph. Returning to Balbec after his grandmother's death, Marcel is struck for the first time by a real sense of loss as he bends down to unbutton his boots and is suddenly confronted by a memory of 'the tender preoccupied, disappointed face of my grandmother' that 'recaptured the living reality in a complete and involuntary recollection' (*S*, 4, p. 180). But rather than having the consoling effect which the experience of involuntary memories will bring about at the close of the *Search*, this raising of the dead confronts Marcel with the irrevocable meaning of the passage of time:

> Lost for ever; I could not understand, and I struggled to endure the anguish of this contradiction: on the one hand an existence, a tenderness, surviving in me as I had known them, that is to say created for me, a love which found in me so totally its complement, its goal, its constant lodestar, that the genius of great men, all the genius that might have existed from the beginning of the world, would have been less precious to my grandmother than a single one of my defects; and on the other hand, as soon as I had relived that bliss, as though it were present, feeling it shot through by the certainty, throbbing like a recurrent pain, of an annihilation that had effaced my image of that tenderness, had destroyed that existence, retrospectively abolished our mutual predestination, made of my grandmother, at the moment when I had found her again as in a mirror, a mere stranger whom chance had allowed to spend a few years with me, as she might have done with anyone else, but to whom, before and after those years, I was and would be nothing.
>
> (*S*, 4, p. 182)

At this point of realisation, it is as if Marcel finds himself interposed between the two sides of the photograph taken by Saint-Loup in Balbec. Rather than presenting the photograph as one of those 'laminated objects whose two leaves cannot be separated without destroying them both',[30] Proust deploys the repetition of this motif to expose the coexistence within that technology of two paradoxical and contradictory tendencies. On the one hand, and in accordance with the wishes of Marcel's grandmother, photography offers its subjects eternal life, or at least, a memory that is not susceptible of oblivion or forgetfulness. As Françoise points out to Marcel in the third episode, what prompted his grandmother to have her photograph taken was the knowledge of being ill and the desire to leave for Marcel an image of herself that would endure beyond death. Yet, as Marcel's mother testifies, the photograph – with the aid of Marcel's wounding words – eventually cannot help but reveal the ravages of time and illness that announced her impending death and which she wished to keep hidden from her grandchild. Through the repetition and revisiting of the motif of the grandmother's photograph the three stages in the hero's development of an understanding of linear time, of death and loss become clearly mapped onto a process of *learning to see* photography and the irrevocable temporality it inscribes.

If photography works in the *Search* as a way of figuring the model of linear time that the text sets out to undo, this process of undoing requires first a familiarisation with the ways in which photography operates. This familiarisation or process of education is effected not just through the vicissitudes of the hero/protagonist's life, but also through writing itself, which in the *Search* becomes a somewhat mechanical generator of more and more writing. As Mieke Bal has argued in the most extensive study of the function played by photography in Proust's text, the recovery of time lost that is the object of the Proustian search requires an 'externalisation of sensation in space' that is achieved by arresting and amplifying those fugitive moments that give access to lost memories.[31] This translation of what is essentially an experience of time into a spatial dimension turns writing into an imitation of the photographic process and thus revolutionises the narratological order. As we saw in the case of the grandmother's photograph, the logic that animates the succession of episodes in the *Search* is not that of a chain of events linked by a relation of causality, but rather that of the repetition of scenes and motifs that are progressively brought into sharper and sharper focus. As Bal points out, this logic of repetition is closer to the mechanical production of the photographic '"contact sheet"'[32] than to the organic return of a rhythm.[33] Its effect is in fact to produce what Bal identifies as a 'serialization'[34] of episodes that are just stopped short of producing their own movement, which is to say that they are photographs caught at the moment before they become cinematic photograms.[35] The logic of this repetition that does not engender its own movement does not represent an attempt at giving birth to an alternative narratological order – that of film – but rather an appropriation of 'a breath-taking seizure of power by the image'[36] in an unprecedented assault on the relentless linearity of 'the purely mathematical order of the years',[37] as Barthes put it.

Bal's invitation to read Proust visually alerts us to the ways in which the response to photography marked by the *Search* differs from the one offered by *The Man Without Qualities*. Where Musil's text goes in search of the historical configuration that made temporality into a spatial category, Proust's takes this form of abstracted temporality as its starting point, as a naturalised structure that is identified with death and the irrecoverable experience of loss. For both texts, the linear temporality of chronology represents the given order that needs to be undone, but the means of this undoing are markedly different. As we saw, Musil deploys the form of the essay to slow down the frenzied temporality of modernity and indefinitely suspend the interval of time between 1913 and 1914. In Proust, though, the chronological order is not so much suspended as radically unravelled through the appropriation of photography's potential for arresting the flow of time and freezing it into isolated scenes or motifs which then become infinitely repeatable and susceptible to return. This is mechanical reproduction put at the service of the work of art, but a mechanical reproduction that is performed by what Bal calls 'effects of language' rather than by technology.[38]

The temporality inscribed by photography is subjected by Proust to a profound transformation that cuts at the heart of the realist conception of the medium. On the one hand, there is the association of photography with a kind of temporality that is geometrical (or mathematical, in Barthes's terms), linear and leading inescapably to death and oblivion. On the other, there is the potential of the photographic process for infinite repetition of the same instant that transforms the aorist of absolute, abstract time into a sort of timeless temporality that abolishes the distinction between past and present. In this second, more innovative conception, photography becomes a technology of repetition that shares with the modernist writing of the *Search* a certain cavalier disregard for grammatical propriety. As Genette points out in *Narrative Discourse*, the *Search* presents its readers with an experience of linguistic disorientation that finds its most obvious expression in Proust's manipulation of verb tenses. In the *Search* the aorist of classical realist narrative is transformed into the imperfect of habitual, repetitive actions, turning individual, 'singulative' scenes into exemplary, 'iterative' ones.[39] This shift in verb tenses produces a paradoxical situation whereby scenes whose 'richness and precision of detail ensure that no reader can seriously believe they occur and reoccur in that manner, several times, without any variations'[40] are in fact transformed into *'pseudo-iterative'* scenes whose repetition is 'intended to be taken in its impossible literalness'.[41] This impossibility – of singular occurrence and repetition in the same scene – is the same impossibility that characterises the Proustian attempt to recover a temporal dimension that is lost and yet always potentially present in a novel which 'is undoubtedly, as it proclaims, a novel of Time lost and found again, but [. . .] also, more secretly perhaps, a novel of Time ruled, captured, bewitched, surreptitiously subverted, or better: *perverted*'.[42]

This transformation of the singulative, marked by the aorist, into the iterative, marked by the imperfect, represents the grammatical scaffolding that supports the serialisation of episodes modelled on the photographic contact sheet analysed by Bal. To adapt Barthes's terms, the photographic in Proust transforms the absolute aorist of historical or novelistic narrative into the imperfect of infinite repetition, not unique, pricking and poignant but rather banal, 'flat' (in Bal's appropriation of the term), an everyday occurrence.[43] It is in this sense that Proust offers for Bal the early emergence of a postmodern rather than modern sensibility for which creativity is not expressed through the original, the unique, but rather through the process of infinite reproducibility that invests both artefacts and experiences, both objects and subjects. Within this new paradigm, the geometric, abstract character of modern temporality is not the mark of a harsh, impersonal view of history (as Barthes would have it in Balzac) but rather the sign of our liberation *from* history, however conceived.

While this liberation from history can be – and has been – read as the kind of irresponsible renunciation that makes of postmodernism 'the cultural logic of late capitalism',[44] it also shares with the Musilian idea of essayism the character of a utopia. Both the pseudo-iterative in the *Search* and the intrusion of essayistic discourse in *The Man Without Qualities* produce an amplification of the interval of time that has a certain delaying effect on the temporality of modernity. In Proust, this delay gives access to an alternative dimension where time can be recaptured and shaped into a circular movement *à rebours* that ties endings and beginnings together. For Musil this resolution into circularity is barred, not least because German, like English and unlike French, does not have separate verbal forms for the preterite and the imperfect.[45] The essay cannot construct an alternative form of temporality to be compared to the Proustian use of the pseudo-iterative, as it is itself part of the dialectic of timelessness and linear temporality for which Proust's text offers the resolution of a 'third form'.[46] There is no liberation from history in *The Man Without Qualities*, but an eternal suspension *of* history in the frozen frame of a photogram.

Despite these remarkable differences in Musil's and Proust's approach to the problematics of historicity, it is clear that both their strategies represent manipulations of the temporal order that would not have been possible before the intervention of photography. Photography gives time a grammar, which opens up time itself to the possibility of manipulation, be it that of the Proustian perversion of French verb tenses or that of Musil's essayistic expansion. This reduction of time to a grammatical category marks the moment of an unprecedented gamble with the historical process, an all-or-nothing game which, as Kracauer pointed out, may well end with an apocalyptic eradication of consciousness and thought. We may shudder with Kracauer at the recklessness of this *Vabanque-Spiel*. Yet without it modernism itself would have remained an unrealised possibility.

Notes

1 Siegfried Kracauer, 'Photography' in *The Mass Ornament: Weimar Essays*, trans. and intro. Thomas Y. Levin (Cambridge: Harvard UP, 1995), p. 61

2 This identification of photography with historicism is not exclusive to Kracauer's writings but can also be found in Benjamin's work, especially in the 'Theses on the Philosophy of History' [1940], sections V, VI and XV (in *Illuminations*, ed. and intro. Hannah Arendt, trans. Harry Zohn (London: Fontana, 1973)). For a sustained study of the relation between photography and historiography in Benjamin see Eduardo Cadava, *Words of Light: Theses on the Photography of History* (Princeton, NJ: Princeton University Press, 1997).

3 Kracauer, 'Photography', p. 49.

4 Kracauer, 'Photography', p. 52.

5 Kracauer, 'Photography', p. 61.

6 For the classical statement of this dialectic of technology, see Walter Benjamin, 'The Work of Art in the Age of Mechanical Reproduction' [1936] in *Illuminations*, ed. and intro. Hannah Arendt, trans. Harry Zohn (London: Fontana, 1973). A feminist reworking of this position is offered by Donna Haraway's 'A Cyborg Manifesto:

Science, Technology and Socialist-Feminism in the Late Twentieth Century' in
Simians, Cyborgs, and Women: The Reinvention of Nature (London: Free Association,
1991), pp. 149-81.

7   The editions I shall be referring to are Marcel Proust, *In Search of Lost Time*, trans. C.
K. Scott Moncrieff and Terence Kilmartin, revised D. J. Enright, 6 vols. (London:
Chatto, 1992); Robert Musil, *The Man Without Qualities*, trans. Sophie Wilkins and
Burton Pike, 2 vols. (London: Picador, 1995). Subsequent references will be
incorporated into the main text as (*S*, vol., p.) and (*MWQ*, ch., p.).

8   See Peter Nicholls, *Modernisms: A Literary Guide* (London: Macmillan, 1995), pp.
273-5 and Franco Moretti, *Opere Mondo: saggio sulla forma epica dal* Faust *a*
Cent'anni di solitudine (Turin: Einaudi, 1994), pp. 194-99.

9   These photographs have been identified by Karl Corino as picturing the tennis player
Suzanne Lenglen in Vienna in 1925 and an unknown swimmer whose disquieting
image was found by Musil in a magazine bought from Ullstein-Bilderdienst. They are
reproduced in Corino's *Robert Musil: Leben und Werken in Bildern und Texten*
(Reinbeck bei Hamburg: Rowholt, 1988) on p. 356 (fig. 1) and 357 (fig. 2)
respectively.

10   Corino has argued that the Vienna in which *The Man Without Qualities* is set
represents a composite amalgam of the city as it was in 1913 (the time of the action)
and in the 1920s (the time of writing). This is particularly clear in the opening
description of city traffic (*MWQ*, 1, p. 3), which Corino shows to be matching
photographs of 1920s Vienna. This superimposition of different historical times is
clearly articulated in the text by the oscillation that characterises the narrative voice, at
times (almost) identical to Ulrich's interior monologue, but very often (especially in
the essayistic chapters) separated from Ulrich's by the subtlest irony, which becomes a
marker of temporal distance (see, e.g., *MWQ*, 8, pp. 26-31).

11   Musil's essayistic practice matches fairly closely Adorno's description of the essay as
the formal equivalent of negative dialectics (in 'The Essay as Form' [1958] in *Notes to
Literature*, trans. Shierry Weber Nicholsen, vol. 1 (New York: Columbia UP, 1991),
pp. 3-23). For a discussion of the essay as the dominant form of twentieth-century
literary practice and critical thinking see Claire de Obaldia, *The Essayistic Spirit:
Literature, Modern Criticism and the Essay* (Oxford: Clarendon, 1995). See also my
study of Virginia Woolf's essayistic practice in *Virginia Woolf's Essays: Sketching the
Past* (London: Macmillan, 2000).

12   Martina Wagner-Egelhaaf has argued that far from representing the dialectical twin of
essayism, photography functions within *The Man Without Qualities* as the privileged
site of reflection on the problem of representation with which Musil's text grapples. In
her reading, photography becomes the medium that embodies 'the condition of "being
without qualities", that conception which postulates a detachment from habitual
attitudes in favour of "another" experience of reality' ('"Wirklichkeitserinnerungen:
Photographie und Text bei Robert Musil', *Poetica*, 23:1-2 (1991), p. 218; my

translation). This alternative experience of reality, Musil's *'der andere Zustand'*, could indeed be identified with the mechanical, abstract dimension of temporality inscribed by photography, but a further transformation is necessary for that dimension to become the location of Musil's utopia. In 'Towards a New Aesthetics' (1925), Musil suggests in fact that it is cinema rather than photography which approximates the 'other' condition (in *Precision and Soul: Essays and Addresses*, ed. and trans. Burton Pike and David S. Luft (Chicago: Chicago University Press, 1990), pp. 193-208).

13   In spite of the concerted attempts at gathering from the *Nachlaß* indications that would lead to its resolution, *The Man Without Qualities* remains radically unfinished. For an overview of the debates around the *Nachlaß* in Musil studies see Christian Rogowski, *Distinguished Outsider: Robert Musil and His Critics* (Columbia: Camden House, 1994), pp. 26-31.

14   Roland Barthes, 'Introduction to the Structural Analysis of Narrative', in *Image-Music-Text*, trans. Stephen Heath (London: Fontana, 1977), p. 98.

15   See, for instance, Walter Benjamin, 'The Storyteller' [1936] in *Illuminations*, ed. and intro. Hannah Arendt, trans. Harry Zohn (London: Fontana, 1973), pp. 83-107.

16   Barthes, 'Structural Analysis', p. 99.

17   On the well-known distinction in French grammar between the system of the preterite (for narrative) and that of the perfect (for discourse), see Emile Benveniste's article, 'The Correlations of Tense in the French Verb' in *Problems in General Linguistics* [1966], trans. Mary Elizabeth Meek (Coral Gables: University of Miami Press, 1971), pp. 205-15.

18   Roland Barthes, *Writing Degree Zero* [1953], trans. Annette Lavers (London: Cape, 1967), p. 27.

19   Barthes, Writing Degree Zero, p. 33.

20   Ann Banfield's compelling analysis of the role played by the existence of the preterite in the development of what we have come to identify as crucial tenets of poststructuralist discourse similarly stresses the ways in which the notion of an impersonal, subject-less *écriture* derives in large part from the French perception 'of division within its own language' between the temporality of novelistic discourse (*le passé simple*), and that of everyday communication, which as Benveniste points out, is marked by the forms of the perfect. See her *'Écriture*, Narration and the Grammar of French' in *Narrative: from Malory to Motion Pictures*, ed. Jeremy Hawthorn (London: Arnold, 1985), p. 17.

21   Roland Barthes, *Camera Lucida: Reflections on Photography*, trans. Richard Howard (London: Cape, 1980), p. 76.

22   Barthes, *Camera Lucida*, p. 87.

23   Barthes, *Camera Lucida*, p. 76.

24   Barthes, *Camera Lucida*, p. 89.

25   Barthes, *Camera Lucida*, p. 90.

26   Barthes, *Camera Lucida*, p. 91.

27   Barthes, *Camera Lucida*, p. 82.

28   The classical analysis of the dialectic between these two types of temporality in Proust is that of J. P. Houston, 'Temporal Patterns in *A la recherche du temps perdu*', *French Studies*, 16 (1962) : 33-45.

29   For Beckett, this is one of the crucial episodes of the *Search* for its exploration of the effects of habit on perception (see *Proust* [1965] (London: Calder, 1999), pp. 27-9). Brassaï also takes this episode as the centre of the Proustian engagement with photography, in *Marcel Proust sous l'emprise de la photographie* (Paris: Gallimard, 1997), p. 92. Mary Price shares with Beckett the sense that this episode illustrates a certain stripping off of the veil of memories which she compares to Benjamin's argument on the loss of the aura through mechanical reproduction (*The Photograph: a Strange Confined Space* (Stanford: Stanford University Press, 1994), pp.150-56).

30   Barthes, *Camera Lucida*, p. 6.

31   Mieke Bal, *The Mottled Screen: Reading Proust Visually*, trans. Anna-Louise Milne (Stanford: Stanford University Press, 1997), pp. 183.

32   Bal, *Mottled Screen*, p. 201.

33   'Rhythm' is the term Barthes takes from Bachelard to designate the narratological innovation performed by Proust's text where '"systems of moments" (Bachelard again) succeed each other, but also correspond to each other' ('*Longtemps je me suis couché de bonne heure . . .*' [1978] in *The Rustle of Language*, trans. Richard Howard (Berkeley: University of California Press, 1986), p. 282).

34   Bal, *Mottled Screen*, p. 213.

35   This reading of Proust's appropriation of the pre-cinematic photogram is supported also by Garret Stewart's study of modernism as being placed 'between film and screen', that is, between the material basis of the cinematic text and its realisation in the projection on screen. For Stewart, the photogram works as the textual/material residue of technology which disrupts narrative cinema and the illusion of realism just as the phonogram in modernist texts undoes narrative sequence and referentiality. See *Between Film and Screen: Modernism's Photo Synthesis* (Chicago: Chicago University Press, 1999).

36   Bal, *Mottled Screen*, p. 213.

37   Barthes, '*Longtemps*', p. 282.

38   Bal, *Mottled Screen*, p. 201. Compare Proust's transformation of writing into a photography of time to the photographic practice of the surrealists who, as Rosalind Krauss has argued, worked to turn photography into (modernist) writing. In surrealism, 'the photographic medium is exploited to produce a paradox: the paradox of reality constituted as a sign – or presence transformed into absence, into representation, into spacing, into writing' ('The Photographic Conditions of Surrealism' in *The Originality of the Avant-Garde and Other Modernist Myths* (Cambridge: MIT, 1985), p. 112).

39   Gérard Genette, *Narrative Discourse: An Essay in Method* [1972], trans. Jane E. Lewin, foreword Jonathan Culler (Ithaca, NY: Cornell University Press, 1980), p. 116.

40 Genette, *Narrative Discourse*, p. 121.

41 Genette, *Narrative Discourse*, p. 122.

42 Genette, *Narrative Discourse*, p. 160.

43 In '*L'Imparfait de l'Objectif*: the Imperfect of the Object Glass' (*Camera Obscura: A Journal of Feminism and Film Theory* 24 (1990) : 65-87), Ann Banfield has proposed that the naming of the photograph as the 'this has been' proposed by Barthes in *Camera Lucida* effectively hides its true verbal referent – the imperfect. Like Bal, Banfield insists that Barthes's interpretation places photography on the same side as Proust's involuntary memory rather than as the 'counter-memory' that Barthes identifies with the aorist/preterite. But she also has to admit that the imperfect of the photograph does not correspond to that of speech but to 'a use of the *imparfait* restricted to written narrative and, specifically to the novel'. As such, this novelistic *imparfait* corresponds to Proust's *perverse* use of the pseudo – iterative and marks 'a perspective unoccupied by any subject, a kind of "camera consciousness"' (p. 76), that is, the impersonal, in-human perspective also marked by the aorist.

44 See Fredric Jameson, *Postmodernism or, the Cultural Logic of Late Capitalism* (London: Verso, 1991), where Jameson in fact identifies the death of historical time explicitly with the use of the aorist, even in languages such as English, where the tense does not exist in isolation from the imperfect and as a separate verbal form. Commenting on Doctorow's *Ragtime*, Jameson claims that it is '*as though* Doctorow had set out systematically to produce the effect or the equivalent, in his language, of a verbal tense we do not possess in English, namely, the French preterite (or *passé simple*), whose "perfective" movement, as Émile Benveniste taught us, serves to separate events from the present of enunciation and to transform the stream of time and action into so many finished, complete, and isolated punctual event objects which find themselves sundered from any present situation (even that of the act of story telling or enunciation)' (p. 24).

45 As Maurice Grevisse, *Le bon usage: grammaire française* (Paris: Duculot, 1980) points out, the French distinction between *passé simple* and *imparfait* is not repeated in the Germanic languages where one single form ('I took' in English, 'Ich nahm' in German) translates both 'Je prenais' and 'Je pris'. Although Grevisse claims that the name of preterite designates only the German and English forms and not the French one of *le passé simple*, both Benveniste and Barthes use either the preterite or the aorist as synonyms for the French form.

46 Once again, Barthes's term for the *Search* which, as he points out, emerged out of 'a crucial period of hesitation' which saw Proust 'at the intersection of two paths, two genres, torn between two "ways" he does not yet know could converge, any more than the Narrator knows, for a very long time – until Gilberte's marriage to Saint-Loup – that Swann's Way meets the Guermantes' Way: the way of the Essay (of Criticism) and the way of the Novel' ('*Longtemps*', p. 278). In this dialectic, photography would either occupy the side of the novel, of narrative and metonymy (as it does in Musil) or

that of an in-between that prevents the opposition of essay and novel from settling into a rigid binary (Proust's solution).

After the Modern

10

How to Read the Image? Beckett's Televisual Memory

Lydia Rainford

Samuel Beckett has long been figured as a ruthless interrogator of linguistic failure. Whether this interrogation is perceived as a project of purposeful reduction and negation, or as something more mired in repetition and proliferation, Beckett's work is invariably read as an attempt to strip away what he referred to as 'the word surface'.[1] Given this critical preoccupation, it is surprising that Beckett's work in the visual media, and in particular his plays for television, has remained relatively unconsidered.

Studies of the late work have tended to assimilate the television plays into more general analyses of Beckett's later, minimalist style.[2] They are considered mainly in spatial terms, as another manifestation of the writer's paring down of characterisation and dialogue and his increasing reliance on gesture, rhythm and movement. When the televisual medium is addressed more directly, it is commonly, and predictably, in the context of asserting Beckett's final abandonment of the communicative possibility of language. Jonathan Kalb argues that the television plays reduce art to an abstract set of movements and images, rather like dance or painting.[3] Enoch Brater, while noting that words and pictures are equally 'canned' in the television plays, nevertheless asserts that Beckett's use of technology 'establishes a truly "concrete" poetry', a 'poetry of form and structure which, in the process of eroding the obvious identity of his characters, restores them, curiously enough, to life.'[4] Martin Esslin describes the shift to visual media as a form of aesthetic purification, writing that the television plays reach the 'point zero of language' and attain,

> the compression of the maximum of experience into the most telling and graphic metaphor which could then be incarnated, made visible and audible, in the most concise and concrete form of a living, moving image: a poem without words.[5]

The emphasis here is on an immediacy and presence enabled by the visual image enables, which verbal communication could never muster. 'Experience' is incarnated and the wayward meanderings of language can be surpassed. Esslin's is clearly a particularly idealised reading, but it gives a strong flavour of the typical critical figuration of the image in Beckett's oeuvre as opponent of and logical successor to the word. A hierarchy comes into play whereby language fades out in the face of the imaginative plenitude of the visual picture.

This characterisation of the visual medium in Beckett's work is understandable given Beckett's defence of film as a serious art form on the grounds of 'the word's inadequacy'.[6] However, it also seems a peculiarly essentialist gesture to attribute such pure representational powers to the image, given that Beckett's preoccupation with expressive failure extends across different literary forms and technologies. Protagonists from Molloy, to Krapp, to the speakers of *Texts for Nothing* battle with the unruly movements of their recorded and represented 'experience', which unpin and deform the integrity of their knowledge and recollections. If attempts to inscribe the truth fail so repeatedly in these narratives and plays, why should they suddenly succeed in the medium of television?

A marked exception to the critical readings of the media plays is provided by the work of Gilles Deleuze. His essay 'L'Épuisé' (in English translation 'The Exhausted'), first published as a coda to the French translation of *Quad*, also interprets the plays in terms of a negation of language, but here negation represents something far more radical than a poised movement towards aesthetic purity and expressive integrity.[7] According to Deleuze, Beckett's work for television functions as an 'exhaustion' of the 'possible', a state of persisting beyond all combinations of goals, plans, preferences and significations. This total exhaustion is the culmination of a gradual decline throughout Beckett's literary oeuvre, which Deleuze divides into three different 'languages'. The first, *language I*, the 'language of names', exhausts what Deleuze calls subjective and objective possibility by combining all the different variables of a particular situation (*E*, p.156). This language is exemplified by the eponymous hero's rigorous ordering of his biscuits in *Murphy*, or, in the *Trilogy*, by Molloy's sucking stones. *Language II* not only exhausts the possible with words, but exhausts the words themselves. This is 'no longer a language of names but of voices', the voices of characters like those in *The Trilogy*, who cannot cease to speak because they can never fully possess or coincide with the words they use or the things they speak about:

> it is always an Other who speaks, since the words have not waited for me, and there is no language other than the foreign. (*E*, p.157).

The third language, *language III*, is the one Deleuze associates with Beckett's late work. Although this language can co-exist with and be 'folded' in words (such as it is in *Imagination Dead Imagine*, or *Worstward Ho*), it 'accomplishes its own mission' in the televisual medium, because it aspires to what Deleuze terms 'Image'. This Image may be aural or visual, but its defining characteristic is that it breaks from the 'calculations and significations, ... intentions and personal memories' which weigh down words, and 'imprison' us (*E*, p. 173). Instead, the Image creates a 'hiatus' or hole in the surface of language which allows for 'the emergence of the void or the visible in itself, the silence or the audible in itself' (Ibid.). Thus *Quad* operates simply as Space and silence; *Ghost Trio*, as Space with voice and music; *...but the clouds...* as Image with voice and poetry; and *Nacht und Traüme* as Image, silence, song and music (*E*, p. 162). Reduced to these components the television plays function as an 'amnesiac witness' to the obliteration of suffocating linguistic content (*E*, p. 170).

Deleuze's reading is an intriguing one, because it is proximate but contrary to other interpretations. While the movement away from language and towards 'image' is clearly traced as a progression in Beckett's work, its final realisation is not read as the breakthrough into concrete representation of experience so much as a complete rupturing of identity and memory. 'Image' signifies exhaustion and 'void' rather than immediacy and presence. This means that the 'human' quality, which according to most readings, resonates through the television plays, is according to Deleuze, completely absent.[8]

So why should the media plays sustain such contrary readings, and how does Deleuze's conception of the image claim to capture Beckett's specific manipulation of the televisual medium? What, precisely, do Beckett's manipulations of the medium suggest about his ideas of visual and verbal mediation? In order to answer these questions, this chapter will seek to sketch the conceptual implications of the different notions of the 'image', and the extent to which they are echoed, or not, by Beckett. I will argue that the habitually oppositional relation between 'word' and 'image' set up by critical interpretations misrepresents the complex picture of mediation which is formed in Beckett's media plays. I will also suggest an alternative idea of verbal and visual technologies – one indebted to the work of Jacques Derrida – which I believe speaks more clearly to the structure and resonance of the plays.

Deleuze, 'image' and exhaustion

Deleuze's concepts of 'exhaustion' and 'Image' are very specific, and stem from his exposition of the 'movement-image' in his two-volume book *Cinema*.[9] Here he defines a modern ontology based on a mechanical notion of movement, as opposed to a Platonic one based on eternal Forms or Ideas (*C1*, p. 7). In keeping with this 'open system', Deleuze follows Bergson's notion of perception, which rejects the philosophical tendency to consider it either as the mental representation of objective matter (materialism) or as the creative consciousness that forms the order of the universe (idealism).[10] While both of these opposed choices construct perception as a point of origin and as distinct from mediated matter, Bergson figures it as part of the constant flux and movement of matter in the universe, and the manifestation of this movement as images.[11] According to Deleuze's definition, movement-images exist on a 'plane of immanence' as part of a 'world of universal variation, of universal undulation' (*C1*, p. 58). Although this undifferentiated universe settles and solidifies into systems which necessitate a place or object to which the movement-image is directed, in their 'mother' state the movement-images are matter which has not yet become, and as such they need no source through which to appear, or thing to which to appear.[12] Movement-images contain their own luminosity, and perception *per se* is simply one point of action and reaction in a long chain of acting and reacting matter. As Deleuze puts it,

> How could my brain contain images since it is one image among others? External images act on me, transmit movement to me, and I return movement: how could images be in my consciousness, since I am myself image, that is, movement? And can I even, at this level, speak of 'ego', of eye, of brain and of body? Only for simple convenience; for nothing can yet be identified in this way. (*C1*, p. 58)

It is this state of unidentified, undifferentiated movement that is most important to Deleuze's assessment of the specificity of cinema, and of Beckett's film and television work. For Deleuze, as for Bergson, subjective perception is 'subtracted' and 'framed' from total, objective perception, and is part of the set of reactions to and sensations of movement that gradually become engraved as a system of habitual and regular responses: the voluntary memory.[13] However, whereas Bergson regards cinema as the corresponding 'snapshot' registration of reality by these responses – and thus too ordered and constrained to reflect the universal flow of movement – Deleuze regards the cinema as having no essential relation to systematised perception (*C1*, p. 57). Rather, it 'lacks a centre of anchorage and of horizon', which may enable an unloosening of subjective responses, and all their perceptions, and a return to 'the matrix or the movement-image as it is in itself, in its acentred purity' (*C1*, pp. 58 & 66).

Thus while Deleuze's analysis of cinema is concerned with the division of the movement-image into three different 'varieties' – the action-image, the perception-image, and the affection-image – his main preoccupation is with the propensity of these living images to de-differentiate into the pure movement-image. Significantly, Beckett's only work for cinema, *Film*, represents for Deleuze the anticipation of one such moment. In *Cinema 1*, Deleuze considers *Film* as the 'exhaustion' of Bishop Berkeley's theory of being as extraneous perception. The film's lone protagonist ('O') is resistant to being perceived by anything. He is pursued, then confronted by the intent perception of the camera-eye ('E'), which, when finally seen from 'O's' perspective, turns out to share his face and black eye patch. In his film script, Beckett describes this action as the 'search of non-being in flight from extraneous perception breaking down in inescapability of self-perception'.[14] Deleuze describes it as the traversal of 'the three great elementary images of the cinema', culminating in a still frame which suggests the 'extinction' of the character's subjectivity and the 'exhaustion' of perception.[15] Yet as far as Deleuze is concerned, this is 'only a means in relation to a more profound end':

> It is a question of attaining once more the world before man, before our own dawn, the position where movement was ... under the régime of universal variation, and where light, always propagating itself, had no need to be revealed.   (*C1*, p. 68)

In other words, although Beckett's film only portrays the systematic wearing out of Berkleyan perception – images in a lived state – it does so as a means of anticipating a form of cinema that would express the pure movement-image. In 'The Greatest Irish Film', Deleuze even echoes the language of Beckett's novel *Murphy*, asserting that with the death of the film's perception, the character will be returned to 'the luminous void' as 'an impersonal yet singular atom'.[16]

Deleuze's reading of Beckett's television plays in 'The Exhausted' develops this analysis in line with his theorisation of the 'time-image' in his second volume on cinema. Here he traces modern cinema's fulfilment of that which classical cinema made possible: the direct, rather than indirect, exposure of 'interval[s] of movement' (*C2*, p. 41).[17] The new time-image shatters the sensory-motor schema 'from the inside', and cinema now operates through non-localizable relations (*C2*, p. 40). Actions and perceptions 'cease to be linked together' and the image is constituted through 'purely optical and sound situations' (*C2*, p. 28). The terms Deleuze uses to describe the effect of this cinema are similar to those of 'The Exhausted' in their emphasis on a pure semiotics of the visual, and direct, degree zero revelation. It 'brings[s] the emancipated senses into direct relation with time and thought' (*C2*, p. 17). It 'makes us grasp, ... something intolerable and unbearable', and thereby seeks to become 'visionary, to produce a means of knowledge and action out of pure vision' (*C2*, p. 18). The 'gaps' and 'hiatuses' in language and memory which Deleuze sees in Beckett's television plays are thus the intervals which open the closed and localised world of 'subjective' perception to the flux and dissonance of 'image' without temporal or spatial enclosure. The persistence of 'possibility' is clearly allied to the persistence of sensory-motor schema and indirect, linguistic semiotics:

> Language 'does not say what is, it says what might be...' (*E*, p. 202)[18]
> Language states the possible, but only by readying it for a realization. ... But the realization of the possible always proceeds through exclusion, because it presupposes preferences and goals that vary, always replacing the proceeding ones. (*E*, pp. 152-3)

Thus where *Film* implied but stopped just short of the complete 'exhaustion of the possible', the television plays inhabit it. Subjective and linguistic perception are methodically obliterated until all that is left are 'opsigns' and 'sonsigns', constituting the 'transparent material' of the pure cinematic / televisual event (*C2*, p. 34). Appropriately, when Deleuze writes about the 1976 play *...but the clouds...* the reference to Beckett's *Murphy* becomes more definite and actualised. Now the image is at the threshold of its lived state, suspended in the very act of self-dissipation, rushing towards '"the dark ... of ... absolute freedom"' (*E*, p. 170).

Resonances and Problems

Deleuze's reading is persuasive in several ways. It chimes with the tone of Beckett's early critical writing on language and memory. In his much-quoted letters to Axel Kaun and in the *Three Dialogues with Georges Duthuit*, Beckett's constant theme was his desire to express the 'nothingness' of expression, to emulate the 'giddy heights' and 'unfathomable abysses' of Beethoven's music, to tear aside the 'veil' of language and 'get at the things (or the Nothingness) behind it.'[19] Although Bergson's influence is indirect, Beckett employs a broadly Bergsonian model of memory in *Proust*, equating the artistic process with involuntary memory, which erupts into and disrupts Habit or voluntary memory.[20] The 'exhaustion' described in Deleuze's theorisation of cinema can thus be equated with Beckett's more unequivocal aesthetic writings. Deleuze's image-ontology also corresponds with the distinctly anti-Platonic nature of Beckett's conception of memory and knowledge. I will say more about this below.

However, Beckett's aesthetic theorising is not necessarily identical with Beckett's artistic practice. For all of Beckett's critical declarations about the inadequacy of language, and for all his characters' attempts to give up speaking and remembering and lapse into the void, traces of language and memory – even if they are only ruined traces – always seem to remain. Deleuze's emphasis on forgetfulness and emptiness does not correlate with this. His references to Murphy's 'absolute freedom' in connection to the cinematic image are a case in point. In Beckett's novel this freedom is never achievable through a systematic 'ridding' of the self by the self, and the state Murphy reaches in dying accidentally is not necessarily the same 'void' he has aspired to through his philosophical techniques. And while Deleuze is careful to write of the void as being 'folded' in language, and of language 'turning against itself', his mapping of the path to the 'void or the visible in itself' seems dialectical in a way which is alien to the movement of Beckett's work.[21] In one particular rhetorical flourish 'The Exhausted' declares 'This is the final word, "nohow"', putting an absolutist twist on the last words of Beckett's *Worstward Ho*, which are, in fact, "nohow on". This curtails the ironic interrelation of Beckett's negated yet ever persistent phrases.[22]

The totalising thrust of Deleuze's reading is, of course, indicative of the scale of his reinterpretation of prevailing visual and ontological categories. Nevertheless, I would argue that the 'amnesiac' break from material language in this late work is not as pure and definite as Deleuze implies, even if it does trouble classical models of mediation. If we are concerned with the significance and specificity of Beckett's use of visual technology, we should be careful not to override the complexity of its relation to subjective memory and language in his television plays.[23] Indeed, a close reading of the very play Deleuze describes in such forgetful terms will suggest this.

...but the clouds...

...but the clouds... was written in 1976 and first televised in 1977, in a programme entitled *Shades*, alongside *Ghost Trio* and the television version of the stage play *Not I*.[24] Like the later *Nacht und Traüme*, *...but the clouds...* and *Ghost Trio* work through a methodical layering of different camera shots in 'shades of grey', but whereas *Nacht und Traüme* and *Ghost Trio* are haunted predominantly by fragments of music (Schubert's Leid and the Largo of Beethoven's Fifth Piano Trio), *...but the clouds...* is haunted by a fragment of poetry.

The play's title is a line from W. B. Yeats' 'The Tower' (1926), a poem which attempts to find some form of reconciliation with decrepitude and death. In Yeats' poem, the old poet sits in his lonely tower, thinking of his lost vigour and youth, and the characters, real and imagined, who inspired his love and poetry. Weary and embittered, he struggles to muster the courage to continue in his 'sedentary trade'. In the last stanza he faces his fears and puts his faith in the transformatory powers of the poetic imagination.

> Now shall I make my soul,
> Compelling it to study
> In a learned school
> Till the wreck of body,

Slow decay of blood,
Testy delirium
Or dull decrepitude,
Or what worse evil come —
The death of friends, or death
Of every brilliant eye
That made a catch in the breath —
Seem but the clouds of the sky
When the horizon fades;
Or a bird's sleepy cry
Among the deepening shades.[25]

The end of Yeats' poem is not without its ironies, for the vast effort of his soul's study cannot fend off the 'slow decay' of his old age, or recapture the breathless brilliance of past visions and events. Nevertheless, a faith persists in the possible transmogrification of the mutable into a state of truth and permanence that transcends loss. This faith pays homage to Blake's insistence on the immortality of the imagination, and reflects Yeats' (Neo-)Platonic ideas of the soul as that which stores and recollects ideal Forms from the eternal world of 'being'.[26] Yeats' modern version of the poetic sublime is evoked in the metaphorical transformation of the final images of the poem. They echo and resolve the preceding stanzas' comparison of the mother bird who builds her 'wild nest' to 'Man' who makes a 'superhuman / Mirror-resembling dream.'[27] The process of anamnesis enacted by the poem is trusted to turn painful introspection into something suggestive of future regeneration.

...*but the clouds*... repeats the themes of Yeats' poem to different ends. Beckett hijacks the last four lines of the poem and by setting them in his new, 'televisual' context, interrogates their redemptive capacity. The play begins with a near shot of a figure (called 'M') dressed in a long grey robe and slumped over an invisible table, so that his face is not visible. This view returns throughout the play. In between, M is repeatedly seen moving in and out of a lighted circle surrounded by darkness, while his voice ('V') explains that these movements are his daily routine: he makes his entrance from the 'west shadow' having 'walked the roads since break of day', he goes to his closet to change into his robe and skull-cap, re-enters, then turns and vanishes 'within' his 'little sanctum' where he crouches in the dark and, as he says, 'begs of her to appear'. This 'her' is a woman ('W'), presumably a lost loved one, whose face appears on the screen for a few seconds whenever he speaks of summoning her.

The play shares the profound sense of mourning evoked in Yeats' poem, and is even more obsessive in its tracing of remembered images. Indeed, there is a duplication of the memorial process, for the man is not only remembering the image of the woman, but is remembering how he remembered her.[28] His voice describes in meticulous, weary detail the four possible 'cases' of his encounter with the ghostly face of the woman: her not appearing, her appearing, her appearing and lingering, and her appearing and speaking. When she appears and speaks, her lips mouth the last lines of the Yeats poem, but cannot be heard. The camera images follow the man's narration and repeat the sequence in silence, when he has finished speaking, until he interjects to begin his recollections again.

The structuration of *...but the clouds...* around the appearing and disappearing image of the woman suggests a further, non-verbal echo of Yeats' poem: the line in 'The Tower' where he wonders 'Does the imagination dwell the most / Upon a woman won or a woman lost.' However, Beckett's play seems to repeat and replicate the won / lost dichotomy to the point where the distinction between the two is confused. The image of the woman's face is what the man is desperate to retrieve, and its presence seems to be as real to him as was the original woman. He speaks of her 'unseeing eyes' which he 'so begged when alive to look at me': the ambiguity of this line blurs the distinction between the live, present, 'won' woman and the dead, absent, 'lost' one. Were her eyes *ever* seeing, was she ever not 'lost' to him? Yet no matter how carefully visual and verbal remembrances are layered, the two remain dissociated. The woman's appearance is arbitrary and unpredictable: she does not come in response to his 'begging of the mind' and when she appears, the luminous close-up image of her face, gazing to the left of the camera-view, is antithetical to the shot of the anonymous crouched man, slumped to the right. Attempts at verbal communication also fail, for while the lines of the Yeats poem seem to be the connecting link between the man and woman, she never mouths more than 'but...the...clouds', and he speaks the lines in a mechanical, monotone way, as if their meaning is unrecognised. The act of recalling and reordering the past so carefully brings no inspiration or reconciliation and fails to promise a transformation of the 'lost' face into a less painful image. We are left only with a continual haunting.

Whatever the final significance these of visual, verbal, cinematic and literary associations, they do seem to undercut Yeats' faith in the process of anamnesis and the retrieval of a 'superhuman' image. The deliberate, 'knowing' memory persistently fails to recall what it seeks, and the image only comes as an involuntary or spontaneous memory, full of affect but without comprehension or true presence. 'M's' predicament is much like the one Beckett describes in *Proust*, where 'Habit' destroys the 'miraculous relief and clarity' of spontaneously remembered visions even as they are recalled, so that 'no effort of deliberate rememoration can impart or restore' them.[29] Past and present, voluntary and involuntary memories are unable to coincide productively. This anti-Platonic current in the play's action, and the disruption it brings to any notion of essential 'soul' or idealised memory, problematises those readings that stress the 'concrete poetry' of the media plays. It might, in turn, lead us to map ...*but the clouds*... onto Deleuze's image-ontology, and regard Beckett's layering of images and poetry as the means to make words 'loosen their grip' (*E*, p.173) and open them up to the 'void' and 'silence', the pure, chaotic movement which lies behind. However, as ever with Beckett, things are not so certain. For while the sequence of images trouble Yeats' Platonism, and Yeats' enduring faith in poetic redemption, they do not exhaust or forget them. Indeed, the verbal exceeds the visual as much as the visual exceeds the verbal. By the end of the play, through their constant repetition, the lines of Yeats' poem have gained a ghostly status equal to that of the image of the woman. They are the last thing we witness as we watch the play, and they seem to comment on the uncanny nature of the televisual image itself, as the play, 'fades out' like Yeats' 'horizon'.

> 53. *Dissolve to* S[long shot of set] *empty. 2 seconds.* M1 *in robe and skullcap emerges from north shadow, advances five steps and stands facing camera. 2 seconds. He turns left and advances five steps to disappear in east shadow. 2 seconds. He emerges in hat and greatcoat from east shadow, advances five steps and stands facing west shadow. 2 seconds. He advances five steps to disappear in west shadow. 2 seconds.*
> 54. V: Right.
> 55. *Dissolve to* M. *5 seconds.*
> 56. *Dissolve to* W. *5 seconds.*
> 57. V: '...but the clouds of the sky ... when the horizon fades...or a bird's sleepy cry ... among the deepening shades...' *5 seconds.*
> 58. *Dissolve to* M. *5 seconds.*
> 59. *Fade out on* M.
> 60. *Dark. 5 seconds.*

> (*CDW*, p. 422)

The particular sense of 'fading out' here is important, because it differs both from Yeats' definition and Deleuze's. Where Yeats' fading horizon implies the resurrection of the natural cycle (day following night, singing following silence), Beckett's implies no change of state. It simply marks another fading of language and image in the sequence of disunified, unnatural fadings. Nevertheless, this does not amount to an exhaustion, because the persistence of the Yeats reference, and its seepage into the visual action, suggests reappearance. The final fade out simply returns the play to its beginning: five seconds of darkness which fade up onto the shot of 'M'. This means that, contrary to Deleuze's reading, the bird and cloud imagery does not announce 'that the end of the possible is at hand for the protagonist' (*E*, p. 170) and the figure 'M', sitting in his 'little sanctum' is not reduced to being an 'amnesiac witness' (*E*, p. 155). Rather, the alteration of the meaning of the 'fade out' achieved by the juxtaposition of literary and televisual effects suggests an interminable memorial process; one which is other to Platonic recollection, with its conscious conjuring of original presence, but which lacks the movement towards the pure exhaustion and forgetting of Deleuze's cinematic 'assemblage'.

Far from escaping or extinguishing language in favour of the image, *...but the clouds...* creates an ironic and mutually contaminating balance between the two media that is central to the play's interrogation of perception, memorial inscription and recollection. The play does, indeed, disrupt the laborious 'habit' of voluntary memory, and deform the process of anamnesis, but it achieves this by troubling the apparent purity and immediacy of the image as much as by revealing the inadequacy and imprecision of the word. Memory in *...but the clouds...* is an endless web of visual and aural impressions whose technical mechanisms confound the sense of it taking place within, and being possessed by, the subjective spirit or 'soul'. Neither, however, can its 'matter' be said to exist in a wholly external, objective frame.[30] The doubling of 'mnemotechnics', and the complex interrelation of the specific forms of the two media, is precisely what reinforces the sense of alterity haunting the play; of the remembered object being not quite itself, happening elsewhere, in another time. To consider the visual and verbal in an oppositional relation, and to privilege one over the other, is to destroy the ghostliness of the play.

How, then, might the specificity of visual technology in Beckett's work for television be theorised without swamping the delicate cross-currents of different forms, texts and media within particular plays? I would like to answer this question by turning to some of Jacques Derrida's comments on the specificity of filmic and televisual technology. Derrida is broadly sympathetic to Deleuze's critical and philosophical projects, but his deconstructive contamination of ontological and epistemological boundaries seems to guard against the teleological and oppositional slant of Deleuze's reading. And although his comments do not address Beckett specifically, they resonate closely with the tone of Beckett's late plays, and with what Beckett seems to be saying about image, mediation and memorial inscription.

Derrida, spectrality and the archive

While writing with a different agenda to Deleuze's, Derrida's work is also embroiled in the technical specificity of philosophical models of perception and memory. His enduring battle with what he calls the 'historical repression and suppression of writing since Plato' challenges the constitution of 'the origin of philosophy as *episteme*, and of truth as the unity of *logos* and *phone*'.[31] The metaphysical tradition has privileged an idea of presence: an essential, revealed truth, encountered by a being in the moment of its origin. The Platonic philosopher relies on the act of anamnesis to recall pre-existing ideas and make them 'present' again. This may be prompted by 'hypomnesic' tools, such as writing, but the technical aspect of recollection always remains external to the 'present' event of the thing remembered: it is merely an aide-mémoire. Derrida's logic of *différance* deconstructs this notion. If, philosophically-speaking, we are waiting for the return of the origin, the pure event, and this event is mediated through a language that is not yet present – in the sense of being essentially true to the thing it describes – to a subjective consciousness who is not (yet) wholly identical to their pure state of being, then it was ever thus. As Derrida says, 'language has started without us, in us and before us' which means that the moment in which we speak is 'always already past, hence without a past present'.[32] This also means that the written trace is not in fact exterior to the act of retrieving knowledge, but is a constitutive part of the process. It is simply being repressed by a philosophical structure frightened of 'that which threatens presence and mastering of absence' (*FS*, p. 197).

Derrida's marking of the repressed *techne* has particular bearing on his analyses of memorial and archival processes. In 'Freud and the Scene of Writing', and in his more recent book, *Archive Fever*, Derrida explores the way in which 'the metaphorics of the written trace' return to haunt Freud's descriptions of his psychoanalytic model of memory, in spite of his attempts to conform to the materialist register of the natural sciences.[33] Freud described the workings of the memory as a series of impressions made on the psychic apparatus. These 'memory traces' differ in the conscious and unconscious realm (what is necessarily forgotten by the conscious can leave an indelible mark on the unconscious) but at the same time the two realms are in constant communication with each other. Faced with the simultaneous 'breach' and connection between conscious and unconscious, Freud attempted to make sense of this complex relation through his analogy of 'the mystic writing pad': a wax slab covered with a transparent sheet that would record an impression made on both surfaces, which could then be made invisible by pulling the sheet away from the slab. For Derrida, this analogy exposes rather than resolves the difficulty Freud has in modelling a fully integrated psychic apparatus because it relies on 'a certain outside' (*AF*, p. 19), a *technical* element which means that what is recorded

> cannot be reduced to memory: neither to memory as conscious reserve, nor to memory as rememoration, as act of recalling. The psychic archive comes neither under *mneme* nor under *anamnesis*.
>
> (*AF*, p. 92)

In other words, the written or technical trace of memory cannot be thought of as an additional, purely external mechanism, and this inevitably alters the status of the psychic material. It ceases to be the preserve of a discrete or 'private' space, and because its 'presence' as a remembered event is open to the contingencies of its technical transcription from its first moment, its recollection is a potentially never-ending process of alterable, reiterable inscriptions and transcriptions. Indeed, it leads Derrida to wonder in *Archive Fever* whether the constitution of the psychic apparatus – the very content of its memorial archive – would be affected by modern technological developments in recording, inscribing and reproducing 'so-called live memory' (*AF*, p. 15).

Derrida approaches this question in relation to visual technological developments in a set of interviews on the subject of television, entitled *Échographies*.[34] Here he speaks about the specificity of televisual technology in double-edged terms. On the one hand, it is unique in its ability to record the singularity and immediacy of the 'live moment' and reproduce it in another time or context. Whereas a scribe in the nineteenth century would 'leave no living trace of his voice, face, hand etc. in his text', now a moment is captured immediately,

> which was live, which is live, which one thinks is simply live, but which will be reproduced *as if live*, with reference to this present and this moment, anywhere and anytime, weeks or years from now, reinscribed in other settings or 'contexts'.
>
> (*ET*, p. 47)

On the other hand, this very capacity to reproduce the 'live moment' in other times and contexts, to repeat a moment that has already been lost, interferes with its temporal and phenomenal presence:

> because this 'live' moment will be able to be, is already, captured by machines which will transport or show them God knows when and God knows where, we already know that death is here. (Ibid.)

Although televisual recording is apparently more immediate, and more accurate, it is still susceptible to the play of différance that Derrida has already associated with 'older' technologies, such as writing. Indeed, the différantial effect seems even more exaggerated here, because of the exaggerated mobility and reiterability of the recorded image.[35] Derrida describes this more 'brilliant' but already deathly quality of the image as the 'spectral', because

> it is at once visible and invisible, at once phenomenal and non-phenomenal: a trace which marks in advance the present of its absence. (*ET*, p. 131)

Thus the contingencies of the technical trace infect the moment-to-moment work of composing and situating the present (and the past present) with an otherness and an absence which is replicated rather than banished by this work. The 'live image' of television is caught up in a spectral movement which cannot be recuperated by the desire for immediacy and authenticity, no matter how well it may fool us into thinking that it is 'the living image of the living' rather than 'the simulacrum of life' (*ET*, p. 47). This spectrality further alters our understanding of memory, because it exposes and exaggerates the diremption between the movements, times and contexts of recording and reproducing remembered material. It conforms to neither the notion of memory 'as conscious reserve' nor to the notion of memory 'as act of recalling', but implies a form of archive which lies at the crossover of immediate and recollected events, spontaneous, internal and repetitive, external experience.

Derrida's reading of television and cinema resembles Deleuze's insofar as it breaks from the metaphysical distinction between 'matter' and 'mediation', and emphasises the mobility of terms within the philosophical structure. Both readings also disrupt the sense of film acting to preserve or recover 'presence'. However, Derrida's delineation of the specificity of the 'new' technology does not amount to a completely other ontology, unlike Deleuze's 'Chaos' of Being. The spectral is not a thing 'in itself', but a haunting and contamination of existing boundaries. Its experience is not of a pure otherness or a pure absence, and therefore it cannot be thought of as that which heralds a pure 'void' or 'exhaustion'. Elsewhere, Derrida describes the abyssal and undecidable element which haunts definitions and decisions as 'the open mouth, *that which speaks* as well as that which signifies hunger.'[36] This also means that cinematic and televisual technologies do not necessarily represent a complete rupture from 'words' and their 'associations', even while the technology radically reconfigures the governance of their destination and content. Throughout *Échographies*, Derrida resists the temptation to think of the televisual image as being phenomenally and temporally purer, more immediate, than other media. And while, in another interview about deconstruction and the visual arts, he asserts that the 'specificity' of the cinematic medium 'is foreign to the word', he also asserts that even silent works of art, including films, 'are already talkative, full of virtual discourses'.[37] According to this definition, film is caught between the mute and the discursive, and its specific relation to the word should be defined in very particular contexts. Different films 'play differently with the relations among discourse, discursivity, and nondiscursivity' and 'a given cinematic method may be closer to a certain type of literature than to another cinematic method'.[38] The echoes, remains and reinscriptions of different technical traces, both written and visual, are precisely what emerge through Derrida's readings of the recorded archive.

Derrida's mode of reading and writing necessarily resists totalising stances and thus, in comparison to Deleuze, may seem to compromise the radical specificity of the filmic medium. However, it is through this very resistance that I would argue Derrida manages to maintain a vigilant regard not only towards the specificity of film technology, but to other technologies in relation to it (in this case, writing) and of particular manifestations of these technologies. While Derrida is not writing directly about Beckett's work, his definition of the spectral, disymmetrical, différantial effects of 'teletechnology', seems to come far closer to describing the *specific* effect of Beckett's *...but the clouds....* than Deleuze's direct analysis of the play. The image of the woman's face, already 'dead', never responding, and haunting the man with its irreducible otherness, epitomises what Derrida calls the spectral. The havoc it plays with the boundaries of 'inner' and 'outer' consciousness and 'private' and 'public' manifestation (is she a voluntary or involuntary memory; does she 'appear' within the 'inner sanctum' of his mind or as some externally transcribed archive?) questions the source and possession of the recorded image.[39] And the simultaneous dislocation and confusion between the different times in the play (the time when 'she' was alive; the time when he used to remember her; and the reconstruction of that time in the present) which is exaggerated through the layering of and fading between different shots, reveals the uncanny, unreliable 'immediacy' of the image. These effects, in turn, work to interrogate the Platonic model of memory maintained by Yeats, for the technical trace, the hypomnesic 'tool' which is meant to awaken recollection, is revealed as a constitutive rather than exterior part of the process of remembering and retrieving past events; which means that the memorial image, far from restoring or resurrecting lost presence, will always be caught in a pattern of anticipation and delay. This applies as much to the verbally-conjured image as the visually-conjured image, which suggests why the lines of poetry and the image of the woman's face operate in perpetual, ironic juxtaposition, forever full of affect but never coincident with settled significance.

In Beckett's other plays for television the relation between discursivity and non-discursivity, visual and non-visual technologies is different again. Like *...but the clouds...*, *Ghost Trio* builds methodically towards a shot of a man waiting for 'her' in a room. This time, however, the literary echoes are from Beckett's own work, for just as in *Waiting for Godot*, a small boy arrives to inform the man (silently) that the woman is not coming. Not even an imaginary image of the woman arrives, and the visual ghost is supplanted by the recurrence of fragments of Beethoven's *Ghost Trio*. The female voice which seems to direct the camera, persistently tells us to 'look again' at the details of the familiar scene, preempting the failure of the man to find revelation (*CDW*, pp. 408-9). In *Nacht und Träume* the only speech is in the brief burst of the Schubert *Lied*, 'Lovely dreams, oh come again' (*CDW*, p. 465-66), but the action of the play echoes the fabular unfolding enacted in several of Beckett's late prose texts, such as *Company*, where a voice in the half-light gains consolation from an imagined figment of himself.[40] *Quad* is the only play which functions completely without verbal language, but the protagonists seem no nearer to reaching 'the void or the visible in itself': they are caught in an interminable sequence of movements, colours and percussion rhythms, and the weary monochrome version of the play, *Quadrat II*, reveals the decay, but stops short of the obliteration of the four figures' individualised signifiers.[41] Each of these late plays is caught in an uncanny realm where images, sounds and words resonate, but never gain full presence or reach the longed-for state of annihilation.

Beckett's reiteration of textual, musical and choreographic memory in the medium of television does violence to the 'veil' of both verbal and visual language, and the revealed presence that they imply, but it exhausts neither. Instead it performs an interminable interrogation of the specific aspirations and betrayals of the different media, and of the misconceptions of prevailing aesthetic and philosophical notions of 'mediation'. By drawing out the ghostly nature of the televisual medium, Beckett troubles our faith in the direct transmission of 'lived' experience, and reveals the impure and irresolvable relations of the technologies of perception, inscription and recollection.

Notes

1   Samuel Beckett, Letter of 1937 to Axel Kaun, in *Disjecta: Miscellaneous Writings and A Dramatic Fragment*, ed. Ruby Cohn (London: John Calder, 1983), p. 172.

2   Anna McMullan's *Theatre on Trial: Samuel Beckett's Later Drama* (New York and London: Routledge, 1993) and James Knowlson's and John Pilling's *Frescoes of the Skull: The Recent Prose and Drama of Samuel Beckett* (London: John Calder, 1979), would be examples of this tendency.

3   Jonathan Kalb, 'The Radio and Television Plays, and 'Film'', in John Pilling (ed.), *The Cambridge Companion to Beckett* (Cambridge: Cambridge University Press,1994), pp. 124-144.

4   Enoch Brater, *Beyond Minimalsim: Beckett's Late Style in the Theater* (New York and Oxford: Oxford University Press, 1987), pp.102, 74 and 87.

5   Martin Esslin, 'Towards the Zero of Language', in James Acheson and Kateryna Arthur (eds.), *Beckett's Later Fiction and Drama* (New York: St. Martins Press, 1987), p. 46, and 'A poetry of moving images', in *Beckett Translating / Translating Beckett*, ed. Alan Warren Friedman, Charles Rossman and Dina Sherzer (University Park: Pennsylvania State University Press, 1987), p. 74.

6   Written in an unpublished notebook dated 26 March, 1937, quoted by James Knowlson in *Damned to Fame: The Life of Samuel Beckett* (London: Bloomsbury, 1996), p. 258.

7   Gilles Deleuze, 'L'épuisé', in Samuel Beckett, *Quad et autres pièces pour la télévision* (Paris: Les Éditions de Minuit, 1992), pp. 55-106; 'The Exhausted', in *Essays Clinical*

and Critical, trans. Daniel W. Smith and Michael A. Greco (London and New York: Verso, 1998), pp. 152-174. Subsequent references will be to the English translation, incorporated into the main text as (*E*, p.)

8   Phyllis Carey, for example, asserts that the media plays explore 'the subtle interrelationship between making meaning and human being, between design and *Dasein*', and says that 'the wordless mime of *Quad*' leads us 'to a silent contemplation of the enigma 'to be'; in 'The Quad Pieces: A Screen for the Unseeable', in Robin J. Davis and Lance St. John Butler (ed.s) *Make Sense Who May: Essays on Samuel Beckett's Later Works* (Gerrards Cross: Colin Smythe, 1988), pp. 145 & 148. Enoch Brater argues that the media plays' 'concern with relief, tone, chiaroscuro, a sense of composition, and placement on the television screen forces us, ironically, to overlook the geometry which makes all of this possible and respond instead to the human quality located in the images themselves', in *Beyond Minimalism*, p. 87.

9   Gilles Deleuze, *Cinema 1: The Movement-Image*, trans. Hugh Tomlinson and Barbara Haberjam (London: The Athlone Press, 1986) and *Cinema 2: The Time-Image*, trans. Hugh Tomlinson and Robert Galeta (London: The Athlone Press, 1989). Subsequent references will be incorporated into the main text as (*C1*, p.) and (*C2*, p.).

10   As Bergson puts it in *Matter and Memory*, 'Of these two opposite doctrines, the one attributes to the body and the other to the intellect a true power of creation, the first insisting that our brain begets representation and the second that our understanding designs the plan of nature'; *Matter and Memory*, trans. N. M. Paul and W. S. Palmer (New York, 1991), p. 181.

11   Bergson describes the world as an 'aggregate of images', where each image is 'merely a road by which pass, in every direction, the modifications propagated throughout the immensity of the universe'; in *Matter and Memory*, p.121. Deleuze insists that the 'in-itself of the image is matter: not something hidden behind the image, but on the contrary the absolute identity of the image and movement', in *Cinema 1*, p. 58 note 6. In other words, 'the *movement-image* and *flowing-matter* are strictly the same thing', Ibid., p.59.

12   The images within this world of flux are determined insofar as they act on others and react to others, but these actions and reactions are 'on all their facets at once' and 'by all their elements', so that there are in effect no 'points of anchorage and center of reference', *Cinema 1*, pp. 59-60. Interactivity and movement are thus the only 'essence' of Deleuze's cosmology.

13   Henri Bergson, *Matter and Memory*, p. 44-5. Anthony Uhlman provides an interesting analysis on Bergsonian memory and Habit in Beckett's work in chapter 2 of his book *Beckett and Poststructuralism* (Cambridge: Cambridge University Press, 1999), pp. 58-90.

14   Samuel Beckett, *Complete Dramatic Works* (London and Boston: Faber and Faber, 1986), p. 323. Subsequent references to this volume will be included in the main text as (*CDW*, p.). Berkeley's famous dictum, '*esse est percipi*' — 'to be is to be perceived'

—is the epigraph to the script of Beckett's film, but the script also warns that 'no truth value attaches to the above, regarded as of merely structural and dramatic convenience.'

15   Gilles Deleuze, 'The Greatest Irish Film' in *Essays Critical and Clinical*, p. 26. This essay posits a condensed, and more rhetorically exuberant version of the argument put forth in the section on the varieties of the movement-image, in *Cinema 1*, pp. 66-69.

16   *Essays Critical and Clinical*, p. 26. The prevailing desire of Murphy in Beckett's novel is to escape the strictures of the actual world and 'float' like a 'mote' in a state of 'absolute freedom' in the zone of his mind which consists of 'a flux of forms, a perpetual coming together and falling asunder of forms'; in Samuel Beckett, *Murphy* (London: John Calder, 1963) p. 79. The action of the novel parodies Murphy's attempts to reach this 'zone' through a Cartesian rational method.

17   Although Deleuze describes the time-image as representing a development or evolution of the movement-image in cinematic terms, it is clear that both types of image have the capacity to reveal the 'matrix of movement', and thus, in ontological terms, relate to the pure movement-image described in volume one of *Cinema*. Deleuze writes ot the relation of the two images as being both developmental and continuous: the 'direct time-image is the phantom which has always haunted the cinema, but it took modern cinema to give a body to this phantom'; Ibid., p. 41.

18   This is taken from footnote 6 of the text, where Deleuze quotes Brice Parain, *Sur la dialectique* (Paris, Gallimard, 1953).

19   Samuel Beckett, Letter of 1937 to Axel Kaun, in *Disjecta: Miscellaneous Writings and a Dramatic Fragment*, p.171-2; 'Three Dialogues' in *Proust and Three Dialogues with Georges Duthuit* (London: John Calder, 1999), p. 102.

20   As *Proust* is a piece of commentary, the model of memory described is obviously for the most part a description of Proust's model of memory. However, Beckett's reading of Proust lays greater stress on the constant return of Habit's 'evil and necessary structure' than on the moments when involuntary memory allows for the perception of objects as 'particular and unique'. See Samuel Beckett, *Proust and Three Dialogues with Georges Duthuit*, pp. 43 & 22.

21   Simon Critchley makes a similar point about Deleuze, without my particular emphasis on Beckett's use of visual media, in his book *Very Little ... Almost Nothing: Death, Philosophy and Literature* (London: Routledge, 1997).

22   Samuel Beckett, 'Worstward Ho', in *Nohow On: Company, Ill Seen Ill Said, Worstward Ho*, (London: John Calder, 1989), p. 128.

23   Martin Schwab points out that since Deleuze relates his readings of films only to the general ontology of the movement-image, he never attends to the aesthetic specificity of the films. In the case of 'Film' this is the 'plurivalence of a "representation" that seems to move in opposite and incompatible directions—differentiation and de-differentiation—in one and the same movement'; Martin Schwab, 'Escape from the Image', in Gregory Flaxman (ed.), *The Brain is the Screen: Deleuze and the*

Philosophy of the Cinema (Minneapolis and London: University of Minnesota Press, 2000), p. 124.

24   The 1977 BBC production of *...but the clouds...* was directed by Donald McWhinnie and acted by Ronald Pickup and Billie Whitelaw.

25   W. B Yeats, *The Collected Poems*, ed. Richard J. Finneran (Basingstoke and London: Macmillan Press, 1983), pp. 199-200.

26   The theme of 'The Tower' is reflected in a letter of Blake's, quoted by Yeats in *Letters to the New Island*, which contrasts the poet's 'feeble and tottering' physical state in old age with his 'imagination which liveth forever'; quoted in T. R. Henn, *The Lonely Tower: Studies in the Poetry of W. B. Yeats* (London: Methuen, 1950), p. 39. The third part of 'The Tower' takes issue with Plato and Plotinus for what he sees as their partial suspicion of the creative imagination (imagination must be modified with knowledge according to their teaching), but the notion of recollection used in the poem is nevertheless Platonic. In his note to the 1933 edition of *Collected Poems*, Yeats corrects his criticism of Plato and Plotinus, quoting Plotinus' asssertion that 'every soul [should] recall ... at the outset the truth that soul is the author of all living things'; in *The Varorium Edition of Yeats' Poems*, ed. Peter Allt and Russell K. Alspach (New York: Macmillan Press, 1957), p. 825.

27   *The Collected Poems*, p. 199.

28   Daniel Katz comments on this 'double' remembrance in his article 'Mirror Resembling Screens: Yeats, Beckett and ...but the clouds...', in *Beckett Today/ Beckett Aujourd'hui*, vol. 4 (1994), 83-91. He draws attention to the implicit temporal distinction between the two presented acts of memory, and the fact that this distinction is increasingly blurred as the play progresses.

29   Beckett, *Proust and Three Dialogues with Georges Duthoit*, p. 43.

30   Deleuze's notion of the 'exhaustion of the possible' encompasses subjective and objective possibility, thus signalling that he is thinking in terms of the universal; *The Exhausted*, p. 152.

31   Jacques Derrida, 'Freud and the Scene of Writing', in *Writing and Difference*, trans. Alan Bass (London: Routledge and Kegan Paul, 1978), p. 196. Subsequent references will be included in the main text as (*FS*, p.).

32   Jacques Derrida, 'How to Avoid Speaking: Denials', in Sanford Budick and Wolfgang Iser (ed.s), *Languages of the Unsayable: The Play of Negativity in Literature and Literary Theory* (New York: Columbia University Press, 1989), p. 29.

33   Jacques Derrida, *Mal d'Archive: une impression freudienne* (Paris: Éditions Galilée, 1995), trans. Eric Prenowitz as *Archive Fever: A Freudian Impression* (Chicago and London: University of Chicago Press, 1996). Subsequent references will be to the English translation, included in the main text as (*AF*, p.).

34   Jacques Derrida & Bernard Stiegler, *Échographies de la télévision; Entretiens filmés* (Paris: Éditions Galilée / Institut national de l'audiovisuel, 1996). Subsequent

references will be included in the main text as (*ET*, p.). Translations into English are mine.

35   Derrida says that if there is a specificity to television, it lies in 'the extent of [the] distance' between the capturing and reproduction of the image. In addition to the other times and contexts available to the televisual image, Derrida remarks on the increased capacity for the manipulation of the image through 'teletechnology': cutting, editing, recomposing, producing synthetic images etc; *Échographies*, pp. 48 & 110.

36   Jacques Derrida, *The Gift of Death*, trans. David Wills (Chicago and London: The University of Chicago Press, 1995), p. 84.

37   Jacques Derrida, 'The Spatial Arts: An Interview with Jacques Derrida', in Peter Brunette and David Wills (ed.s), *Deconstruction and the Visual Arts: Art, Media, Architecture* (Cambridge: Cambridge University Press, 1994), p. 13.

38   Ibid., pp. 13-14.

39   This question in particular is tied to the televisual medium, rather than the cinematic medium, as the undecidability of source and possession stems from the play being broadcast on the small screen. This creates an intimacy and proximity which reinforce the sense of the play enacting an interminable interrogation of the mind (the audience sit in their own 'little sanctum' witnessing the 'begging of the mind'), but it also troubles the intimacy and proximity it creates, because the image of the woman's face is so clearly already mediated.

40   Andrew Renton makes similar comments in relation to Beckett's later prose piece, *Stirrings still*, in his essay, 'Disabled figures: from the *Residua* to *Stirrings still*', in John Pilling (ed.), *The Cambridge Companion to Beckett*, p. 172.

41   When the text of *Quad* was produced as a television play by Süddeutscher Rundfunk in Stuttgart in 1981, it was transmitted in two versions, *Quadrat 1* and *Quadrat 2*. *Quadrat 1* was shot in colour and *Quadrat 2* in black and white, at a slower speed and with the percussion beats removed. Beckett apparently commented that the second version was the same play taking place 'a hundred thousand years later'; quoted by Martin Esslin, 'Towards the Zero of Language', in James Acheson and Kateryna Arthur, *Beckett's Later Drama and Fiction*, p. 44.

11

Writing Images, Images of Writing: Tom Phillips's *A Humument* and Peter Greenaway's Textual Cinema

Paula Geyh and Arkady Plotnitsky

... when you read text, you see image, when you view the image, you read text. Would not this be an exciting module, a template, a basis on which to reconsider some cinema practice?[1]

Peter Greenaway

Writing and Writing-Image: From Derrida to Phillips and Greenaway, From Phillips and Greenaway to Derrida

In recent years, artists' books – texts that self-consciously investigate the conceptual and material form of the book – have become a focus of study for the insights they offer into the history and future of the book as a medium of information transmission. Artists' books complement more conventional literary practices by using visual and other 'non-literary' elements. By so doing, they exemplify and illuminate the complex relationships between (print) literature and other visual media, as we shall illustrate here by considering Tom Phillips's *A Humument*.[2] Ultimately, however, and in order to pursue this task more effectively, we would like in this essay to explore a richer and more complex case of the interaction between literature and other media. In particular, we will discuss the conjunction, defined by Jacques Derrida's concept of 'writing' and its extensions, of the artists' book, as exemplified by *A Humument,* and postmodern cinema, as exemplified by Peter Greenaway's films. Greenaway's cinema has been intimately connected to literature and the idea of writing and related concepts, such as the book, throughout his career. Phillips's and Greenaway's works may be seen as reflecting and engaging with the process that Derrida defined in 1967 in *Of Grammatology* as 'the end of the book and the beginning of writing,' using the latter term in the extended and radical sense Derrida gave to it.[3] So conceived, 'writing' can no longer be understood conventionally as a representation of speech. The concept of speech itself is also reconfigured, along with other classical concepts involved in our understanding of writing, beginning with 'thought' (often seen as better represented by speech than writing) and 'language.' Ultimately, Derrida's 'writing' replaces language (as traditionally understood from Plato to Saussure and beyond) with a more complex dynamics of meaning production and communication. In 'Signature Event Context,' Derrida specifies the 'nuclear traits of all writing' as follows:

> (1) the break with the horizon of communication as the communication of consciousnesses and presences, and as the linguistic or semantic transport of meaning; (2) the subtraction of all writing from the semantic horizon or the hermeneutic horizon which, at least as a horizon of meaning, lets itself be punctured by writing [thus making writing irreducible, contrary to the claims of the programs based on these conceptions]; (3) the necessity of, in a way, *separating* the concept of polysemia [as a controlled plurality of meaning] from the concept I have elsewhere named *dissemination* [the uncontrollable plurality of meaning], which is also the concept of writing; (4) the disqualification or the limit of the concept of the 'real' or 'linguistic' context, whose theoretical determination or empirical saturation are, strictly speaking, rendered impossible or insufficient by writing.[4]

Derrida's deconstructive matrix (which, in addition to writing itself, involves other Derridean structures, such as *dissemination, trace, différance,* and so forth) has tremendous theoretical and practical potential. Specifically and most significantly for our purposes here, it allows one to attach writing, as a reconfigurative operator, to other (conventionally conceived) denominations, writing itself included, and transform them. There may be *writing*-thought, *writing*-speech, *writing*-writing, *writing*-reading, *writing*-philosophy, *writing*-literature, *writing*-painting, *writing*-cinema, and so forth.[5]

Both Phillips's and Greenaway's works enact this transition to writing in their respective art forms, cross the boundaries between them, and link them as writing. Thus, these works become the art of what may be called '*writing*-image,' using this latter term by analogy with (and extending) Gilles Deleuze's concepts of 'movement-image' and, especially, 'time-image,' through which he approaches modern cinema. We will also suggest here that these cinematic practices are supplanted by the '*writing*-image' of Greenaway's cinema.[6] According to Deleuze, the history of modern cinema is defined not so much by its specifically cinematographic (as opposed to, say, literary or photographic) portrayal of things, characters, events, and so forth. Instead it is defined, first (prior roughly to the Second World War), by the image of movement itself (whatever is in motion), movement occurring in time, and, then (after the Second World War), by the image of time itself, rather than of anything, now including even movement, that occurs in time. On the other hand, a crucial part of Derrida's deconstructive project is his deconstruction of the concept(s) of time and the rethinking of these concepts in terms of and specifically as the effects of writing in Derrida's sense, which may, we would argue, also be applied to the time-image of modern cinema. It is beyond the scope of this chapter to consider Derrida's analysis itself of time and writing, and is not necessary for our purposes. Our argument is instead that Greenaway's films enact the image of writing in Derrida's sense, the *writing*-image, in part by way of a cinematic deconstruction in practice (where Phillips-like techniques are often employed) of the time-image of modern cinema. Accordingly Greenaway's work may be seen as postmodern at least in this sense of being the art of *writing*-image rather than the time-image (or earlier movement-image) of modern cinema. This view may be linked to Greenaway's remark, 'I've made comments about cinema not reaching Cubism yet, but there hasn't even been an awareness of Joyce. When these other art forms have taken great imaginative leaps, cinema tragically has remained very conventional and backward-looking.'[7] A forward-looking cinema may require the *writing*-image. (We will return to the significance of Cubism in Greenaway below.)

The relationships between Phillips's and Greenaway's art manifest themselves most directly and most graphically in their collaborative project *A TV Dante*, a 1989 television version of Dante's *Inferno*, based on Phillips's annotations (derived from *A Humument*) of his illustrated translation of Dante's *Inferno*.[8] We will argue that it has much greater significance both in the work of these two artists and for understanding the evolving relationship between the newer visual media, especially cinema, and older literary forms. This collaboration, we argue, significantly affected Greenaway's subsequent work, such as *Prospero's Books* and especially *The Pillow Book*, on which, in addition to the *Inferno*, we shall primarily focus here. While all of Greenaway's work is a practice of *writing*-image, the influence of Phillips's work led to the introduction of more radical inscriptive elements into Greenaway's art and a more radical form of transformation of the movement-image and time-image of modern cinema into the *writing*-image of postmodern cinema.[9]

The art of '*writing*-image' is both the art of *writing* images and the art of *images* of writing, and of their fusion in, one might say, the *writing* of 'writing' in Derrida's sense. At the same time, both a (new) art of the book and a (new) art of cinema (re)emerge, rather than disappear. This type of reemergence, however, may have been implied in Derrida's argument concerning 'the end of the book and the beginning of writing' as well, given the way it is inscribed in the textual and conceptual network of his works. Derrida's statement should not be read in the ontological or historical sense, but in the sense that writing, as Derrida understands it, is a condition or even *the* condition of the possibility of the book. As he further explains in *Positions* (the point is more implicit elsewhere in earlier works), human culture has been defined by 'the end of the book' and 'the beginning of writing' throughout its history, even though the character of the relationships between the book and writing has been different.[10] Rigorously considered, the specific character of these relationships is different each time, or rather each time is defined by the irreducible interplay of more or less general and more or less particular traits. In other words, Derrida's writing or the transitions (in either direction) between the book and writing cannot be fully defined by a general concept. At the same time, some measure of conceptual generality is required as well, since the field of writing cannot be absolutely singular either, even though each event of writing is singular, unique. Accordingly, a very different relationship between the particular and the general emerges, both in this *particular* case and *in general*.

In the present case, too, on the one hand, there is both a (more or less) general determination of Phillips's and Greenaway's work as '*writing*-image,' as explained above, and, we will argue, as a particular formation of their '*writing*-images' through the conjunction of the city, the body, and the book in their irreducible relation to writing. (We will be tracing this formation throughout this essay.) On the other hand, these two determinations, general and particular, cannot ultimately be dissociated, although they can, of course, and often must be considered separately, for strategic or analytic purposes. The conjunction of the city, the body, and the book appears to be not merely a particular case of writing, but instead the primary, if not the only, way to enact writing in its post-Derridean sense at this point of history. That is, there may be no other writing in our – let us say, postmodern – world. The main reason for this is that in the postmodern world it no longer appears to be possible, virtually anywhere, to avoid the impact of the materiality of the city, of the body, and of the book, especially insofar as we see all three in relation to and as forms of writing (in Derrida's sense) and as conjoined within writing. First of all, it is difficult, under 'the postmodern condition,' to think, either in terms of theory or in terms of practice, of a disembodied mind or subjectivity in general, free either from the materiality of the body (extending even beyond the brain) or from the materiality of language and/as writing, although both ideas or, one might say, ideologies persist along different lines.[11] Secondly, however, given the postmodern condition, the city (broadly conceived) becomes an irreducible part of the materiality/ies in question, Derrida's writing included. It goes without saying that this view does not abolish mind or subjectivity, conscious or unconscious, but resituates them, along with materiality itself. Materiality is now in turn *reinscribed*, also in the sense of being irreducibly linked to writing, as Derrida makes clear in *Positions*.[12] The present essay is an attempt to argue this case by using Phillips's and Greenaway's work, in which this particular economy of writing and of writing-image appears as defining our world (it would be difficult to speak of mimetic representation in this case). Accordingly, we shall explain and justify the claims just made as we proceed. It may be briefly noted here that the city and the book, especially as writing in Derrida's sense, inhabit one's existence virtually everywhere. Or, more accurately, the city and the book become the habitat of the world and the subject, dislocating or deconstructing both the world and the subject. This happens in part by virtue of the specifically postmodern dissemination of information, beginning with the very means of information (cinema, television, computers and other forms of digital technology, such as fax machines). As we will explain by using Greenaway's works as allegories of this postmodern dynamics, the body reciprocally participates in this process of interactively disseminating inscription. The term 'dissemination' is used here in Derrida's sense, the sense correlatively interactive with *writing*, as explained earlier. Even though defined by the conjunction in question, this dynamics is itself multiple, in part because each of the elements involved (the city, the body, and the book) of the interactions between them may take a different and even singular, unique form at each point, in each place, and so may such entities as 'points' or 'places.'

The Workings of Writing and Writing-Image: From Phillips to Greenaway, from Greenway to Phillips

Tom Phillips's work probably needs some introduction, since it may be less familiar than that of Greenaway. Tom Phillips is a British artist, writer, translator, filmmaker, photographer and composer who studied Anglo-Saxon literature at Oxford and art at the Ruskin School of Drawing and Fine Art. Inspired by William S. Burroughs's use of the 'cut-up' technique as a way of critiquing existing systems of thought, Phillips began work on the ongoing project that is *A Humument* in the mid-1960s. He started by materially 'reworking' an obscure and undistinguished Victorian novel, W. H. Mallock's *A Human Document*. Painting and otherwise 'treating' the pages of the novel using acrylic gouache, pen and ink, type, and collage, Phillips fashioned a text that drew its 'material' from the pages of Mallock's original. By linking selected words on the existing pages to create 'rivers' of text that flow through fields of images, Phillips produced a new narrative that was related to yet quite distinct from the original. This 'reworking' of Mallock's novel formed the first edition of *A Humument*.

In the years since the publication of its first edition, *A Humument* has become the center of a massive web of literary and multimedia intertextuality. The novel itself currently exists in three editions – a fourth is underway – with each new edition featuring from sixty to a hundred new pages replacing those in the first edition. Its literary offspring include *The Heart of A Humument*, a tiny book measuring 3' x 4' and created from the central core of the rectangles of *A Human Document*'s pages; a book called *Trailer* that was taken from 'the cutting room floor' of *A Humument*; and *DOC*, yet another *Humument*-generated narrative in the form of a series of affidavits and testimonies about a lecherous doctor. Phillips has based multiple series of paintings, numbering over 300 individual works, on *A Humument*. He has recast it into a ballet scenario, *The Quest for Grenville*, and into the full-length opera *IRMA*, 'whose libretto, music, staging instructions and costume designs all come from *A Human Document*.'[13] (One of Greenaway's most recent works is an opera-libretto as well, *Writing to Vermeer.*)[14] Finally, Phillips has generated a hundred 'parallel texts' from *A Humument* and used them to annotate his own illustrated translation of Dante's *Inferno*, which he subsequently made into *A TV Dante* with Greenaway.

A Humument is a dramatic bringing together of the genre of the artists' book and the history of modernist and postmodernist art. Artists' books have come of age in the 20th century. The genre, however, has not only coexisted with but has also been part of virtually every major artistic movement of the past 100 years, from Cubism to Futurism to the Russian Avant-Garde to Conceptual art. As we explained from the outset, the artists' book complements conventional literary genres by visual and other 'non-literary' elements and contributes to a deeper understanding of the materiality of the book – those elements such as typeface, paper, binding, and design that constitute the book as a physical, material object. They often do so, moreover, by utilizing the resources supplied by modernist and postmodernist art. Over the past few decades, this concept of the book as a material object has helped to redefine the phenomenon of literature itself and the nature of writing in general (including in Derrida's sense), and to illuminate the complex relationships between literature and other media, especially in more radically mixed works of recent decades. The conjunction of Phillips's work and Greenaway's cinema of *writing*-image are a particularly dramatic example of these interrelations, where, through the workings of writing, the key elements defining the work of both artists effectively come together, and enrich and redefine both works and both art forms.

For Phillips, his book or, as it has been called, this 'dynamic generator and receiver of words, images, and ideas,' has become a machine to think with.[15] It 'writes' in Derrida's sense, as thinking is itself superimposed upon and is an effect of generalized textuality, a process itself allegorized by Phillips's book as a 'book *after* writing.' Phillips himself speaks of *A Humument* in more traditional terms as producing the 'structures, connections, correspondences, and systems that link the sensual, visual and intellectual worlds.'[16] These systems have undeniable game-like aspects to them ('is / book / game?' the unnamed narrator of *A Humument* asks on page 257), from the rules Phillips has imposed upon himself (including retaining the original page numbers and structure of the original book, and using only material from the text itself rather than importing material from other sources) to color codes that link pages thematically, various numerological structures and symbols, and an assortment of visual references to chess, checkers, jigsaw puzzles, and crossword puzzles in the text.[17] Similarly, as part of his effort to create 'a cinema of ideas, not plots' (or, to put it another way, to move from the cinema of the time-image into the cinema of the *writing*-image), Greenaway often structures his films using systems of classification – numbers, alphabets, color-codes, taxonomies, categories, catalogues, and games – that relate to his broad artistic, musical, and literary interests, which he describes as being 'strong on lists, classifying, encyclopedias, and the nouvelle roman' (qtd. in Woods, p. 18). The oeuvres of both Phillips and Greenaway are distinguished by their immense, ever-expanding networks of intertextuality – the massive interlinking of characters, motifs, visual and literary references, themes, and concepts of different works of their own and of others – which is one of the most pronounced and, in recent years, well-examined effects of writing in Derrida's sense. In order to relate these structures, connections, and correspondences within the books and films discussed here to the ongoing, dynamic, and open-ended operation of writing in Derrida's more radical sense, we shall briefly examine the mechanisms by which they are created.

First, *A Humument*'s text contains an extensive range of visual references – Van Gogh, Seurat, the Dadaists, Klee, Jasper Johns, Roy Lichtenstein, Francis Bacon, Julian Schnabel, A.J. Kitaj, and others. The Cubists are particularly significant, among them Braque, Gris, Léger, and Picasso. Beyond visual references and allusions, their works also serve as conceptual models for Phillips's, as, it can be shown, they do for Greenaway and for Derrida. In particular, such models provide certain disassembling and reassembling techniques of the kind we have become familiar with in Derrida. These techniques may be used either directly or in exposing previously hidden elements and relations, which one can then reassemble into a new configuration. (It would be difficult to speak of the same object after such a reassemblage.)[18] *A Humument* also interlinks with literary works such as the *Aeneid*, *Hamlet*, and *Ulysses*, all of which find their way into Phillips and Greenaway's version of Dante's *Inferno*, for which the *Aeneid* and the *Odyssey* are obviously crucial. We shall consider how these multiple links function in the book presently. Before we do so, however, we want to briefly examine the relationship between *A Humument* and Mallock's original, which may, again, be seen as a parodic reenactment of the relationships between Dante's *Inferno* and Virgil's *Aeneid*. In his notes to the text, Phillips observes that *A Humument* seems a good title for 'a book exhumed from…another.'[19] This idea of bringing something to the surface, uncovering the hidden or buried, is reiterated on the first page of the text: 'sing / I / a / book / a book of art / of / mind / art / and / that / which / he / hid / reveal I' (1987, 1997, p. 1). In this model, the text of *A Humument* in effect lies beneath that of *A Human Document*. More immediately, Phillips's superimposition of paint and other materials on the pages of Mallock's text might easily suggest the opposite idea: that it is *A Humument* that lies atop *A Human Document*. Neither, however, seems to adequately describe what is in fact happening here. In part contrary to Phillips's own view, it appears that any vertical or hierarchical model (whichever text governs the relationship) is inadequate. Rather, one is inclined to think along the lines of, speaking in Deleuze and Guattari's terms, a rhizomatic or horizontal model of interactive networks of relationships ungoverned by any single hierarchy.[20] From this perspective, in particular, the model is not a palimpsest but a hypertext or, more generally and more accurately, a parallel-interactive text, a text open to parallel-interactive processing, which type of model hypertexts realize. As we will see shortly, Phillips and Greenaway's *A TV Dante* deploys a similar hypertextual model.

On a page interlaced with wandering networks of lines converging on and diverging from nodes, Phillips's text offers its own rendition of this idea. '[A] / door opened / on / a glitter of / fanciful / passages, and / rooms,' one page begins, 'on / the / net; his mean / mosaic / and / suite of / night / routine' (1997, p. 97). The 'night routine' obliquely refers to the book's many equations of the creative process with dreaming. Very early in the text, Phillips glosses his own text as 'my / pillow / -book; the / puzzled / sheets' bringing together the page and his bed linens (possibly 'written upon' by the movements of his body) in both images (1987, 1997, p. 3). Later an unnamed 'I' observes: 'I dream with my pen balanced in my hand, fragments of poetry / fragments' (1987, 1997, p. 159). Arguably, the concept of 'the pillow book' of Greenaway's film is defined by analogous economies of fragmentation and inscription, although it also has, as does Phillips's book, other, much older, genealogies.

Phillips defines *A Humument* as a 'forgettive recycler,' a term that opens up the question of the interactive roles of memory and forgetting in the workings of literary and artistic imagination. To create the text of *A Humument*, Phillips had to detach Mallock's words from their original context, to 'forget' the plot of the original novel while remembering the words themselves. The original is simultaneously forgotten (negated), remembered (conserved), and exceeded (superceded) – many of the 'rivers' (both narrative and material) of Phillips's text extend beyond the boundaries of the printed pages of *A Human Document*. Depending upon one's reading, one can see this machinery either as that of the Hegelian *Aufhebung* (defined by this triple action), or as a Nietzschean or Derridean deconstruction of this Hegelian operation, as Nietzsche's 'active forgetting' or Derrida's 'iterability,' another of the key aspects of writing in his sense. This same mechanism of forgetting yet remembering is deployed in Phillips and Greenaway's *A TV Dante*, where, for example, clips from nature documentaries are iterated so as to act as commentary on the text.[21] These clips are frequently presented as 'windows' opening inside the visual field of the other images, in effect creating a simultaneous, hypertextual-like link. In these aspects, too, *A TV Dante* recapitulates the structure of Dante's *Inferno*. As Greenaway has observed, 'There's a way in which Dante's *Inferno* is forever a chopped narrative…always developing new leads, wandering off in different directions, full of side-events, small stories in brackets' (qtd. in Woods, p. 227).

The ways in which all of these texts – Phillips's *A Humument*, Phillips and Greenaway's *A TV Dante*, and Greenaway's *Prospero's Books* and *The Pillow Book*, among others – overflow their own boundaries and stream into other texts and contexts is signaled by the broken, shifting frames and borders of their images. The borders of *A TV Dante*'s images, like those of *Prospero's Books* and *The Pillow Book*, are in perpetual flux. They disintegrate along their outer edges and are interrupted by inserts, titles, and subtitles. Again and again, image is superimposed upon image, frame opens into frame. The worlds of these films are all much as Greenaway has described Prospero's island in *Prospero's Books: a film of Shakespeare's the Tempest*:

> [a] world [that] is appreciated and referenced with…architecture, paintings, and classical literature…. With such a fabric, it will be no surprise that it is an island full of superimposed images, of shifting mirrors and mirror-images – true mirages – where pictures conjured by text can be as tantalisingly substantial as objects and facts and events, constantly framed and re-framed. This framing and reframing becomes like the text itself – a motif – reminding the viewer that it is all an illusion constantly fitted into a rectangle…into a picture frame, a film frame.[22]

Like Greenaway's films, Phillips's *A Humument* is a thoroughly self-conscious text, and it is, therefore, not surprising that it contains numerous allusions to these processes of forgetting, remembering, and exceeding (or superceding). 'Dogma / the words of / some miraculous source?' one page asks, 'the truth of / infallible traditions?' '*[B]etrayal* / take a new turn,' the text urges, addressing, one surmises, the agnostic author himself (1997, p. 243). Many of the literary allusions in *A Humument* practice this betrayal, 'a new turn' or détournement of the source text. Forster's 'only connect,' an injunction that captures Phillips's creative spirit, is echoed and then transformed into the equally apt 'oddly connect' (1987, 1997, p. 251). Stein's famous modernist dictum: 'A rose is a rose is a rose' is rendered 'like / a rose / is / a / boast / is / a / boast' (1987, 1997, p. 159). 'Now / the / arts / connect' another page observes, 'so the changes made / the / book / continue' (1987, 1997, p. 7). 'The air seemed full / of dead generations,' another page observes, 'I / ring / arms, and / the woman' – one of multiple references and renditions of the opening lines of Virgil's *Aeneid*: 'Of arms and the man I sing' (1987, 1997, p. 141). Even the first page of *A Humument*, which begins 'Sing I a book / a book of art / of mind art,' might be read as a very askew rendition of Virgil's invocation. Such references and renditions open up yet another series of links – another river of remembering/forgetting in the text – to Dante's *Inferno*, to which we will return presently.

Cultures of Writing and Writing-Image: The City, the Body, and the Book From Phillips and Greenaway to Dante, from Dante to Phillips and Greenaway

Whether the relationships to or dislocation of the classical tradition, or the radical fragmenting of the work itself are at stake, both modernist and postmodernist techniques are used by Phillips in *making* and/as *un*-making *A Humument*. The list of precursors and influences upon the book here would extend from Cubism and Surrealism to Rauschenberg in the visual arts, to T. S. Eliot's 'The Waste Land' and William S. Burroughs's 'cut-ups' in literature, to John Cage in music. It is these modernist and postmodernist strategies of fragmentation, collage, détournement and pastiche that enable Phillips to investigate the materiality and the very concept of the book. On the other hand, his collaboration with Greenaway on *A TV Dante* (which is a similar deployment of modernist and postmodernist aesthetic or counter-aesthetic machinery) and other offspring of Phillips's book or *un*-book, establish, as we mentioned earlier, the way in which the genre of the artists' book reciprocally shapes other forms of artistic endeavour. It is not only or even primarily a matter of reference and allusion to *A Humument* itself in the film, but rather a transfer of key structural or constructional elements of Phillips's project. It is quite apparent that the very same elements affect Greenaway's other works, in particular *Prospero's Books*, *The Pillow Book*, and, most recently, his libretto for the opera *Writing to Vermeer*. Like Phillips's *A Humument*, Greenaway's films commonly spawn numerous offspring, and they, too, are shaped by the same or related structural elements. The progeny of *Prospero's Books*, for example, include the book *Prospero's Books: a film of Shakespeare's the Tempest*; *Ex Libris Prospero*, a collection of images from the film; *Miranda*, a play about *The Tempest*'s characters' voyage back to Milan; and a novel entitled *Prospero's Creatures* that takes up the 'allegorical creatures that dart about in the penumbra areas of the film'.[23] Such assemblages of interconnected texts might be seen as postmodern transformations or translations of Wagner's modernist ideal of the *Gesamtkunstwerk*.

Writing to Vermeer would require a separate analysis, but, as the title indicates, it brings together writing and painting yet again, in ways analogous to the

Derridean and post-Derridean analysis and deconstruction of writing. (It would, of course, be naïve to read the title only in epistolary terms of a letter to Vermeer, unless one in turn brings the whole thematic of writing into such a reading, which one might ultimately need to do in any event.) Indeed, while these elements are enhanced in Greenaway's work in the wake of his collaborations with Phillips, they are found in all of his work, which, as these titles indicate, is fundamentally concerned with the problematics of the book and/as writing. These relationships, while in many ways unique, are also in many ways exemplary of the reciprocal economy of the relationships between the artists' book and modernist or postmodernist art. We may also see these relationships as beginning with Dante and his relationships with medieval illuminated manuscripts, an important reference and in turn a model for Phillips. It would difficult to say, however, which one is written upon which.

We will now trace, within the limits a single essay permits, the relationships between the general practice of writing in Derrida's sense and the conjunction of the city, the body, and the book in Greenaway's work. *A TV Dante* offers a paradigmatic case here, by the same token reflecting (on) and expanding the celebrated encyclopedic or (this is less commented upon and less well understood) *written*-encyclopedic complexity of Dante's *Comedia*. According to Greenaway, '...each canto lends itself to twelve-minute news summary timings, but it has vast complexity. Some have seen it as a compendium of all known information of the world, circa 1300. An encyclopaedic work – and we wanted to be lexicographers in sympathy with it' (qtd. in Woods, p. 225). The city-body-book-writing economy is manifest through the film, both thematically and, more significantly, inscriptively – that is, insofar as the content, too, is defined by the form of this conjunction. *A TV Dante* is replete with shots of conflagrations consuming cities, of bodies descending the stairs of the various levels of hell, of vast libraries, of major military and political conflicts that defined the very concept of the European and, eventually, geo-political city from Ancient Rome, to Dante's Florence, to Mussolini's Rome, to name some of them. This conjunction may be traced as well throughout many of Greenaway's earlier and subsequent films, including *The Belly of an Architect* (1987), in which the Roman cityscape is punctuated by classical statues inscribed with graffiti, much as the architect Kracklite scribbles on photocopies of the belly of a statue of the Emperor Augustus – an action that prefigures the inscribed bodies in their conjunction with the *writing*-image of the city in *A TV Dante* (1989), *Prospero's Books* (1991), and *The Pillow Book* (1996).

The conjunction is even more important in *Prospero's Books*. When the pages of *The Book of Architecture and Other Music* are opened, Greenaway writes, 'plans and diagrams spring up fully-formed. There are definitive models of buildings constantly shaded by moving cloud-shadow. Noontime piazzas fill and empty with noisy crowds, lights flicker in nocturnal urban landscapes and music is played in the halls and towers. With this book, Prospero rebuilt the island into a palace of libraries that recapitulate all the architectural ideas of the Renaissance' (*Prospero's Books*, p. 21). When the pages of another of the books, *The Vesalius Anatomy of Birth*, are opened, they move and throb and bleed. To generate the books' images and effects, Greenaway makes extensive use of the digital, electronic Graphic Paintbox, which he refers to as 'the newest Gutenberg technology' (*Prospero's Books*, p. 28). 'This machine,' Greenaway observes, 'as its name suggests, links the vocabulary of electronic picture-taking with the traditions of the artist's pen, palette and brush, and like them permits a personal signature,' (*Prospero's Books*, p. 28) thus bringing together the city, the cinematic 'book,' writing, and the body (the 'personal signature' and the pages that bleed).

Within *A TV Dante*, this conjunction of the city, the body, and the book is of course also motivated, if not overdetermined, by the equally irreducible role of an analogous conjunction in Dante's text.[24] This is the case at the very least thematically but, one might argue, inscriptively as well, even though the (more conventionally literary) character of this inscription is different and is differently historically determined. Dante's hell is a complex superposition of the city and the body of Satan, through the inside of which Dante and Virgil travel on their way out, to Purgatorio. It may also be seen as a kind of body without organs in Deleuze and Guattari's sense.[25]

Upon this body without organs, the fragmented bodies of the sinners, the sinners as forever unfulfilled and forever Oedipalized desiring machines, and the fragmented books are inscribed and continuously superimposed, both thematically and in the inscriptions of Dante's text itself. The Phillips and Greenaway's film takes advantage of this economy by using the short format to convey and enhance some of these elements visually rather than through a comprehensive reading of Dante's text, of which, in fact, a very limited portion is presented (Cantos 1-8). There is, however, yet another level of fusion, perhaps most crucial to Dante's work and its long-term impact on modern and even postmodern culture: the fusion of the city, the body, and the book is *interfused* with the processes and workings of writing. It is not possible, within the confines of this chapter, to address the question of the political in Dante and in the film (and specifically in relation to the question of writing, which is always irreducibly political even though never quite reducible to politics alone.) It is, however, clearly germane to the film, from the visual depictions of and commentaries on the political struggles in Dante's Florence to those of Mussolini and beyond to the contemporary references.

We also stress the fact that both movement-images and time-images in Deleuze's sense in the film are consistently enacted as emerging from the textual working of writing, rather than structuring the work in the way they do in most modern cinema, as analyzed by Deleuze, or to some degree in Dante, whose

Comedia can be seen in terms of the time-images of Dante's journey – its many interfused movements and temporalities. In the latter case, we encounter the time of Dante's journey through Hell, and then Purgatory and Paradise, his historical time, the overarching history of Europe from Virgil's Rome to Dante's Florence, and ultimately cosmological history. Phillips and Greenaway sometimes take advantage of Dante's own deployment of various textual elements and sometimes add their own. This process is indicated as allegorized, for example, by the quasi-digitalized and textualized image of the clock opening each segment.[26] It inscribes the time-points of Dante's journey, almost in the manner of (and perhaps alluding to) Einstein's relativity theory, as derivatives, as the *effects* of the clock, rather than as anything existing independently and self-sufficiently (in the manner of Newtonian physics) and merely measured or shown by a clock. This clock also symbolically measures, that is, generates the accelerated tempo of the film's own inscription, even though it can of course also be read as measuring the beating of Dante's heart, if one ignores the inscriptive elements just mentioned.

This also anticipates the more vastly techno-textual, and digitalized, elements of *Prospero's Books*. According to Peter S. Donaldson, '*Prospero's Books* is an anticipatory or proleptic allegory of the digital future, figuring destruction of libraries and their rebirth as 'magically' enhanced electronic books.'[27] It is significant that John Gielgud is both Virgil in Dante's *Inferno* and Prospero. Beyond the fact that Virgil's *Aeneid* was a written epic, a book, as opposed to Homer's works, Gielgud's appearance in both roles may also be read as a deliberate link between both works, similar to many such links in Greenaway's other works, or those in Phillips's interconnected texts.

The Pillow Book is a text (in either sense) of inscribed bodies and body parts, from the inscription of 'the book of silence' on the tongue of a messenger, to a more radical bodily mutilation (which is also a form of textual synthesis) of the inscribed skin of Jerome, the dead lover of both the female protagonist and the male book publisher. Jerome (not unlike St. Jerome) is both a writer and a translator, whose skin is now made into a book. All these events take place against the background of, and are fused with, the city. This city is already inscribed or, more accurately, it emerges as a city reciprocally with multiple fields of inscription, and in the process forms the cityscape of writing in Derrida's sense. This proliferation of city writing, shaping and defining the city and culture, is, it is true, found elsewhere. English city inscription appears throughout *The Pillow Book* as well, beginning with the very word 'books,' 'English books,' the name of the bookstore owned by the publisher, who is also the lover of the protagonist's father (also a writer). In Japanese cities, however, such as Kyoto (which is fittingly the main Japanese site of the story, as the rest takes place in Hong Kong), this inscription is especially pronounced as an irreducible, constitutive part of city architecture and city life, rather than merely a supplement to it. Multiple inscriptions are not merely added to the buildings, but actively shape and even define the city as a space. Accordingly, one must here think in terms of Derrida's supplementarity as the possibility that (through writing) produces, as an effect, that to which it is supposed to be added on. In this case, it may appear that inscriptions are merely added to the city, but in fact they also make the city the city; they produce the city as much as they are produced by it.[28] We also recall that, in Derrida, supplementarity is also, and in turn irreducibly, linked to sexuality, as both reciprocally define each other. The point is made especially clear in his famous reading of Rousseau in *Of Grammatology*, but is implicit throughout.[29]

The same situation is both thematized in and inscriptively enacted throughout *The Pillow Book*. The protagonist's sexuality and her own body, to the degree we can even distinguish them, are as indissociable from the inscribed city as they are from the inscription on the body, or from the body as an inscription. One of Greenaway's or Derrida's points is that we cannot dissociate an object or any entity, such as the body, from inscription. That is, there is no uninscribed (or unfragmented) body, city, book, or anything else. Or, more rigorously, the body, the city, and the book, with which we are especially concerned here, or anything else, are effects of inscription or/as fragmentation, just as time is the effect of the inscribed clock, provided of course that we extend the concept of inscription to Derrida's sense of writing. Here, of course, we argue that in *The Pillow Book* and in the postmodern world it reflects, the actuality or materiality of the city/ies, the body/ies, and the book/s, and, most especially, of their irreducible interactions is the primary dynamics enabling the workings of writing.

The film opens with the ideographic painting upon the face and the body of the protagonist, Nagiko, showing (in either sense) that the face and the body emerge from inscription (the cosmology accompanying the event allegorizes this). The sequence inescapably and probably deliberately (especially given other events of the film) reminds one of Kafka's inscription on/as the body in 'In the Penal Colony.'[30] From here it moves – or, as it were, 'movies' – to a lavish fashion show against the background of the cityscape, defined (along with the show itself) by the irreducible and irreducibly counter-cultural translation. (A reference to the Vatican fashion show in Fellini's *Roma* is equally inescapable.) This translation in the sense of Derrida's writing precedes (again, logically rather than ontologically) and gives rise to any possible original. Superimposed upon the images of the fashion show is the ideographic text of Section 150 of *The Pillow Book of Sei Shonagon*, and upon it, images of the Empress and her court and nearby (in a temporal elision), Nagiko's aunt narrating Shonagon's detailed description of the Empress's formal robes. What arises here is the sense that there may be no such thing as an absolutely naked, undressed and un-cross-dressed, body, any more than an uninscribed or unfragmented body, a body that would not be always already a book, a *writing*-image, and a city. As we have indicated above, this formulation is transposable to, say, the city that is always already an inscription, a fragmented body, a fashion show of cross-dressing, and so forth.

The inscribed body, in the sense just outlined, becomes Nagiko's ultimate project and art form. In addition to the inscriptive complexities just discussed, in this art form we can no longer distinguish between the dead and the alive either. We recall that, as Derrida's reading of Blanchot in 'Living on: Border Lines' and related works shows, writing is always 'living on,' sur-vivre, and indeed life-death, *'la vie la mort.'*[31] This gives a radically deconstructive or perhaps post-deconstructive sense to the association of death and writing (or of both with woman and sexuality), which has, in its classical (undeconstructed form) defined the history of both. This transition is itself clearly allegorized by the film in linking the original 999 *Pillow Book* by the lady-in-waiting Sei Shonagon and the protagonist's (both of whom have the same name, Nagiko) pillow book, which is allegorically converted into a *writing*-book as the city, the body, and book aggregate in 1996. '9' is of course also the number assigned by Dante to Beatrice.

The concept of the artists' book is here engaged and redefined throughout, since Nagiko's writing and (they are the same) her body, her clothes, her city – all of her life practices – are that of the artists' book, as they continuously refine and redefine the genre and make it a defining art form of our culture.[32] In the process the book is made into an effect of, interactively, both writing and of the interfusion of the city, the body, and the book. It also follows that it also produces or contributes to the production of the city and the body, and even to writing in Derrida's sense.

There may ultimately be no way out of this double-bind entanglement, which *The Pillow Book* multiply allegorizes. But then perhaps, while this entanglement makes our life difficult and even intolerable, it also makes our life possible--at least our intellectual and cultural life. One could, though, make a case for our biological life as well, say, the life of the body, assuming that we can distinguish between or at least disentangle them. Modern biology and genetics tell us that life, too, is a form of inscription. In any event, it appears that these entanglements and their many double-binds are inevitable at least in the case of the always already inscribed body, city, and book, which are, at least for now, our inescapable habitat – the book and the city of the body, the city of the body and the book, the body of the city and the book.... All of these permutations and still others, for example, those of literature and other media, appear to be unavoidable.

Notes

1   Paula Willoquet-Maricondi, 'Fleshing the Text: Greenaway's *Pillow Book* and the Erasure of the Body,' *Postmodern Culture* 9.2 (January 1999): 34.

2   Tom Phillips, *A Humument*, 2nd ed. (London: Thames and Hudson, 1987) and Tom
     Phillips, *A Humument*, 3rd ed. (London: Thames and Hudson, 1997). Subsequent
     references will be made in brackets in the main text.

3   Jacques Derrida, *Of Grammatology*, trans. Gayatri Chakravorty Spivak (Baltimore:
     Johns Hopkins University Press, 1974) pp. 6-26.

4   Jacques Derrida, *Margins of Philosophy*, trans. Alan Bass (Chicago: University of
     Chicago Press, 1982) p.316.

5   On this point, see especially Derrida's reading of Stéphane Mallarmé in 'The Double
     Session,' *Dissemination*, trans. Barbara Johnson (Chicago: University of Chicago
     Press, 1981), pp. 173-285. The essay also shows or in turn *inscribes* Mallarmé's text
     as arguably the best example of an 'enactment' of writing in Derrida's sense by a
     literary text found in Derrida's work. It may well also be the best example of Derrida's
     usage of literature to build his philosophical conceptuality, including, in particular,
     'dissemination,' as defined above. Both Phillips's and Greenaway's art work in this
     way as well, specifically by coupling literature to visual media and technologies, which
     are also found in Mallarmé's writing (in either sense), cinematic technologies included.

6   See Gilles Deleuze, *Cinema 1: The Time-Image*, trans. Hugh Tomlinson and Barbara
     Habberjam (Minneapolis: University of Minnesota Press, 1986) and *Cinema 2: The
     Movement-Image*, trans. Hugh Tomlinson and Robert Galta (Minneapolis: University
     of Minnesota Press, 1989).

7   Marlene Rodgers, 'Prospero's Books—Word and Spectacle: An Interview with Peter
     Greenaway,' *Film Quarterly* 45:2 (Winter 1991-92) 13.

8   Tom Phillips and Peter Greenaway, dir, *A TV Dante*, Channel 4, 1989.

9   For a discussion of the commonalities between Phillips and Greenaway's multimedia
     artistic practices, see Alan Woods, *Being Naked—Playing Dead: The Art of Peter
     Greenaway* (Manchester: Manchester University Press, 1996) pp. 128-29. Subsequent
     references will be made in brackets in the main text.

10   Jacques Derrida, *Positions*, trans. Alan Bass (Chicago: University of Chicago Press,
     1981) pp. 13-14. Subsequent references will be made in brackets in the main text.

11   We use the phrase 'the postmodern condition' (in singular) in the sense of the
     condition defined by postmodernity itself, following Jean-François Lyotard's argument
     in *The Postmodern Condition: A Report of Knowledge*, trans. Geoffrey Bennington and
     Brian Massumi (Minneapolis: University of Minnesota Press, 1984).

12   Derrida, *Positions*, p. 64.

13   Tom Phillips, *A Humument*, 1987, page three of unnumbered pages of 'Notes on *A
     Humument*.' (Also on page four of unnumbered pages in 1997 edition.)

14   'Writing to Vermeer,' music by Louis Andriessen, libretto by Peter Greenaway,
     directed by Saskia Boddeke and Peter Greenaway, Asko Ensemble and Schönberg
     Ensemble, conducted by Reinbert de Leeuw. U.S. Premiere, Lincoln Center Festival,
     July 2000.

15 Elizabeth Elsas, 'Treatment and Transformation: Tom Phillips's *A Humument*' (unpublished honors thesis, Harvard University), 3.

16 Tom Phillips, *Works, Texts to 1974* (Stuttgart: Edition Hansjörg Mayer, 1983), p. 17.

17 See in particular the play with the number seven on page 199 of *A Humument* (1987, 1997).

18 The second version of the approach just described virtually defines deconstruction and is found throughout Derrida. But one may also consider, for example, Derrida's assemblage of *différance*, arguably his most famous neologism, out of the elements of the discourses of, among others, Nietzsche, Saussure, Freud, Heidegger, Bataille, Levinas, and Lacan, which does not involve deconstruction. See Jacques Derrida, 'Différance,' *Margins of Philosophy*, pp. 1-28. One finds the key elements of this approach throughout Greenaway's work, and, as we have seen, Greenaway specifically appeals to Cubism as something not yet reached by cinema. His reassembling of Shakespeare in *Prospero's Books* is especially illustrative here. As will be seen presently, Phillips, too, deploys these reassembling strategies throughout, at every textual or signifying level. Analogous and related paradigms, such as Dadaism or certain versions of symbolist literature, such as Mallarmé, are pertinent here (or in Derrida) as well, as they exemplify and deploy the workings of writing in Derrida's sense, which is our main point here. Alan Woods offers a nice example of a multiple intertextual juncture, involving Cubism (here Marcel Duchamp's), in *A TV Dante*: 'In *A TV Dante*, Greenaway and Tom Phillips also animated them [Muybridge's figures], including his hound and his (male) nude descending a staircase. 'We regarded Muybridge's figures as the timeless abstracts of being and moving.' In using them within what is a kind of video history painting, a contemporary addition to a tradition of visualizing Dante that stretches back to the Renaissance, Greenaway and Phillips were both using Muybridge in the way he would have envisaged, moving from his supposedly neutral 'abstract' of motion to the work of art in which it was given a new artistic meaning and context: so that the hound becomes Dante's world (and later in the same canto, the Great Hound of Virgil's prophecy) and the nude an angel descending, as Christ did, from heaven. They simultaneously acknowledged Muybridge's own status as an image-maker, even if it is a status largely conferred through just such appropriations' (p. 58).

19 Tom Phillips, *A Humument*, 1997, page three of unnumbered pages of 'Notes on *A Humument*.'

20 See Gilles Deleuze and Félix Guattari, *A Thousand Plateaus: Capitalism and Schizophrenia*, trans. Brian Massumi (Minneapolis: University of Minneapolis Press, 1987).

21 Quoted in Rodgers pp. 11-19, 14. Greenaway also used Attenborough's *Life on Earth* in *A Zed and Two Noughts*.

22 Peter Greenaway, *Prospero's Books: a film of Shakespeare's the Tempest* (New York: Four Walls Eight Windows, 1991) p. 12.

23   Quoted in Rodgers, pp. 11-19, 14. Greenaway also observes in this interview that, 'Prospero has become an industry'; Ibid.

24   We keep in mind the transformation of each—the city, the body, and the book—and of the interaction between them in our own world.

25   See Gilles Deleuze and Félix Guattari, *Anti-Oedipus: Capitalism and Schizophrenia*, trans. Robert Hurley, Mark Seem, and Helen R. Lane (Minneapolis: University of Minnesota Press, 1983).

26   The text of *A Humument* similarly evidences an ongoing preoccupation with instruments of time measurement (clocks and sundials) and with time itself—time that stops ('time I can plead for you, / you/ still/ thing' (p. 223)), and time that circles back upon itself ('this / hour / and these / followed by hours of / time / And yet—and yet— / / / repeating / time is / until / afterwards' (p. 233)). Quotations appear on the same pages in both the 1987 and 1997 editions.

27   Peter S. Donaldson, 'Digital Archives,' *Postmodern Culture* 8:2 (May 1998), 2.

28   This analysis also extends and radicalizes Fredric Jameson's influential discussion of postmodern architecture in 'Postmodernism, or the Cultural Logic of Late Capitalism,' *Postmodernism, or the Cultural of Late Capitalism* (Durham, NC: Duke University Press, 1991), pp. 1-84, which does not consider the irreducible textuality of postmodern spaces.

29   See especially the chapter '... That Dangerous Supplement ...,' Jacques Derrida, *Of Grammatology*, pp. 141-64.

30   Franz Kafka, 'In The Penal Colony,' *Kafka: The Complete Stories*, ed. Nahum N. Glatzer (New York: Schocken Books, 1976) pp. 140-67.

31   Jacques Derrida, 'Living on: Border Lines,' Harold Bloom et al, *Deconstruction and Criticism* (New York: Continuum, 1979) pp. 75-176.

32   It would, accordingly, be difficult to avoid the significance of Greenaway's earlier collaboration with Phillips on Dante, even though and because one can trace other genealogies of this throughout his work, at least from *The Draughtsman's Contract* on.

Index

215